C463748100

Local

WITHDRAWN

# NORT
# CHURC WALKS

## Peter Donaghy and John Laidler

**Copyright** © Peter Donaghy and John Laidler, 2002
*Reprinted with minor corrections, 2003*

**All Rights Reserved.** No part of this publication may be reproduced, stored in a retrieval system, or transmitted in any form or by any means – electronic, mechanical, photocopying, recording, or otherwise – without prior written permission from the publisher or a licence permitting restricted copying issued by the Copyright Licensing Agency, 90 Tottenham Court Road, London W1P 0LA. This book may not be lent, resold, hired out or otherwise disposed of by trade in any form of binding or cover other than that in which it is published, without the prior consent of the publisher.

**Published by** Sigma Leisure – an imprint of
Sigma Press, 5 Alton Road, Wilmslow, Cheshire SK9 5DY, England.

**British Library Cataloguing in Publication Data**
A CIP record for this book is available from the British Library.

**ISBN:** 1-85058-768-X


**Typesetting and Design by:** Sigma Press, Wilmslow, Cheshire.

**Edited by:** Vanessa Betts

**Cover photograph:** St Aidan's statue, Lindisfarne *(photograph by Graeme Peacock – www.graeme-peacock.com)*

**Maps:** Jeremy Semmens

**Photographs:** the authors

**Printed by:** Bell & Bain Ltd, Glasgow

NEWCASTLE UPON TYN
CITY LIBRARIES

914.288

ACC No.

Issued

**Disclaimer:** the information in this book is given in good faith and is believed to be correct at the time of publication. No responsibility is accepted by either the authors or publisher for errors or omissions, or for any loss or injury howsoever caused. Only you can judge your own fitness, competence and experience.

# Foreword – by *Sting*

In the North East there is a piece of local advice often given to those setting out on a journey: "gan canny", they'll tell you. "Gan" from the Norse, meaning to walk and "canny" which has a number of interpretations: agreeable, sagacious, perceptive and cautious. For me, "gan canny" means to walk with awareness.

There is something in the nature of walking that soothes the mind, something in the binary rhythms of stepping and breathing that calms troubled and chaotic thoughts, where their randomness can be ordered and slowed. Almost all of the solutions to the problems that my own life has inevitably thrown up have presented themselves on long solitary walks.

How exhilarating it is, however, to be walking in natural beauty or to come across a country church. Such places have an irresistible attraction. The charitable grace of an unlocked door invites us into the sanctuary of stones that have witnessed countless joys and sorrows in the cycles of life from birth to death. Emotion and memory are distilled in the silence.

This book details some 50 churches on 30 circular walks throughout the ancient Kingdom of Northumbria. This is a region which was fought over by ancient Britons, Picts, Romans, Celts, Saxons, Norsemen, the Scots and the English for so many centuries, that those of us who were born there, feel in the fierceness of our regional identity that we belong to no-one but ourselves.

Peter Donaghy and John Laidler have done well to encourage us to walk here. To walk in Northumbria is to walk in the footsteps of scholars and saints, warriors and brigands, men and women who created the future in their own imaginations, just as we do, whenever we think, whenever we breathe, whenever we place one foot in front of the other. So, enjoy this book and "gan canny".

# Preface

The idea for this book arose as a result of the authors' family rambles over many years in the north of England between the Tweed and the Tees, the North Sea to the east and the Cheviots and North Pennines to the west. Here the fertile valleys, the rolling hillsides, the desolate moorlands and the magnificent coastline offer an abundant variety of walking opportunities. It was also soon apparent that these landscapes provide the backcloth to the long and interesting history of the ancient Kingdom of Northumbria. However, it was when, for the first time, we tentatively pushed open the door of a remote northern church, that we became aware of the rich social, political and religious history that lay within reach of our boots. Here was part of what Simon Jenkins in *England's Thousand Best Churches* has aptly called "the museum of England".

The tales that can be found within the walls and graveyards of our churches are part of our heritage and are there for all to appreciate. The fact that churches are kept open is precisely because ministers and congregations want to share what they have with the wider community. What we hope to do in this book, therefore, is to give more people the confidence to enter these buildings in order to enjoy this rich source of cultural and historical information and to discover some of the architectural and spiritual significance of Northumbria's many churches.

We have chosen churches which are spread geographically throughout Northumbria, which for the purposes of this volume we have defined as the present geographical counties of Northumberland and Durham. Most importantly, all the churches used as the focal point of the walks are known to be open for visitors but, in a few exceptional cases, it might be necessary to obtain the key for a church encountered on the route. Several walks incorporate visits to more than one church so that, in all, more than 50 churches are described.

The descriptions of the churches are clearly subjective accounts of what we feel is merit worthy with reference to historical events and persons and aspects of architectural and cultural interest. Where appropriate, we have incorporated in the text, highlighted vignettes of some of the fascinating people, places and events associated with the churches and localities visited. It will soon become apparent that some characters and artists have come to have a special appeal to us! Hopefully, the information we have supplied will serve to whet the reader's appetite to discover more.

All the walks are circular with a variety of landscapes and points of interest, on established rights of way and permissive paths without foreseeable hazards. Distances range from three miles to ten miles. Where possible, particularly for the longer routes, alternative, shorter walks have been presented. However, it has to be recognised that these shorter walks might still retain one or more difficult features, for example, a long ascent; an indication of this is given under the heading "terrain" in each section. Users are advised to read through the walk in advance in order to obtain a fuller idea of the nature of the route. At the same time, we know that some people may enjoy an "armchair" walk or a short stroll around the church grounds. The bullet points of interesting features may also serve as the basis of a "treasure hunt" for younger visitors. We trust, therefore, that there is something for everyone in this book.

As in the companion volume, *Lakeland Church Walks*, this book is divided into 30 sections each covering one walk together with alternative routes or short-cuts where appropriate. For each walk, details are given for location, distance, map, terrain and car parking. Under 'location', the Ordnance Survey (OS) reference given is for the church where the walk begins. Each section also contains a description of the church or churches, instructions for the walk and an indicative sketch map, cross-referenced to the description of the walk by alphabetical symbols. The instructions for the walks include reference to gates, stiles and other features where these are expected to be helpful to the user.

We have tried to ensure that the instructions for the walks and the information about the churches are correct. However, it is inevitable that changes will occur – for example, signs fall into disrepair, gates and stiles are replaced, paths are diverted, trees are felled, new vegetation is grown, restoration work is carried out in churches and some churches are fortunate enough to acquire new furnishings or windows. The reader needs to make allowance for these changed situations. In addition, adequate time should be allowed for visits to the churches.

Finally, a word about respect. Do be careful to respect yourself by ensuring that you are properly clothed, shod and equipped for the conditions you might encounter. It is always advisable to carry the appropriate Ordnance Survey map, as this can be particularly important in case of unforeseen circumstances. Respect the environment in which you are walking by following the country code. For the exploration of the churches, removal of muddy boots might be necessary and visits might have to be deferred if a service is taking place. It may also be helpful to have a torch in order to appreciate some of the finer details of the interior of a church. The fact that so many churches remain open for visitors is largely because of the efforts of the local clergy and congregation – which often means just a few people. Their contribution to the maintenance of this part of our heritage deserves our thanks, which we can express by making a suitable donation to their church funds, purchasing the church guidebook and signing the visitors' book.

*Peter Donaghy and John Laidler*

# Acknowledgements

In describing the churches and personalities contained in this volume, we have had recourse to a number of works of reference which we have listed in the bibliography. We are also indebted to the writers of the numerous church guidebooks to which we have had access. These have been listed under the specific church descriptions to which they refer and the authors, where known, have been duly acknowledged. Naturally, we would be happy to include in a future edition any further names brought to our attention.

We are grateful to the many people who literally helped us on our way, especially all those ministers and parishioners who so willing responded to our queries. We are indebted to the countryside officers of Northumberland and Durham County Councils and officers of the Northumberland National Park for their assistance. The route to publication is often as arduous as any long distance walk and so we are grateful to Graham Beech and his staff at Sigma Leisure for their admirable and patient assistance with this venture.

Last, but certainly not least, this book would have been impossible without the support and encouragement of our families and, in particular, our wives Jeanne and Gillian who have visited every church and walked every mile at least once!

# Contents

## Introduction

## The Walks

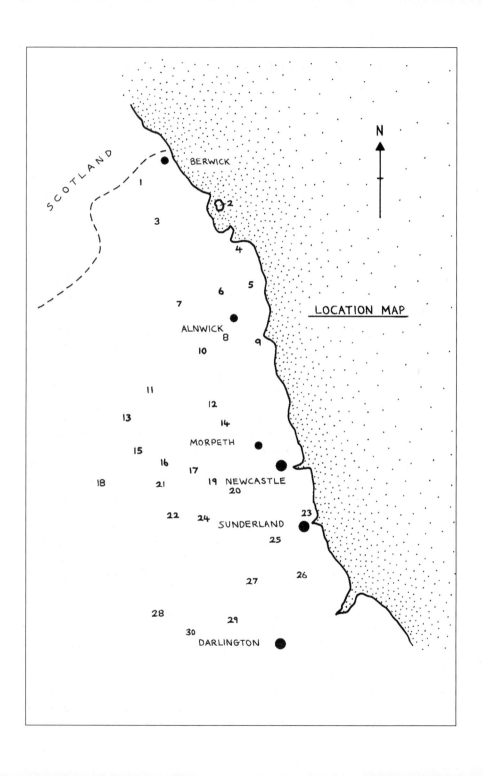

LOCATION MAP

# Religious and social background

Two thousand years ago, at the dawn of the Christian era, Britain was populated by a number of independent, often competing, kingdoms, with surviving pockets from earlier civilisations, and had neither political nor cultural
unity. Christianity was brought to these people during the Roman occupa-
tion, but there is a great deal of uncertainty about the starting point and the
extent of the Christian presence in these early times. By the turn of the 4th
century, there were the beginnings of church organisation, but virtually
nothing is known about Northumbrian Christians. It is likely that the early
Celtic saints, even those whose presence was real and not simply mythical,
would have had little or no influence in the north–east – the only reference
in the churches in this volume being to Kentigern (see Walk 15, Simonburn).

Following the fall of the Roman Empire and invasions by Jutes, Saxons
and Angles, there emerged, in the 6th century, a number of independent,
non-Christian, Anglo-Saxon kingdoms, the northern-most being
Northumbria. Two missions brought about its conversion to Christianity.

First, in 625, came Paulinus, a monk of the Roman tradition from the
Augustinian monastery in Kent. His successful evangelising included, in
627, the baptism of King Edwin. However, when Edwin was killed in battle,
Paulinus had to flee south, leaving a flickering flame of Christianity in the
hands of James the Deacon, at Catterick. The year of brutal heathen rule that
followed was brought to an end when Edwin's kinsman, Oswald, defeated
Cadwalla at Heavenfield (Walk 16). Oswald turned to the Celtic monks of
Iona, where he had been converted during a period of exile, to provide a new
mission. Aidan (see Walk 4, Bamburgh) was sent, and set up a monastery on
Holy Island. His and his successors' achievements are the reason why Holy
Island is often referred to as the "cradle of Christianity". In 664, the differ-
ences between the Roman and the Celtic traditions were debated at the
Synod of Whitby where Wilfrid (see Walk 21, St John Lee and Hexham) suc-
cessfully promoted the Roman cause.

As Christianity spread, more monasteries were established, including
twin monasteries at Jarrow and Monkwearmouth. They became famous for
their libraries and learning. The Venerable Bede (see Walk 23, Roker and
Whitburn) wrote his *Ecclesiastical History* at Jarrow. Another monastic
achievement, at Lindisfarne, was the production of the beautiful *Lindisfarne
Gospels* at the end of the 7th century.

From the 8th century, the Church experienced a period of consolidation
and growth. The parish system was developed under local lords of the
manor and new parish churches were built. A series of Viking invasions cut
short these developments and many ecclesiastical buildings were
destroyed. Subsequently, there was a slow recovery in church fortunes
including the building of abbeys and the establishment of cathedral priories.

One of the oldest surviving examples of Saxon church architecture is at
Escomb (Walk 27). Fortunately, the Saxon builders used stones from a

nearby Roman fort, rather than the wood from which their churches would usually be built at the time, so that this church from 1,300 years ago can still be appreciated. Only traces remain of the early Northumbrian Saxon abbey churches and monastic buildings, but Hexham Abbey (Walk 21) retains its original 7th-century crypt. Saxon stone crosses, possibly set up to signify the presence of a Christian mission in a place, also survive. One of the best preserved is at Rothbury (Walk 10). Later Saxon churches often had sturdy defensive towers, such as those at Bolam (Walk 12) and Ovingham (Walk 20).

Following the Norman Conquest, in the second half of the 11th century, the Church grew under the new king, William I, who introduced organisational changes and a new architectural style. Many Anglo-Saxon churches were pulled down and rebuilt. Monasticism was encouraged. Often, Norman abbots were appointed and continental religious orders established monasteries in England (see, for example, Walk 22, Blanchland). As part of his defensive strategy, William set up special areas along the Scottish and Welsh borders, delegating considerable powers to local lords – in the case of Durham to the Prince Bishops (see Walk 25).

Many churches in present-day Northumberland and Durham date back to Norman times but have been subject to much renovation over the last 950 years. Examples include Old Bewick (Walk 6) and Romaldkirk (Walk 28). On a grander scale, the magnificent Durham Cathedral (Walk 25) represents the pinnacle of achievement of the Anglo-Norman builders in the country.

The 14th and 15th centuries saw a move away from making financial endowments to cathedrals and monasteries, to supporting the rebuilding of parish churches in evolving architectural styles. In the border area during the time of the English/Scots wars, this could include protective additions such as the unique fireproof stone roof at Bellingham (Walk 13). A parish church would often be the most impressive building in the village, surrounded by the poor dwellings of the local people. The parish priest might be a poorly educated local man paid a low stipend to fulfil the duties of an absentee incumbent, who, maybe, had a plurality of livings. Usually, there were no seats for the congregation and, in the early part of the period, no sermons; the Christian message being conveyed pictorially by wall paintings and decorated windows. Preaching in the parishes was not the norm until the advent of orders of mendicant friars, mainly Franciscans and Dominicans, around the middle of the 13th century. From around 1340, pulpits became an addition to church furnishings.

From the early 16th century, much church property was destroyed or damaged as a result of the Dissolution of the Monasteries (1535-1539) and by various changes in allegiance by Henry VIII's successors. All of this culminated in the abolition of the Church of England as an entity during the Commonwealth (1649-1660).

With the restoration of the Church of England came the requirement to conform to its practices. Under the Clarendon Code, non-conformists were forbidden to hold their own services. However, churches such as Baptists, Congregationalists and Quakers continued to develop and the Toleration Act of 1659 granted freedom of worship to non-conformists – with the exception of Roman Catholics.

After the Restoration many churches were restored and refurnished. In an age when preaching and church music were encouraged, three-decker pulpits, western galleries for singers and (especially in town churches) organs were introduced. An example of the three "decks" of a three-decker pulpit can be seen at Romaldkirk Church (Walk 28).

The second half of the 18th century saw the development of Methodism, following the tireless preaching journeys of John Wesley and a revival of Evangelism within and outside of the Church of England.

In the early 19th century, reform was in the air. Freedom for Roman Catholics came with the Catholic Emancipation Act of 1829 and was followed by the building of Catholic churches, especially later in the century, to meet the needs of the influx of immigrants from Ireland. The growth in population in the industrial centres made it necessary to look at the organisation of the established church. A new body, the Ecclesiastical Commissioners, made sweeping changes in the redistribution of the wealth of the Church and established new dioceses to accommodate population changes. In 1882, the northern half of the Durham Diocese, stretching from the Tyne to the Tweed, became the new Diocese of Newcastle with St Nicholas, one of the largest parish churches in England, becoming its cathedral.

The 1850s witnessed a great revival in the life of the Church, including the building of new churches in the developing urban areas together with a vast amount of renovation and refurbishing of existing buildings. According to J.H.R. Moorman (*A History of the Church in England*), "Scarcely a church in England escaped the attention of the Victorian 'reformers'". In an age that was waking up to the necessity for social reform, the Church of England and the other churches, including The Salvation Army founded in 1864, continued to be involved in education and social issues.

The 20th century undoubtedly saw a general fall off in church attendance, resulting in the closure of some buildings and the merger of various national churches. The different branches of Methodism amalgamated in 1932 and, in 1972, the Congregationalist and Presbyterian churches combined to form the United Reformed Church. In addition, there has been a reduction in candidates for ordination but, in most traditions, there has been a greater lay involvement in church services and pastoral work.

At the beginning of the third millennium, in spite of falling numbers in some areas, the efforts of local clergy and parishioners have enabled the vast majority of churches to remain open for their worshipping congregations and their welcome visitors.

# Church Architecture

## Basic church structure

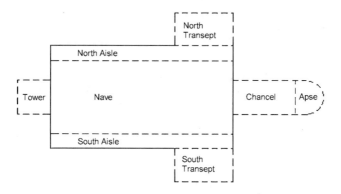

## Architectural terms

**Apse:** a semi-circular addition to the chancel at the east end of a church.

**Arcade:** a number of arches sustained by columns usually dividing the nave from the aisles.

**Bellcote:** a turret on the roof where bells are hung.

**Capital:** the top of a column, usually carved.

**Chancel:** the eastern end of the church where the main altar is situated. It is often divided from the nave by an arch (chancel arch).

**Gothic:** a style of architecture found approximately between the 12th and 16th centuries. Its most significant feature being pointed arches. This style became increasingly popular again in the Victorian period.

**Hatchment:** a diamond-shaped tablet showing the coat of arms of a deceased person.

**Lancet:** a narrow window with a pointed top.

**Light:** the individual compartment of a window.

**Misericord:** a shelf under a hinged choir seat to support a person when standing.

**Nave:** the body or main part of the church.

**Norman:** a style of architecture introduced into England following the Norman Conquest of 1066. Its most significant feature being rounded arches.

**Piscina:** basin in or on a wall in which church vessels are washed.

**Reredos:** a decorated panel behind an altar.

**Sanctuary:** the part of the chancel containing the altar.

**Sedilia:** a group of seats for clergy, built into the chancel wall.

**Tracery:** ribbed stonework in upper part of windows.

**Transepts:** extensions on the north and south of the church, which give a church a cross (cruciform) shape.

# Walk 1: Norham
## *Tweed, Till and Twizel*

**Location:** St Cuthbert's Church (NT897474) is at Norham. Norham is on the A698, 6½ miles west of Berwick-upon-Tweed.

**Distance:** Walk 1(a), Norham and Twizel: 9½ miles; Walk 1(b), Norham only: 3 miles.

**Map:** OS Explorer 339: Kelso, Coldstream and Lower Tweed Valley.

**Terrain:** Both walks are mainly on the level along riverbanks and field paths. There is one short section on a fairly busy road on Walk 1(a).

**Church:** St Cuthbert.

**Car parking:** There is limited parking outside the church and street parking in the village.

## The Church

This impressive church is situated in an extensive churchyard at the west end of Norham between the River Tweed and the village. It is a large stone building, light grey in colour, with a west tower and an extremely long nave and chancel. It has the distinction of being the English church which is closest to Scotland. Norham, set on a bend in the River Tweed, is overlooked by the ruins of Norham Castle from its high commanding position. The church and castle, built around the middle of the 12th century, were designed by the same architect for Bishop Puiset, one of the Prince Bishops of Durham – Norham being the northernmost outpost of the See of Durham at that time (see Walk 25, Durham). Over the centuries, damage caused by border fighting and river flooding has necessitated much rebuilding and restoration but the impressive "princely" dimensions of the Norman church still provide the basis for the imposing structure that is seen today.

Bishop Puiset's church replaced an earlier stone church built in 830. It is probable that this in turn was a replacement for a wooden church. It is interesting to note that St Aidan crossed the Tweed at Norham in 615 on his way to set up his mission at Lindisfarne. In 875 Norham was one of the resting-places for St Cuthbert's body, borne by his monks on their flight from the Vikings.

A glass door, with an engraving of St Cuthbert's Cross, leads into the south-west entrance from which you enter the nave. Standing at the west end, looking east towards the altar, it can be seen just how big this church is. Four pillars on the left and four on the right support the massive, wide arches which separate the north and south aisles from the nave. Beyond the pillars, a splendid arch leads into the long chancel. The overall form of the building follows the Norman plan, but the only major features surviving from the 12th-century church are the pillars and arches of the south aisle, the chancel (excluding the sanctuary), and the chancel arch which has alternate red and white stones – a rare style also found at St Mary's, Holy Island (Walk 2). The

St Cuthbert, Norham – a Prince Bishop's church

impressive arches on the south side were bricked up for over 200 years until restored to their full glory in a restoration of 1846. Light is provided not only through the windows but, somewhat unusually, from two skylights in the roof.

Some beautiful 17th-century furniture – including the pulpit, lectern and priest's stall – contributes to the almost sumptuous ambience of this church. These items were acquired from Durham Cathedral by the Revd Dr Gilly, vicar from 1831-1855. Norham's historical association with Durham and the Prince Bishops makes it an appropriate place to house these splendid pieces.

### *Among the other features of interest are:*

❖ At the north-west corner, a single window, plain with a stained-glass insert. This is one of four which formed a memorial in the local Presbyterian church, now a private house. On the right is a simple tablet in memory of a soldier from the 1914-1918 War, originally in another parish church which has now closed. Two simple items, for which a fitting place has been found.

❖ On the south-aisle wall, a memorial to Daniel Laidlaw, The Piper of Loos, who was awarded the VC in 1915. He died in 1950 and for many years lay in an unmarked grave. Recently, a simple headstone has been erected to mark his last resting place.

❖ The 1950s wrought-iron communion rail in front of the altar. It incorporates emblems of the three saints to whom the pre-Norman church was dedicated: St Peter, cross keys; St Cuthbert, an eider duck; and St

Ceolwulf, a crown. St Ceolwulf was a King of Northumbria who became a monk at Lindisfarne. Bede dedicated his work *A History of the English Church and People* to him.

❖ In the north wall of the chancel an effigy of Dr Gilly, by John Graham Lough (see Walk 24, Edmundbyres and Muggleswick).

❖ On the north wall of the sanctuary, the stained-glass window by Kempe (see Walk 15, Simonburn).

❖ Outside, the tower clock made to celebrate Queen Victoria's Jubilee in 1897 by a famous Northumbrian clockmaker, Charles Taylor of Earsden. His grave is at the foot of the tower near the north-west porch. In accordance with his wishes, he was buried as near as possible to one of his favourite clocks.

### Information available in the church:

❶ *St Cuthbert's Church Norham.*

# The Walks

## Walk 1(a), Norham and Twizel: 9½ miles

Leave the church **(A)** by the glass door in the porch, walk around the south and east walls of the building and head diagonally left across the graveyard to exit by a stone stile onto a narrow track. Walk straight ahead to join a path running alongside the River Tweed. Turn left and walk along the path with the river on your right. The border runs in the middle of the river here, so you are looking at Scotland on the opposite bank. The next part of the walk follows the rivers Tweed and Till and so you simply need to follow the riverside paths. However, just in case here are some guidelines.

The path goes through two kissing gates. At the bridge, turn left, go up the waymarked steps and, taking care, go over the stone stile and cross the road. To the left are road signs for England and Northumberland. Go over the wall and descend by the steps. Ignore the ladder stile immediately after the bridge and proceed for several hundred metres to cross a stile on your right. Continue in the same direction with the fence now on your left. After about 200 metres, go through a gate to emerge onto a minor road. Turn right and proceed to where there is a house on the left near a public footpath sign showing "Twizel Bridge 4" **(B)**.

Follow the path straight ahead to go through a waymarked gate then continue ahead. Eventually, turn right to arrive at a footbridge **(C)**.

The river banks have been taken over by giant hogweed in a number of places but praiseworthy efforts have been made to keep the footpaths clear of this. However, take care not to touch this as it can cause serious skin irritation. In addition, there are a number of short sections where native nettles and thistles try to make their presence felt, so shorts might not be the best apparel in summertime.

Cross the footbridge, turn right and follow the path over a plank bridge. Where the path divides, with two waymarks, take the right-hand path down steps and go over another plank bridge to arrive at a public footpath sign showing "Twizel Bridge 3½". Proceed in the same direction and eventually go over a waymarked ladder stile into woods. Continue ahead as the path wends its way through the woodland, climbing at one stage before dropping back to the river bank to pass through an area with a new planting of young trees in their protective tubes. Go over a little plank bridge and carry on along the path as it passes between the trees, going up and/or down a series of user-friendly steps cut into some tricky sections. The nearby islands of Kippie and Dreeper are over to the right for much of this part of the route. Go over two wooden footbridges. Climb up out of the wood and turn right at a waymark post to walk along a field edge towards a house on the left and a public footpath sign showing "Twizel Bridge 1¾" **(D)**.

Take the broad path to the right and follow it as it swings back to the river. Proceed ahead to the property known as Twizel Boathouse. Go through the stile to the right of the property and follow the path as it comes to the meeting of the waters of the Tweed and Till. Over the river bank ahead are the ruins of St Cuthbert's Chapel, which was built in the 18th century on the site of an earlier chapel **(E)**.

The path is now a broad, grassy track running alongside the Till on your right and soon passing under the high arches of the bridge carrying the dismantled railway over the river. Continue to where the path comes to a metal gate leading to the old Twizel Bridge with the replacement bridge a few metres away **(F)**.

*Twizel Bridge was used by the Earl of Surrey to move his artillery to a superior position prior to the battle between the English and Scots at Flodden Field in 1513 – described by Tomlinson (Comprehensive Guide to Northumberland) as the "last and most sanguinary struggle between the two nations". It is worth going onto the old bridge to appreciate the beauty of this spot, with the river below and the wooded hill above. To the south you can see the Tillmouth Park Hotel.*

Return back through the metal gate and take the public footpath to "Twizel Castle ¼". Climb up the hill and follow the path as it bears left and, after a few metres, go over a ladder stile into a field. Turn left and walk to the castle ruins.

*Twizel Castle ruins are magnificently situated and look romantic, but the unromantic truth is that Sir Francis Blake commenced building around 1770 and the castle was never completed. However, it was said to have reached five stories by 1812 and was probably a useful quarry for the construction in 1882 of the building now occupied by the Tillmouth Park Hotel.*

Continue past the castle ruins, bearing slightly right to exit the grounds via a stile onto a minor road. Turn right, proceed along this road and carry on to come to a main road with Twizel Smithy on your right. Turn left and walk

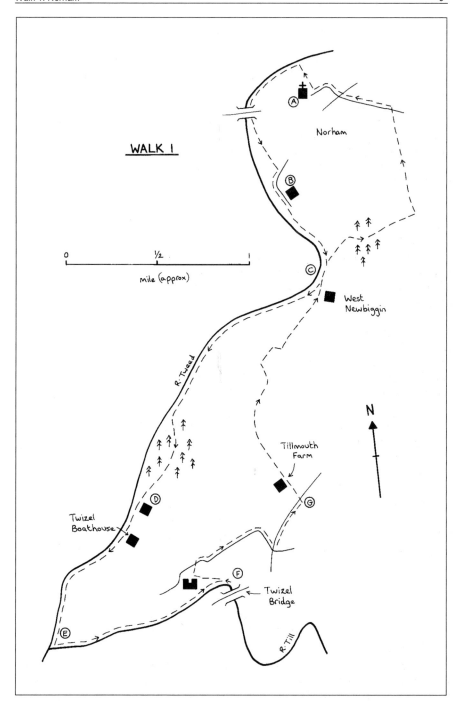

up this busy road for a few hundred metres to the entrance to Tillmouth Farm **(G)**.

There is a public footpath sign showing "Tillmouth Farm ¼, River Tweed 1½". Go up the metalled road, past bungalows on the right, to the main farm buildings ahead. Proceed through the farm area; there are waymarks and stiles at the entry and exit gates. At the end of the area of farm buildings, go onto the waymarked path almost straight ahead and walk in the same direction onto a field just past the vestiges of the track of the dismantled railway. You need to walk diagonally right, across the field, to a waymarked ladder stile. Go over the stile, turn left and walk for a few metres then turn right. Proceed across the field with the new hedge plantings in their protective tubes on your left. In the distance, you can see the silo and other structures of West Newbiggin farm to which you are heading. Go over the waymarked stile and carry on in the same direction with the hedge on your right. At the end of the hedge a waymark directs you to walk straight ahead, keeping to the left of the farm fence, until you go over a stile leading onto a farm track. Follow the track to go through a metal gate and walk up a few metres to public footpath signs. Take the path to the left, shown as "Riverside Path", and walk to a waymark post. This post was passed earlier in the walk. Turn right to retrace your steps, via a plank bridge, to arrive back at the footbridge **(C)**.

Cross the footbridge and turn right to go through the waymarked gate and walk to where the path divides. Climb up the steps as indicated by the waymark and continue to a junction of paths at a waymark post. Turn right and proceed under a railway arch, then through the trees at the top of Newbiggin Dean to reach a ladder stile. Cross the stile and come to public footpath signs. Take the path to the left for "Norham ¾". Walk ahead and follow the path, keeping the hedge on your right. The raised path turns along the perimeter of the large field and then straightens out to ascend, then descend, and exits at a road on the outskirts of Norham. Turn left and walk to the village. Carry on to the village green, with its ancient market cross, the church and the end of the walk.

### Walk 1(b), Norham only: 3 miles

Follow Walk 1(a) to **(C)** in the third paragraph. Do not cross the footbridge but walk straight ahead to go through the waymarked gate and follow the remaining instructions in the last paragraph of Walk 1(a).

# Walk 2: Holy Island (Lindisfarne)
## *Cradle, centre and Catholic camp*

**Location:** St Mary the Virgin's Church (NU126418) is on Holy Island, 5 miles off the A1, 60 miles from Newcastle and 14 miles from Berwick. It is cut off from the mainland twice a day by the tide and it is very important to check the crossing times, which vary daily. There are timetables at each end of the causeway. Advance information may be obtained from the coastguard (Tel 0126-2672317).

**Distance:** 4¼ miles.

**Map:** OS Explorer 340: Holy Island & Bamburgh.

**Terrain:** This is mainly an easy stroll along tracks and grassy paths. There is one short, steep ascent but this could be avoided.

**Churches:** St Cuthbert's Centre (The United Reformed Church on Holy Island); Lindisfarne Priory; St Mary the Virgin; St Aidan RC Church.

**Car parking:** Except in low season, all private cars have to be parked in the public car park at the entrance to the village; hence the walk is described from this point.

## The Churches
### St Cuthbert's Centre (The United Reformed Church on Holy Island)

In the 1990s, the church (dating from 1892) was converted into St Cuthbert's Holy Island Project (now St Cuthbert's Centre) as a focus for local cultural and religious information, as well as a place for worship, meetings and fellowship. Today, in addition to offering a welcome to all visitors with a series of displays about life on Holy Island, it organises a number of activities including guided pilgrimages around the island.

The interior has been very tastefully refurbished and it is also worth climbing up to the gallery to read about the beautifully embroidered communion cloth displayed there.

The Old Boiler House Chapel attached to the side of the church is a further example of "conversion". It is a tiny cell containing little more than a solitary bench and a mosaic in the form of a Celtic cross made from broken pottery. It merits a visit.

*Information available in the church:*

❶ There are numerous leaflets about the island available in the church.

### Lindisfarne Priory

St Aidan (see Walk 4, Bamburgh), whose statue stands proudly near the entrance, founded a monastery here in about 635. It was largely as a result of his work and that of one of his successors, St Cuthbert (see below), that Lindisfarne became the "cradle of Christianity" and earned the name Holy Island. During a "golden age" in the 7th and 8th centuries, this and other monasteries in Northumbria – inspired by an array of northern saints – produced wonderful religious artefacts and books. These included the richly illuminated manuscripts the Lindisfarne Gospels, produced in honour of St Cuthbert after his death. Unfortunately, such treasures were to prove too

The church of St Mary the Virgin and the ruins of Lindisfarne Priory

attractive to invaders and the monastic settlement was largely destroyed by the Vikings towards the end of the 8th century.

It was not until the late 11th century that the Bishops of Durham saw fit to re-establish an important religious settlement here in the form of a priory, thought to be on the site where both St Aidan and St Cuthbert were originally buried. The Norman priory church and monastic buildings survived until the Dissolution of the Monasteries in 1537 but then fell into disrepair. What you see now is a glorious ruin, helped by some 19th- and 20th-century restoration work. The grounds are well cared for and there are helpful explanatory notices. In 2001, St Cuthbert returned home here in the form of an evocative bronze statue by Fenwick Lawson (formerly Head of Sculpture at what is now the University of Northumbria). If time allows, you may wish to obtain admission tickets and also inspect the exhibits in the adjacent English Heritage Lindisfarne Priory Museum. Otherwise, you may have to be content to admire its substantial walls and towering archways from a little distance. The Celtic spirituality fostered within this precinct so long ago, is still strongly manifested on Holy Island in many ways.

*St Cuthbert (c.634-687), was a shepherd boy who became Prior of Lindisfarne and eventually, with reluctance, Bishop. His reputation as a holy man and miracle worker soon ensured that Holy Island and the shrine of St Cuthbert became a place of pilgrimage. Nearly two centuries after his death, with the threat of Viking invasion, his body was removed from Lindisfarne. The head of St Oswald was also placed in the coffin for safety, and this is the reason why many depictions of St Cuthbert show him holding the head of St Oswald. Eventually, in 995, the coffin arrived in Durham where a cathedral was built and to which pilgrims once again flocked to visit his shrine.*

## St Mary the Virgin

The parish church is superbly positioned next to the ruins of the priory and within sight of the castle. Externally it consists of a nave and chancel, a bell-cote and a south-west porch, all in attractive sandstone. Entrance is via the porch and down some steps. Inside, you immediately come across the 18th-century font with its pleasing modern cover and then, once accustomed to the light, the eye is drawn to the high timbered ceiling, divided by elegant north and south arcades.

The origins of the church are the subject of debate and it has clearly been altered over a long period of time. Although its main structure was completed in the 13th century, it does seem probable that there was a church on this site in Saxon times and a small arch in the wall above the chancel arch seems to provide evidence of this. The Norman period is reflected in the three rounded arches in the north aisle, which have alternating red and white stones, a rare feature in Northumberland (see Walk 1, Norham). The pointed arches on the south side, on the other hand, are 14th-century early Gothic style. Interestingly, the bases of the pillars have disappeared as a result of the floor being raised 60 centimetres in Victorian times. The wide nave leads to a long narrow chancel, the walls of which deliberately lean outwards like a haystack to channel rainwater away from the sides.

Here there are strong Celtic resonances. In a showcase in the south aisle of the church, you will find a facsimile copy of the Lindisfarne Gospels. In addition, the church boasts two beautiful carpets with Celtic designs: an abstract illustration or "carpet page" used to decorate St Mark's Gospel in front of the high altar; and St Luke's "carpet page" in the north-east "Fisherman's" chapel. These carpets, as well as a series of attractive kneelers with Celtic designs, were made by the women of the island.

While opinions on the architectural merit of this church may differ, it is, as Simon Jenkins (*England's Thousand Best Churches*) suggests, on "a remarkable site", one clearly evocative of early saints and religious art and culture.

### Among the other features of interest are:

❖ Two stained-glass windows in the west wall by Leonard Evetts (see Walk 12, Bolam and Hartburn). One, depicting St Aidan, is in memory of Edward de Stein and his sister Gladys who gave Lindisfarne Castle to the National Trust. The other, depicting St Cuthbert, honours the memory of Kathleen Parbury who designed the carpet which lies in front of the high altar.

❖ The interpretations of the decorations found on St Cuthbert's coffin on the north wall of the nave.

❖ The reredos behind the main altar which includes depictions of several northern saints.

❖ The small replica of a sculpture of St Olaf, in a glass case in the south aisle.

*Information available in the church:*

❶ Numerous displays, books and pamphlets.

❶ *A guide to the church of St Mary the Virgin.*

## St Aidan RC Church

This very plain, rendered building has served as a church for visitors since 1959. A camp for young people is attached to the church and so, not surprisingly, there are usually displays appropriate to their needs and interests. An unusual statue of St Aidan stands near the back of the church and there are plaques illustrating the lives of northern saints on the north wall. A movable screen divides the sanctuary and its small stone altar from the body of the building, thus facilitating a multi-purpose use. This is a peaceful spot in which to pause and reflect before leaving the island and one verse in particular on a wall seems to sum up the history of Lindisfarne:

> *Well known to warriors*
> *Crossed to by kings*
> *Prayed-in place of princes*
> *Made holy by early monks*

# The Walk

This walk begins and ends in the public car park at the entrance to the village of Holy Island **(A)**. Given the question of the tides, you are advised to complete the walk before deciding whether or not you have sufficient time at your disposal to visit the many other places of interest on the island.

From the public car park walk up the road to the T-junction at Marygate, the main street on the island. Turn right, pass the Lindisfarne Heritage Centre and turn left at the top of the street. Walk past the Craft Centre and then turn left to visit the URC church, now the St Cuthbert's Centre **(B)**.

On leaving the church turn left past the winery, famed for its mead, to reach the market place, the village green and the Celtic cross rebuilt in 1828 by John Dobson (see Walk 14, Whalton and Meldon). Turn right, and after passing the English Heritage Lindisfarne Priory Museum you will find yourself in the grounds of the parish church within sight of the statue of St Aidan, the ruins of Lindisfarne Priory and the church of St Mary the Virgin **(C)**.

Admire the priory, and then follow the path for a few metres to the entrance to the church. After visiting the church, turn right and follow the path to a wooden gate. Go through the gate, cross the lane and go through the gate opposite. Proceed a short distance across the field and through a kissing gate onto the seashore. Turn left to an English Nature information board. A few metres to the west is a very small rocky islet where St Cuthbert used to seek solitude. If the tide permits you can clamber across the rocks to the wooden cross and see the scant traces of a medieval chapel. Otherwise continue a little further to a second information board. Now follow the path which climbs steeply over rocks to the coastguard lookout at the top of the ridge known as The Heugh. (If you wish to avoid this climb, return via the

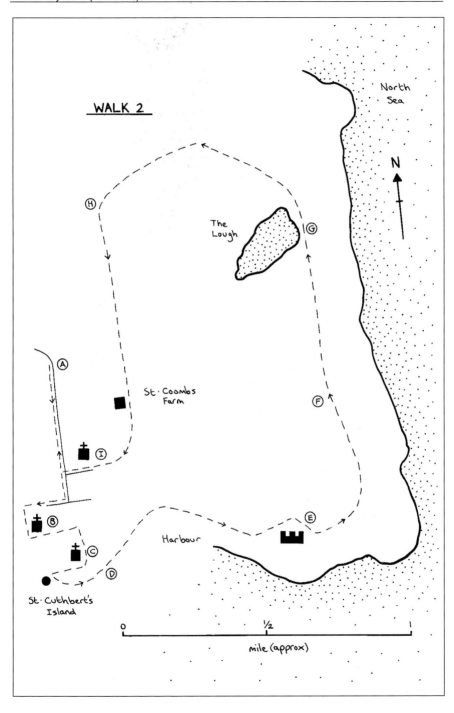

WALK 2

North Sea

N

The Lough

H

G

A

St·Coombs Farm

F

I

B

C

E

Harbour

D

St·Cuthbert's Island

0 ½ 1

mile (approx)

church to the centre of the village and follow the signs to the castle). From here you can look down into the ruins of the priory where you will see the modern *Cuthbert of Farne* statue; ahead are the Farne Islands so loved by the saint and on the mainland to the south lies Bamburgh Castle. Just beyond the coastguard lookout is the war memorial designed by Sir Edwin Lutyens. Continue along The Heugh right to its eastern end where a few stones are all that now remain of a 17$^{th}$-century fort **(D)**.

Descend to the harbour side and make your way round the bay towards the castle, passing the old upturned boats, which the fishermen now use for storage. You will join a metalled road and reach a kissing gate in close proximity to Lindisfarne Castle perched on its rocky base.

> *Lindisfarne Castle dates from the 16$^{th}$ century and it served as a garrison until 1819, after which it was used for some time as a coastguard station. One of the most eventful moments in its history was its brief capture by two local Jacobites in 1715. At the beginning of the 20$^{th}$ century, it was sensitively converted into a private dwelling by Sir Edwin Lutyens for Edward Hudson, the proprietor of Country Life. It was given to the National Trust in 1944 by the then owners Edward de Stein and his sister (both of who are remembered in the stained-glass windows in the parish church).*

Go through the kissing gate, bear left and follow the track beyond the castle to some stone steps beside a footbridge **(E)**. Climb the steps but do not cross the footbridge, unless you wish to visit the old limekilns dating from the 1860s and read about their history on the National Trust information board at their foot. You are now on the old wagon-way that was once used to transport coal to the limekilns. The raised grassy track heads towards the sea and then bears left, passing through two gates before it reaches a public right of way on the left known as the Crooked Lonnen **(F)**.

Ignore this, unless you need to take a short cut that brings you to St Coombs Farm. Continue straight ahead to the next landmark: a fresh water lake and bird sanctuary called The Lough, believed to have been created by the monks about the time of St Cuthbert to provide water and fish. Here you can pause in the hide and, with the help of the information boards, learn a little more about the migratory birds **(G)**.

Continue along the wagon-way, cross the stile and go through a kissing gate to an English Nature information board. To the right you may already have glimpsed what appears to be a white sail, but what, in fact, is a marker to warn shipping off Emmanuel Head. Turn left and follow the path with the wall on your left, until you eventually reach a fingerpost **(H)**.

The fingerpost directs you left, back towards the village down a public right of way known as the Straight Lonnen. This is a pleasant walk between hedgerows as far as St Coombs Farm where the lane becomes a metalled road. Follow the road as it bears right round the coach park to St Aidan's RC Church **(I)**. After visiting the church, turn right and walk to the T-junction at the Lindisfarne Hotel. Turn right and retrace your steps back to the car park and the end of the walk.

# Walk 3: Ford and Etal

## Model village, mortuary chapel and mill house

**Location:** St Michael and All Angels Church (NT945374) is just east of Ford village which is on the B6353 near its junction with the B6354. The B6354 runs east from the A697 Wooler to Cornhill-on-Tweed road, about 5 miles north of Wooler.

**Distance:** 5 miles.

**Map:** OS Explorer 339: Kelso, Coldstream & Lower Tweed Valley.

**Terrain:** Mainly on the level along field paths, with short sections on quiet roads.

**Churches:** St Michael and All Angels, Ford; St Mary, Etal.

**Car parking:** In Ford village. There is a limited amount of parking near the church. Walkers may wish to visit the church then drive to the village to park. The walk is described from the church.

## The Churches

### St Michael and All Angels, Ford

The church is set in pleasant, gentle countryside with a good view of Cheviot from the porch. It is located just outside Ford village, near to the castle, with which it has had close association since at least 1255 – the patrons having always been the owners of Ford Estate, now the Ford and Etal Estates (see below). The main approach is over a mounting block, adjacent to the wrought-iron churchyard gates. These were made by local blacksmiths in

St Michael and All Angels, near Ford Castle

1971 and incorporate the cross of St Michael and the arms of the Joicey family.

Perhaps the most striking feature from the outside is the unusually large buttressed bellcote at the west end, described by Pevsner (*The Buildings of England: Northumberland*) as "a sturdy masculine structure". The building consists of the bellcote, a nave, a lower chancel, north and south aisles and a porch. Much of this dates back to the 13<sup>th</sup> century, but the north aisle was added in an extensive restoration by John Dobson (see Walk 14, Whalton and Meldon) in 1853, which did not meet with Pevsner's approval.

Inside, looking east are the nave and the two aisles, separated by three arcades with supporting circular pillars, the two pillars on the south side are 13<sup>th</sup> century. Each aisle has six lancet windows, part of the 1853 restoration. Those on the south and two on the north side are of stained glass. The windows on the south side appear to be the work of William Wailes (see Walk 19, Bywell). An arch leads into a fairly long chancel. Above, the roof beams are exposed, with wooden-clad ceilings in the aisles and chancel.

Overall, there is a pleasing symmetry, with Dobson's additions now seeming to blend in well with the original 13<sup>th</sup>-century work. Visitors are made welcome here and there is much for them to see.

### Among the other features of interest are:

❖ On the floor at the west end, several medieval grave slabs, brought in from the churchyard about 100 years ago. The adjacent information board identifies one showing a set of Northumbrian pipes.

❖ In the middle of the north aisle wall, the brightly coloured stained-glass window showing St Francis. It is from 1972 and is by Douglas Hogg of Kelso, the winner of a competition held that year.

❖ The elaborate First World War memorial on the south-aisle wall, with the plainer 1939-45 memorial below.

❖ The stone pulpit decorated with statuettes of the four Gospel writers, installed in 1897 to commemorate Queen Victoria's Jubilee.

❖ The window at the east end of the north aisle, dedicated in 1996 to the memory of Lord Michael Joicey, 4th Baron Joicey of Chester-le-Street (1925-1993).

### Information available in the church:

❶ *St Michael & All Angels, Ford, Northumberland.*

❶ Information folder *Ford Parish. Historical notes prepared by the Right Honourable Lord Joicey.*

*The Ford and Etal Estates were originally separate. Ford Castle (see below) was acquired by Lord Delaval about 1768. He left it to his granddaughter who married the 2<sup>nd</sup> Marquis of Waterford. The widow of the 3<sup>rd</sup> Marquis, Louisa (nee Stuart) inherited the estate on his early death in 1859. She restored the castle and lived there until her death in 1891. In the 1860s she built Ford vil-*

lage, usually referred to as a model village, and took a great interest in village life. She was an accomplished watercolourist and decorated the school with biblical scenes. In 1907, the estate was sold to the Joicey family and, shortly after, the Etal Estate was also acquired. Today, the Ford and Etal Estates, in addition to their traditional landowning role, are an important feature of the tourist industry in north Northumberland.

### St Mary, Etal

This is a delightful little church in the grounds of Etal Manor, close by the tiny village of Etal. White-painted houses, a pub with a thatched roof and the ruins of Etal Castle combine to produce a picturesque setting to the church. It is a small sandstone building consisting of a single-chamber nave and chancel, surmounted by a centrally placed bellcote, together with an entrance porch on the north wall and a separate chapel on the south, all with steeply sloping slate roofs. Overall, these blend to produce an attractive building which fits in well with its august neighbour, Etal Manor.

In the mid 1850s the Manor was the home of Lord Frederick Fitzclarence, one of the ten children of William IV and Mrs Jordan, and his wife Lady Augusta. Lord Frederick, a soldier, died in India in 1854 and his wife engaged William Butterfield to build a church, incorporating a mortuary chapel, in memory of her husband. It was consecrated as The Chapel of the Blessed Virgin Mary in 1859, taking the same dedication as a former chantry chapel, established in 1345 on the nearby banks of the River Till. The new

St Mary, Etal – a church of remembrance

church had no district attached to it, the chaplain's only responsibility was to hold regular services; hence, it enjoyed the rare classification of a "sinecure". This is no longer the case, the church is now a chapel-of-ease within the parish of Ford and Etal.

Inside, the nave leads to the chancel through an arch and there is a succession of different finishes in the ceiling: exposed beams with plaster between in the nave; wooden boarding painted in red and green stripes in the chancel; and, in the sanctuary, a ceiling painted with stars each in its own blue background. On the floor are patterned coloured tiles. The overall effect is harmonious and pleasing. The mortuary chapel is separated from the main body of the church by a screen of glass and oak, installed in 1971. This effectively cuts off the chapel from the rest of the church, although it was originally incorporated into the building by means of a series of arches.

Visitors are made welcome to this small, unusual church.

### *Among the other features of interest are:*

❖ On the west wall, a notice setting out details of the consecration of the church.

❖ The original wrought-ironwork of the chancel screen and communion rail.

❖ A dedication, on the first choir stall on the south side, in memory of David Hugh Joicey, killed in action in 1943 aged 21.

❖ In the mortuary chapel, on the east wall, the church's only stained-glass window which depicts the Crucifixion with the Blessed Virgin Mary, St John and two angels.

❖ In the mortuary chapel, a tomb monument to Lord Fitzclarence. His coat of arms is shown in a memorial to him, his wife and their daughter, who are also interred here.

### *Information available in the church:*

❶ A leaflet, *The Chapel of the Blessed Virgin Mary, Etal.*

## The Walk

Leave the church **(A)** by the mounting-block near the gates. Behind the church is Ford Castle.

> *Ford Castle was built about 1282 by Odonel de Ford, whose daughter married Sir William Heron, High Sheriff of Northumberland. He transformed Ford into a courtyard castle and added crenellations – some of this early work remains. Two disputed stories link James IV of Scotland with the castle. The first has it that he stayed there before the battle of Flodden in 1513, in dalliance with Lady Heron; in contrast, another tale suggests that he set fire to the place! Whatever the truth of the matter, by the mid-16th century the castle was falling into disrepair. A succession of restorations, culminating in an extensive programme by Lady Waterford in 1861-5, produced the castle that is seen*

*today. It is used by Northumberland Education Committee for residential courses and is not open to the public.*

Turn left to walk 400 metres to a sign directing you to Lady Waterford Gallery and Moss Nurseries. Go down the road on your left into Ford village. At the end of the road is the Lady Waterford Hall, open to the public, originally the school founded by Lady Waterford, which houses the biblical murals she painted for the children. Turn right and walk to the junction, with Jubilee Cottage (1897) ahead, then turn left and proceed ahead, passing the aptly named Horse Shoe Forge on your right and, in a few hundred metres, the Ford and Etal Estates Office on your left. Go through the gate on your left onto the waymarked public footpath to "Hay Farm ½". Just after the gate bear left, and walk ahead to cross a footbridge. Go through the gate ahead and, as indicated by the waymark on the telegraph post, bear left and go along the field edge with the woods on your left. Bear right at the waymark and continue along the field edge. At the top of the field, go through the waymarked gate on your left and straight across the field to exit through a gate onto a metalled track. Walk for about 80 metres, passing cottages on your left and turn right at the waymark and continue to the end of the barn on your left. Turn right and walk 30 metres to go via a gate on the left onto the waymarked footpath to Heatherslaw and Letham Hill **(B)**.

Proceed ahead for 50 metres or so then bear left and follow the line of the overhead wires to a telegraph post with a waymark. Bear right as indicated and walk ahead with the wire fence on your left. Carry on past a couple of waymarks then through open country almost surrounded by distant plantations to arrive at a waymarked gate at a field corner. Go through the gate, over the footbridge, up the bank and turn left at the waymark. Walk along the field edge with a wood on your left. At a signpost bear right to proceed towards Letham Hill. Walk ahead with the wood on your left, passing a waymark. Continue on the now broader path, past the sawmill on your right, to emerge onto a road, opposite Errol Hut Smithy and Woodwork Shop, at Letham Hill Cottages **(C)**.

Turn left and proceed along this quiet country road for about 600 metres. On your right, just before you reach a road junction, you pass the wide tree-lined ride leading to Etal Manor where Etal Church is located. At the junction turn right and walk along the pavement for 400 metres or so, with Etal Church visible ahead on the right. At the crossroads, turn right and walk the short distance to the church **(D)**.

After visiting the church, retrace your steps to the crossroads and cross the road into the delightful Etal village. Walk along the village street noticing, or entering, the thatched-roofed Black Bull inn. Ahead are the ruins of Etal Castle.

*Etal Castle, now in the care of English Heritage, was built about 1340 by Sir Robert Manners, who is thought also to have founded a chantry chapel in about 1345 on the banks of the Till nearby. The castle was severely damaged by James IV of Scotland in his ravaging forays in the years before the battle of Flodden Field in 1513. Pevsner (The Buildings of England: Northumberland) considers that "The remains are not generous, yet of great interest".*

Just before you reach the castle, follow the road as it bears to the right at a public footpath sign for Taylor and Green, River Till. As you approach the river, more or less opposite the premises of Taylor and Green furniture-makers, turn right onto the public bridleway to Tindal House. Walk along the narrow path which takes you above the river. There is a waymark indicating that you are now on a circular walk. Continue for 200 metres or so and then turn right to go through a gate with the circular walk waymark. Walk in the direction of the waymark across the field, aiming just to the left of the last white house on the left, to a gate and exit onto a road. Turn right as indicated and walk the short distance to the crossroads at the entrance to Etal village **(E)**.

Retrace your steps along the pavement on the left-hand side for 400 metres to the road on the left that leads to Errol Hut Smithy. Do not turn left, instead carry straight on in the same direction. You need to take care as you walk along this stretch of road for about 800 metres, before turning right at the sign for Heatherslaw Light Railway and Heatherslaw Cornmill. The light railway runs between Heatherslaw and Etal. Walk past the entrance to the railway on your left and cross the bridge to walk to Heatherslaw Mill ahead. This is a working mill, producing over ten tons of flour a year on a site which goes back 1000 years. During the summer months you can visit the mill and take refreshments in the café whose fare includes goodies from the adjacent bakery. Carry on along the metalled road, passing, just after the mill, a sculpture of an otter by David Edwick (1992). Continue along the road, passing The Steward's Cottage and, just past a post box, you come to a footpath on your left to Ford Bridge **(F)**.

Go through the gate and walk ahead for 10 metres then bear left to go through a waymarked gate. Walk diagonally across the field to the waymarked gate in the corner. Go through the gate and walk along the field edge with the river on your left. Continue, past a series of waymarks and gates, as the path follows the line of the river to exit via a gate on your left onto a road. Turn left and, with care, cross Ford Bridge. At the junction turn right and walk along the pavement for 800 metres to Ford Church and the end of the walk.

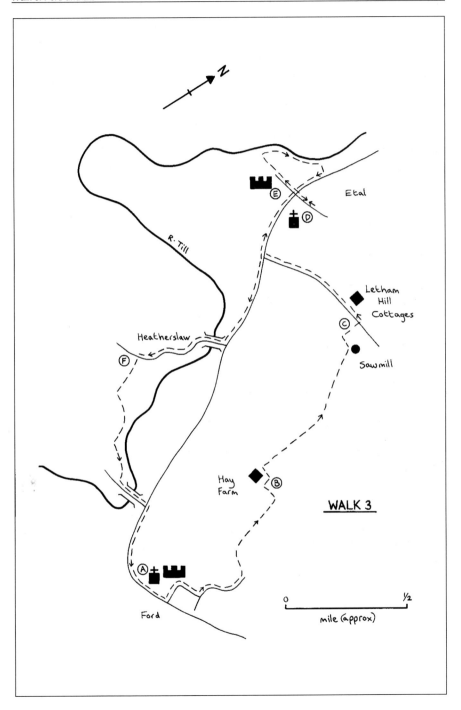

N

Etal

R. Till

Letham
Hill
Cottages

Heatherslaw

Sawmill

Hay
Farm

WALK 3

Ford

0            ½

mile (approx)

# Walk 4: Bamburgh

## *Saint, saver and serpent*

**Location:** St Aidan's Church (NU 179350) is in Bamburgh. Bamburgh is on the coast about 4 miles from the A1, approximately 19 miles from Berwick and 54 miles from Newcastle.

**Distance:** Walk 4(a), Bamburgh and Glororum: 9 miles; Walk 4(b), Bamburgh only: 5 miles.

**Map:** OS Explorer 340: Holy Island & Bamburgh.

**Terrain:** A walk mainly on the level with stretches on a beautiful beach, minor roads and public footpaths.

**Church:** St Aidan.

**Car parking:** A limited amount of street parking is available near the church. There is a large pay and display car park on the Seahouses road just beyond the castle.

## The Church

This is the only ancient church in England dedicated to St Aidan, the first bishop of Lindisfarne (see below). It is in a spacious, exposed position near the impressive bulk of Bamburgh Castle. The church building itself gives an impression of no-nonsense solidity – a sturdy, crenellated west tower together with a flat-roofed nave and a long chancel.

There has been a Christian presence here for over 1300 years but nothing is left of either the mission church built by Aidan in 635 or any subsequent

Anglo-Saxon buildings – although local tradition suggests that a beam in the baptistry is a relic from Aidan's original church. The present building is Norman in origin, dating back to a monastery church built in the late 12th or early 13th century, with 14th and 15th-century additions. Following the Dissolution of the Monasteries in the 16th century the monks were dispersed and the church became the parish church of Bamburgh. Inevitably, over the centuries, a

St Aidan, Bamburgh – a solid presence

great deal of repair and renovation has been necessary, including a major restoration in 1895. Nevertheless, what remains today is mainly a 13th-century church.

A notice on the door is addressed to the "most welcome visitor" and it engenders a feeling of being wanted here. Inside, the church is well organised for visitors. The history of this place is evident in the pillars and arcades dividing the aisles from the nave and, what Pevsner (*The Buildings of England: Northumberland*) considers as its finest piece of architecture, the 13th-century chancel with its attractive choir stalls and stunning ceiling. It is over 18 metres in length and thought to be one of the longest in the country. Throughout the church there are many memorials in the form of tablets, funeral hatchments and stained-glass windows, including several to members of local notable families; in particular the Forsters who had strong connections with Bamburgh.

Overall, there is a feeling of peacefulness, which is enhanced when the sun streams in through the vivid colours of the Netherlands stained-glass windows above the altar at the east end.

### *Among the other features of interest are:*

❖ On the west wall, two large tablets inscribed with the Ten Commandments. Such textual items were introduced by 16th-century reformers who, at a time of increasing literacy, often used them to replace the primitive and colourful medieval wall murals, which they considered superstitious.

❖ In the north aisle, an effigy of Grace Darling (see below).

❖ St Oswald's Chapel in the north aisle. A small panel on the window on the west side gives details of its restoration.

❖ On the north side of the chancel, a simple reminder marking the spot where St Aidan is thought to have died.

❖ A splendid carved Caen stone reredos contrasting with the simplicity of the plain altar.

❖ On the south wall, a stained-glass window depicting 'The joyful song of spring". An explanation of its symbolism is provided.

❖ In the churchyard, to the south-west of the church, the grave of Grace Darling. Her parents and brother are buried close by.

### *Information available in the church:*

❶ *St Aidan's Church Bamburgh*, John Bird.

❶ Hand-held information board.

❶ Booklets relating to local families and events.

*St Aidan (c.600-651) came, in 635, from Iona to Bamburgh, the northern stronghold of King Oswald of Northumbria (see Walk 16, Heavenfield and Wall). He came, at Oswald's request, to convert the people to Christianity. A church was built at Bamburgh but Oswald gave him the island of Lindisfarne (Holy Island) to start his mission. Working mainly in the northern part of*

*Northumbria and usually on foot, he travelled widely to preach and baptise. He founded a monastery on Lindisfarne as well as churches and other monasteries in Northumbria but also sent missionaries to the other ancient kingdoms throughout the land. Firmly rooted in the Celtic tradition, he lived mostly in poverty, seeking Lentern solitude on Inner Farne Island and encouraging the laity to include fasting and meditation in their Christian observance.*

*Grace Darling (1815- 1842) and her father's story of the gallant rescue of nine people from the wreck of the Forfarshire in 1838 is told in the Museum opposite the church. Grace came from a family of lighthouse keepers. She died of tuberculosis aged only 26. One happier outcome of this sad event was that the national publicity following the rescue led to improvements in the inspection system for ships.*

# The Walks
## Walk 4(a), Bamburgh and Glororum: 9 miles

Leave the church and grounds **(A)** and walk down Church Street towards Bamburgh Castle.

*Bamburgh Castle occupies a natural defensive site – high up on an outcrop of the Whin Sill – and overlooking the sea. Saxon kings of Northumbria made this place their northern stronghold. The present building is Norman and suffered much from siege and warfare. It was given to the Forster family in the 17th century and was bought by Lord Crewe (see Walk 22, Blanchland) in 1704. It was later much altered and restored by Lord Armstrong (see Walk 10, Rothbury) who bought it in 1890.*

Before reaching the castle go onto the path round the cricket field, walk past the pavilion and turn left below the castle walls. Follow the direction of a waymark to walk through the grassy area to arrive at a small car park.

Over the sea to your left is Holy Island. Go onto the beach and turn right to walk on the firm sand, with the massive walls of Bamburgh Castle on your right. The walk continues along the sands for the next two miles. Carry on, now with high dunes on your right and views of the Farne Islands on the left. The nearest island, with the white tower, is Inner Farne. Inland, in the dunes to the right, a coastguard lookout comes into view and ahead, spread across the sands, are Greenhill Rocks. From the beginning of the rocky area, walk the remaining 1,000 metres on the sand and/or rocks until you arrive at the cottages at Monks House **(B)**.

Cross the water flowing to the sea from the Clashope Burn. Turn right and go through dunes to reach the corner of a fence. Follow the line of the fence, with properties on your right, to reach a road. Across the road, just to the left of the bus stop, go into the field at a point just to the right of a burn. Follow the line of the Clashope Burn, keeping the fence and burn on your left, until you come to a T-junction of minor roads just to the right of a farm cottage **(C)**.

Turn right and walk along the minor road. Carry on as it bears left and passes Saddlershall. The road bends to the right towards Fowberry, but you need to

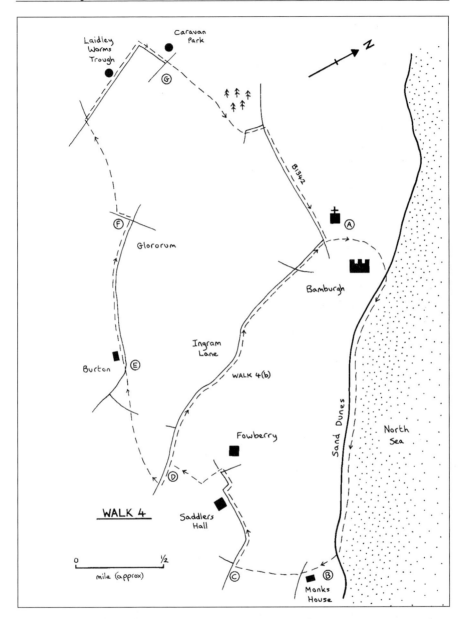

turn left onto the public footpath to "Ingram Lane ½ mile". Through the gate turn left as indicated by the waymark and, keeping the hedge on your left, proceed to the field boundary. Take a 90-degree turn to follow the field edge to arrive at a concrete pill-box. Go past the pill-box to emerge onto Ingram Lane **(D)**.

Turn left and go along this minor road for a few hundred metres until you reach the public footpath sign "Burton ¾" on your right (this is opposite the road to New Shoreston). Leave the minor road, cross the stile and, bearing right as indicated by the fingerpost, head diagonally to the corner of the field. Go over the stile into the next field and, continuing in the same direction, walk towards a public footpath sign on the field edge. This is to the left of the copse of trees on the skyline. Exit from this field via a stile, cross the road and go into the next field, and cross in a diagonal line making for the rooftops visible on the left. The footpath comes out onto a road. Exit via a waymarked gate and turn right to proceed to Burton **(E)**.

Keep on this road, ignoring farm tracks and footpath signs. After about 1,000 metres, the road is crossed by a public footpath with a sign for "Bamburgh 1¼" to the right. Continue on the road for 500 metres until you reach crossroads at Glororum **(F)**.

Turn left in the direction of Newcastle. Just after the last house on the right, go through the gate to take the public footpath. Ahead is a caravan park – aim for a point to the left of this. Continue past the corner of the fence in the direction of the footpath sign to reach the field corner. Go through the gate, follow the footpath to the right, and go along the field edge with the fence on your left. At the corner turn left to follow the hedge, go through the gate and up the slope to emerge at a junction. Turn sharp right and follow the road as it gradually climbs. Where the road reaches its high point, before the entrance to Waren caravan park, there is a small escarpment on the left and just beyond this there is a slight depression known as the "Laidley Worm's Trough" (see below). Follow the road past the entrance to the caravan park. At the T-junction turn left, and after a few metres come to a rough stone stile with a public footpath sign for "Bamburgh 1½ miles" **(G)**.

*The Laidley Worm (= loathsome serpent) is one of the north country legends involving someone being turned into a huge serpent and, subsequently, being rescued. In this case, a 6th-century princess of Bamburgh, whose brother saved her by kissing the serpent three times.*

Cross the stile and walk ahead keeping the field edge on your right. At the end of the field go over a stile. Follow the line of the plantation, keeping to the right of the trees, and descend to cross a waymarked stile. Continue ahead keeping to the right of the shrubs as you cross the field to exit via a stile onto a minor road. Turn left and almost immediately turn right onto the B1342, Make use of the generous verges as you walk for about 800 metres back to Bamburgh, the church and the end of the walk.

### Walk 4(b), Bamburgh only: 5 miles

Follow the directions for Walk 4(a) as far as **(D)**. Turn right and walk for about 1½ miles back to Bamburgh, the church and the end of the walk.

# Walk 5: Embleton and Craster

*Creighton, castle and fishy catch*

**Location:** Holy Trinity Church (NU231225) is at Embleton on the B1339 about 8 miles from the A1 and Alnwick.

**Distance:** Walk 5(a), Embleton and Craster: 6½ miles; Walk 5(b), Embleton only: 2½ miles.

**Map:** OS Explorer 332: Alnwick & Amble.

**Terrain:** Both walks are on the level with sections on the beach. Walk 5(a) includes about 1½ miles on minor roads.

**Churches:** Holy Trinity, Embleton; St Peter the Fisherman, Craster.

**Car parking:** There is limited parking outside the church or by the Creighton Memorial Hall opposite.

## The Churches

### Holy Trinity, Embleton

Holy Trinity, Embleton, with its ornamental tower

Holy Trinity Church lies in a neat churchyard just off the road at the south entrance to the small village of Embleton, a short distance from the coast. The church owes its origins to the creation of a Norman barony, belonging at one time to Simon de Montfort. In 1274 the patronage of the church was granted to Merton College, Oxford, a connection that has been very beneficial, especially through contributions to the alterations and restoration work carried out over the centuries. Being close to the Scottish border the church was attacked and damaged on a number of occasions. So, in 1395, the adjacent pele tower (now converted into a private residence) was erected to provide some protection for the minister and his flock.

The most notable external feature of the church is the

upper part of the tower with its rather unusual ornamental parapet and small pinnacles. Entrance to the church is by the south-west porch, above which is a niche containing an interesting modern sculpture, *The Trinity* (1999), by Christopher Hall of Jedburgh. The general appearance of the interior of the building is light and airy, with an abundance of attractive, well-dressed yellow and pink stone. The nave arcades are marked with an attractive dog-tooth decoration and there are several decorative figureheads and niches.

However, what you now see is the result of many changes, and little, apart from the lower stage of the tower and the arcades in the nave, survives from the 13th-century church. And although substantial alterations were made in the mid-19th century, some of them by John Dobson (see Walk 14, Whalton and Meldon), the chancel continues to preserve a marked slant to the north, believed to be based on the inclination of the head of Christ on the cross.

Two families of particular importance to the church have their own memorial corners. The "Grey Gallery", in the north-west aisle, contains several wall tablets which recall the lives and the travels of the Grey family, notably Sir Edward Grey (1862-1933), whose life story is told in *Embleton Eminences* available in the church. In the north-east aisle, the "Craster Porch", contains wall tablets of this other noted local family, the Crasters. Entry is beneath the low 14th-century arch, above which are two hatchments of Shafto Craster (died 1837).

Although Holy Trinity houses many fine tributes to the great and the good, it remains in essence a pleasant parish church and a place in which to find peace and purpose.

### Among the other features of interest are:

❖ The west window, commemorating the Coronation of Elizabeth II in 1952 and recalling the granting of the patronage of the church to Merton College in 1274.

❖ The window in the north wall by Leonard Evetts (see Walk 12, Bolam and Hartburn) dedicated to a former vicar from Merton College.

❖ The stained-glass windows in the chancel and sanctuary in memory of Sir George Grey, by Kempe (see Walk 15, Simonburn). There is a helpful explanation of the symbolism of the windows by the side of the memorial on the south wall of the chancel.

❖ The tablet on the south wall of the chancel arch in memory of Mandell Creighton, vicar from 1875 to 1884. A bronze bust of him stands in the Grey Gallery in the north-west corner. His distinguished academic and ecclesiastical career is recounted in a leaflet available in the church.

❖ The attractive Mothers' Union banner on the wall of the south aisle showing a Celtic cross, three fishes representing The Trinity and the three castles of the coat of arms of the Diocese of Newcastle.

## Information available in the church:

❶ *A history of Embleton parish church*, Oswin Craster.

❶ A leaflet, *Embleton Eminences*, AMM.

❶ A leaflet, *Mandell Creighton Vicar of Embleton 1875-1884.*

### St Peter the Fisherman, Craster

This is a small, plain, stone church surrounded by cottages and houses in the fishing and holiday village of Craster. The Crasters of nearby Craster Tower trace their lineage back to the 12th century and, while they worshipped over the centuries in Holy Trinity Church at Embleton, they decided to save the villagers the need for the journey there by building a mission church. The church was built in memory of Thomas Wood Craster who is remembered in the stonework above the entrance porch and also on a brass plaque inside on the south wall. The Bishop of Newcastle dedicated the church to St Peter the Fisherman on the centenary of the church in 1977.

The interior is as simple as the exterior. It is a single-chamber building with dark pews surrounded by pine panelling with pine screens on either side of the sanctuary. Although the church is generally locked outside of service times, the key is readily available at the village shop and post office that you pass en route, near the Jolly Fisherman pub. It is certainly well-worthwhile visiting this lovingly cared for little church.

The simple interior of St Peter the Fisherman, Craster (with kind permission from the vicar)

*Among the other features of interest are:*

❖ A plaque on the north wall which recalls the tragic death of a young man.

❖ The sanctuary screens, the war memorials and rolls of honour which provide much evidence of the participation and sacrifice of relatively large numbers of local people from this small community.

❖ The stained-glass window in the south wall, the last window by Leonard Evetts (see Walk 12, Bolam and Hartburn), assisted by his wife Phyl, a very short time before his death in 1997. An adjacent information board provides a detailed explanation of what is reputed to be one of his finest works.

# The Walks

## Walk 5(a), Embleton and Craster: 6½ miles

Leave the churchyard by the main gate **(A)**, cross the road with care and turn left. Walk along the pavement passing the Dunstanburgh Castle Hotel and the school. After the 30 mile per hour de-restriction sign and a lay-by, leave the road via the stone stile on the right **(B)**.

The right of way is straight across the field towards the sea. When you reach the fence bear left to the corner and then turn right as indicated by the waymark. Proceed down the side of the field with the fence on your right, to where a fence ahead meets a stone wall. Cross the stone stile and continue straight ahead. When the fence on your right disappears, continue ahead on a raised path between two fields. A broken wall appears on your left and the village of Low Newton-by-the-Sea is visible ahead on the left. You pass the perimeter fence of the Newton Pool Nature Reserve on your left and then the edge of Dunstanburgh Castle Golf Course on your right. Watch out for flying golf balls and wait if play is in progress nearby. Just beyond a Golf Club noticeboard, you arrive at a junction of paths **(C)**.

Turn right and follow the clear path as it skirts the golf course and climbs towards some cabins. Here, depending on the state of the tide, you can either walk along the beach towards the castle or proceed along the top of the sand dunes. However, the National Trust prefers that you use the beach route wherever possible, in order to protect the dunes and the flora. There are several ways between the cabins to the beach but again you should follow the routes indicated by signs directing you to "steps to beach". Once on the beach continue along the sands in the direction of the castle until you reach what is known as The Skaith, where the Embleton Burn flows across the beach out to the sea **(D)**.

Assuming it is possible, cross the burn and continue ahead along the beach. (Generally, the burn is easily crossed; however, if it is high tide or in flood then bear right and follow the burn to a footbridge. Do not cross this bridge, but instead continue for about another 150 metres to a second footbridge. Cross here, bear right and proceed on the path through the dunes

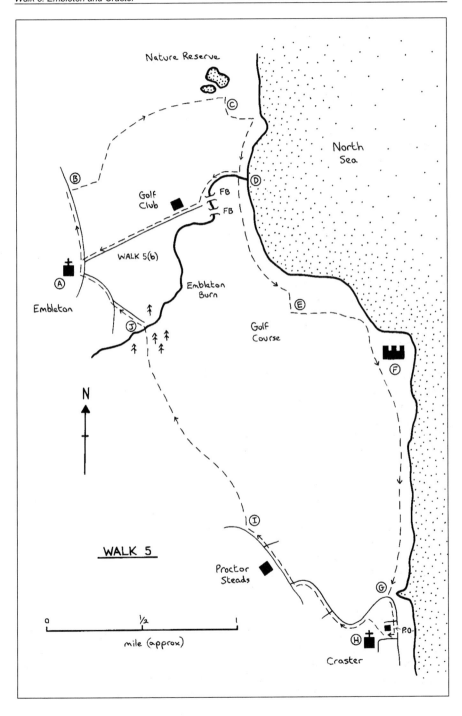

Nature Reserve

North Sea

© C

® B

Golf Club

FB

FB

© D

WALK 5(b)

© A

Embleton

Embleton Burn

© E

Golf Course

© F

© J

N

© I

WALK 5

Proctor Steads

© G

0        ½        1

mile (approx)

© H

P.O.

Craster

back to the beach). Shortly after the appearance of some substantial volcanic rocks, about 100 metres before the end of the beach with the ruins of Dunstanburgh Castle looming ahead, bear right to leave the beach and climb up to the top of the dunes near some short sections of fencing **(E)**.

Now continue along the dunes with the golf course on your right. You will see a fine example of the Whin Sill, the ridge of rock which traverses Northumberland. Then after passing through a kissing gate, you leave the golf course behind. Keep to the lower path which makes its way below the castle following the waymarks, unless you wish to make a detour to visit Dunstanburgh Castle on your left **(F)**.

> *Dunstanburgh Castle (a National Trust property maintained and managed by English Heritage) was built in the 14$^{th}$ century, probably on the site of an Iron Age fort. Unlike many of the other local castles it has not been subject to rebuilding since it fell into decay as early as the 16$^{th}$ century. Its stark, abandoned appearance, silhouetted against the skyline, evokes its place in history in the Anglo-Scottish conflicts and in the Wars of the Roses.*

Follow the path as it winds beyond the castle towards the sea to go through a kissing gate. Now you can continue straight ahead on the clear path and enjoy the coastal views along this popular route until you eventually meet a road above the harbour at the village of Craster **(G)**.

Bear left and walk along the road, passing the harbour with its lobster pots, Robsons' famous kipper-curing factory and restaurant and The Jolly Fisherman pub. The village shop and post office is a little further ahead on the right. Call in here and collect the key for St Peter the Fisherman's Church, which is about 100 metres beyond the shop on the first road on the right **(H)**.

After visiting the church and returning the key, walk about 50 metres back towards the harbour and take the first street on the left. Turn right at the junction, cross the gravelled access road and bear left down the narrow track. You need to exit onto the main road, either after visiting the welcoming Bark Pots Tea Room which appears on your right, or some 100 metres further on, at the Tourist Information Office. Cross the road with care and turn left. Now proceed along the pavement to pass a stone sculpture erected in 2001, reflecting the significance locally of the crab and the lobster. Ignore footpaths that go off on either side, as well as the road on the left to Alnwick, Longhoughton and Howick, and instead continue ahead for about 800 metres to a T-junction at which you turn right for Embleton. Walk along this minor road passing Proctor Steads Caravan and Camping Park and (about 150 metres beyond a sign for the cycle route to Embleton) leave the road to go through a gate on the right next to a public footpath sign "Dunstan Steads 1½ Embleton 1¾" **(I)**.

Walk straight ahead on the broad, green track and bear right at the end of the track to go over a waymarked stile. Turn left and walk round the perimeter of the field with a wire fence and a hedgerow on your left until you reach a gate. Go through the gate and continue ahead towards the wood. Cross the waymarked stile into the wood, go over the footbridge and bear right. Keep on the clear path with the burn on your right and, after about 300 metres, at the edge of the wood bear left to leave via a waymarked stile next to a gate. Follow the faint path across the field to take a stile next to a gate. Continue on the path as it descends to the diagonally opposite corner of the field with the Embleton Burn on your left. Go through the gate, turn left, immediately go through another gate, cross the footbridge and then exit onto a lane at Shirewater Low Mill **(J)**.

Turn left and proceed up the lane to the T-junction. Bear right, cross the road and follow the pavement, as it passes some cottages and accompanies the road via the Blue Bell Inn and the Creighton Memorial Hall, back to the church and the end of the walk.

## Walk 5(b), Embleton only: 2½ miles

Follow Walk 5(a) as far as The Skaith where the Embleton Burn flows across the beach out to the sea **(D)**.

Do not cross the burn but instead bear right and follow the burn to a footbridge. Do not cross this first footbridge but continue for about another 150 metres as far as a second footbridge. Again, do not cross the footbridge, but instead turn right and follow the path past the golf course clubhouse (open to visitors for refreshments) and onto a lane that leads you back into Embleton at the Dunstanburgh Castle Hotel. Turn left and walk a few hundred metres back to the church and the end of the walk.

# Walk 6: Eglingham and Old Bewick

*Archdeacon's base, open space and old place*

**Location:** St Maurice's Church (NU106195) is in Eglingham, which is on the B6346 7 miles north-west of Alnwick.

**Distance:** Walk 6(a), Eglingham and Old Bewick: 10 miles; Walk 6(b), Eglingham only: 3 miles.

**Map:** OS Explorer 332: Alnwick & Amble.

**Terrain:** Mainly on undulating open moorland and field paths with three short sections on country roads.

**Churches:** St Maurice, Eglingham; Holy Trinity, Old Bewick.

**Car parking:** In the lane outside the church.

## The Churches

### St Maurice, Eglingham

The 13th-century west tower of St Maurice, Eglingham

This church is located in its well-maintained churchyard at the end of a lane in the quiet village of Eglingham. There has been a church here for over 1200 years. A Saxon church was built following the gift of land at Eglingham to the monastery at Lindisfarne by the Northumbrian king, Ceolwulf, when he became a monk there. However, virtually nothing remains of either this or the Norman church which succeeded it. What is now seen is a sturdy 13th-century west tower, no doubt providing a useful retreat for the villagers in times of Border raids, together with a nave and chancel and various extensions from different periods. The nave and chancel were completely rebuilt in the 17th century following their virtual destruction in 1596 by an invading Scottish army. Victorian additions include the south transept, and the porch and vestry on the north side. Quite a mixture but everything blends together to produce an attractive country church. Pevsner (*The Buildings of England: Northumberland*) provides an apposite summing up: "much restored but picturesque".

Interesting items can also be seen inside the church. Entrance is through the north-west porch, where a gravestone with skull and crossbones and other relics are displayed. The nave leads through a simple arch to a fairly long chancel with a wooden-boarded ceiling and a nicely proportioned east window. There are many memorials here, principally to members of three prominent local families and to past vicars, many of whom served as Archdeacon of Lindisfarne (see below).

In the south transept are many tablets in memory of the Carr-Ellison family as well as their box pews. The Ogle family (see Walk 14, Whalton and Meldon), once Lords of the Manor of Eglingham, is remembered by the designation of the tiny north transept as the "Ogle Pew" and under which is the Ogle Vault. Another vault, the Collingwood Vault, is under the chancel. Admiral Collingwood who fought with Nelson at Trafalgar is the most famous member of the family although he himself is not buried here.

### Among the other features of interest are:

❖ The octagonal, stone font of 1663.

❖ A wall plaque near the tower setting out information about a young soldier in whose memory the steeple was built.

❖ At the end of the south transept, the Lady Chapel. A grave slab on the south wall, in memory of the minister of a Dissenting Congregation and his wife and children, represents a true act of charity by the incumbent at that time.

❖ On the south wall of the sanctuary, a modern stained-glass window commemorating members of the Collingwood family, by the Glasgow designer Gordon Webster.

❖ The east window, with its restrained colouring, depicting the Resurrection.

### Information available in the church:

❶ An information board in the porch.

❶ A leaflet, *St Maurice, Eglingham*.

> *Archdeacons are appointed to assist a diocesan bishop. By the 1830s, demographic changes made it necessary to establish a new archdeaconry (Lindisfarne) to oversee the north part of the area previously covered by the Archdeacon of Northumberland (an ancient title dating back to the 13th century). From 1842 to 1980, Eglingham's vicar served as Archdeacon of Lindisfarne. Presumably Eglingham was chosen because it had a convenient location, adequate accommodation and a vicar who would be able to devote the necessary time to his wider responsibilities.*

## Holy Trinity, Old Bewick

This old church is tucked away at the end of a country lane in its wooded churchyard, by the side of the aptly named Kirk Burn. It is a quiet, peaceful place and it is easy to agree with the traditional belief that this has been a place of Christian worship since Saxon times. From the outside you see an essentially Norman style building, a low nave and a lower chancel, but the larger blocks in the lower courses of the north and west walls appear to be Anglo-Saxon, while the upper parts of the walls and the roof are Victorian. These structural differences reflect the rebuilding that has taken place over centuries. According to tradition, much of this was to repair damage caused by invading Scottish armies in the late-13th and mid-17th centuries. In the 1860s, after the church had stood in a roofless and ruinous state for more than 150 years, Mr J.C. Langlands had the church restored. This major but sensitive renovation enabled the church to be reopened for services in 1867.

The essentially Norman "feeling" is continued inside, with the nave leading through the chancel arch with its decorated capitals; the one on the north side having two crudely depicted grinning faces, possibly representations of a pre-Christian deity. A similar arch leads into the sanctuary. From inside, the sanctuary is seen as a semi-circular apse but, from the outside, it has been squared off to conform to a later architectural style. The apse makes an attractive focal point. Its decorated ceiling, above bare stone walls, contrasts with the wooden ceilings in the nave and chancel and the stained glass of the small Norman window draws the eye to the east end and the small reredos and altar.

Holy Trinity, Old Bewick – Norman in essence

This old church with its one metre thick lower walls and other reminders of its antiquity remains a place of worship with a welcome for visitors and pilgrims.

### Among the other features of interest are:

❖ In the south-west corner a picture of the church in its ruinous state in 1826. From this the extent of the 1860s restoration can be gauged.

❖ The drum-shaped font.

❖ On the south side of the chancel arch, three plaques recalling J.C.Langlands, his wife and son and two other relatives.

❖ On the north side of the chancel, an effigy of a lady in 14th-century costume. This might be from sculptors who had a workshop in Alnwick until about 1340.

### Information available in the church:

❶ Information board in the church porch.

❶ Information folder.

❶ A leaflet, *Holy Trinity, Old Bewick*.

## The Walks

### Walk 6(a), Eglingham and Old Bewick: 10 miles

Leave the grounds of Eglingham Church (**A**) by the gate at the north end and walk up the lane to the junction with the road through the village. Cross over the road, turn left and walk the few metres to a narrow road on your right. There is a "no through road" sign here. Turn right and walk up the steep road passing woods on the left. Where the woods end, there are fingerposts on both sides of the road. The route you follow is to the left, as indicated by the sign "Harehope 1¼". However, before proceeding you might like to stand on the right-hand side of the road, beyond the hedge, and look back over the fields to gain an appreciation of the sheltered and secluded position occupied by Eglingham at the bottom of the hill. Now, go through the gate to walk on the bridleway to Harehope and come to a waymarked metal gate. The Cheviot Hills come into view ahead. Follow the track as it bears to the right and goes through a metal gate and then towards a stone wall, with a plantation beyond the wall. When you reach the wall go through the gate (**B**).

Follow the grassy track as it bears to the left, initially running parallel to the wall which is about 50 metres over to your left. Proceed down the hill as the track winds its way to a waymarked gate and go over a footbridge. Walk up the slope and follow the line of the stone wall on your left as it heads towards Harehope Farm in front of you. Go through two waymarked metal gates and walk to a junction with another track (**C**).

Turn right and go through the metal gate and up the farm track to a waymarked metal gate in the stone wall on your left. Go through the gate.

Turn right and walk parallel to the wall on your right to the waymark post ahead. Keep on the path as it follows the line of the fence on the right for about 100 metres and then cuts across to the left, to the other side of the depression. The fence on the right is now higher above you and there is the line of an old wall above you on the left. Ahead is a footbridge and the rutted track winds its way there via a waymark post. Cross the bridge and look for a better defined path which goes slightly left and follow this as it goes towards the left- hand edge of the line of trees ahead. Bear round the trees on your right to reach a stile which has blue and yellow waymarks set into the step. Cross the stile into the flat, open area **(D)**.

You need to go straight ahead over the wide, fairly featureless ground. The path is indistinct and there are several boggy sections to be negotiated. Looking ahead, there are hills on both sides with a small hilly area in the middle, which you aim for. As you near its high point, you will pick up a more defined path. Follow this as it carries on in the same direction. The path eventually heads, via a number of waymark posts, towards the ruins of Blawearie. Just before Blawearie you reach a track descending from the ruined farmhouse. Turn left onto the broad track and follow this. In 200 metres or so you come to what appears to be the ruins of a sheepfold, but is actually an ancient burial site, up a little rise on your right **(E)**.

Continue on the track as it descends past a kissing gate next to a metal gate To the left above are the tree-topped heights of Hanging Crag. Carry on to another metal gate **(F)**. Go through the gate and proceed down the track as it descends quite steeply. Immediately after a metal gate, just before you reach the cottages at Old Bewick, there is a public footpath sign next to a gate on the right "Bewick Folly ¾" **(G)**.

The walk goes over the field to the church. However, if conditions are not suitable, you may choose to follow an alternative route by continuing ahead to the road. You then turn right to walk a short distance along the road until a sign directs you to Old Bewick Church.

To continue the walk from **(G)**, go through the gate and walk in the direction of the fingerpost towards the third telegraph post in the field. Continue ahead to make for the left-hand corner of the plantation. Descend to a ladder stile. Cross the stile. You are now in the church grounds. Turn immediately to the left to walk along the path adjacent to the wall on your left. In a few metres turn right, cross the stream by the stone footbridge and walk the short distance to the church **(H)**.

After your visit, leave the church and turn right to walk to the gate leading to a narrow road. Walk along this road to a junction where there is a Celtic cross, erected in 1874 in memory of Mr J. C. Langlands. Turn left and walk the few hundred metres to the hamlet of Old Bewick. Take the public footpath on the left to "Blawearie 1½, Quarry House 3½". Walk past the houses to come to a metal gate. Go through the gate and walk up the well-defined path to arrive at a metal gate, which you passed earlier at **(F)**.

Go through the gate and turn right with a stone wall on your right. Walk

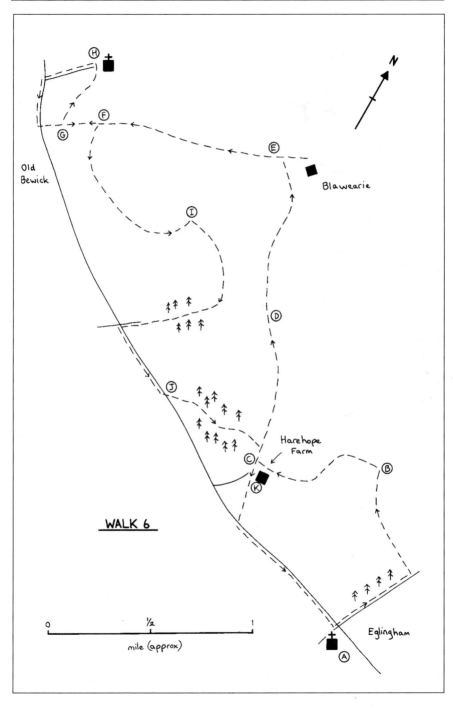

Old Bewick

Blawearie

Harehope Farm

WALK 6

Eglingham

0 ½ 1
mile (approx)

along the track which leads to an open area with several gates. Continue ahead through a metal gate and follow the track as it bears left to skirt the hill above. The track starts to climb and you pass a wood on your right. Keep on the track as it continues to follow the line of the hill. It can be very boggy here. In May and June there is a blaze of colour from the rhododendrons on this hill. As you come to the end of the hill and the end of the rhododendrons, about 100 metres before the stone wall ahead, bear left and climb steeply to find another track making for the stone wall coming up from your right. When you reach the wall, go beyond the stepped corner to come to a small wooden gate **(I)**.

Go through the gate and proceed straight ahead following the line of the fence on your right. After about 400 metres there is a waymark on a fence post and the fence turns to the right. You need to continue straight ahead for about 50 metres, then bear right onto another path. This path runs parallel to the fence over to your right for a few metres, then meanders somewhat as it descends to rejoin the fence at the bottom of the hill by a gate. Go through the gate and follow the broad track towards the woods ahead. Enter the woods by the gate and walk down the path to come out at a metalled road. Walk down the road to a junction, turn left and walk along this busier road for about 600 metres to a public footpath sign on the left **(J)**.

Enter the woods and follow the faint path as it climbs to the right. The path passes two trees with overhanging branches and skirts an area of newly planted trees in their protective tubes. At the highest point of the newly planted area go straight up to join the main woodland path. Turn right and walk to the end of the wood. Leaving the trees, bear left to go uphill and arrive at a metal gate near to the corner of a stone wall. Turn right and then almost immediately left to proceed to climb up the track, close to the wall on your right. Follow the track as it bears right then descends to a waymarked gate. Go through the gate, turn right and walk, via a further waymarked gate, past the farm cottages and barns on your left. Carry on in the same direction to reach a public footpath sign on the left, just past the farmhouse **(K)**.

Go through the gate and go across the paddock to a gate in the opposite corner. Go through the gate and bear right to walk along the top of the ridge. Continue in the same direction until the path descends gradually to a gate leading onto a road. Go through the gate. This is one of the main roads into Eglingham, so take care as you turn left and walk 800 metres to the village, the church and the end of the walk.

### Walk 6(b), Eglingham only: 3 miles

Follow Walk 6(a) as far as **(C)**. Turn left and walk to a public footpath sign on the left just past the farmhouse. Follow the directions from **(K)** back to Eglingham, the church and the end of the walk.

# Walk 7: Ingram and Alnham

## *Park, pele and plateau*

**Location:** St Michael's Church (NU019163) is in Ingram. Ingram is 45 miles north-west of Newcastle on a minor road off the A697.

**Distance:** Walk 7(a), Ingram, Prendwick and Alnham: 10 miles; Walk 7(b), Ingram only: 4 miles.

**Map:** OS Outdoor Leisure 16: The Cheviot Hills.

**Terrain:** Walk 7(a) is mainly on gently undulating tracks through open country with several steady climbs; there are two sections on quiet country roads. Walk 7(b) is on tracks through open country and includes one steady ascent and descent.

**Churches:** St Michael, Ingram; St Michael and All Angels, Alnham.

**Car parking:** In one of two Northumberland National Park car parks at Ingram.

## The Churches

### St Michael, Ingram

This church is in the secluded hamlet of Ingram in the beautiful Breamish Valley. The church is close by the Northumberland National Park Information Centre, a reminder that tourism as well as farming plays an important part in the economy of this unspoilt rural area. Entry to the churchyard is through the lych-gate, built in 1928 as a First World War memorial. The church is an attractive, grey, stone building, quite compact with its west

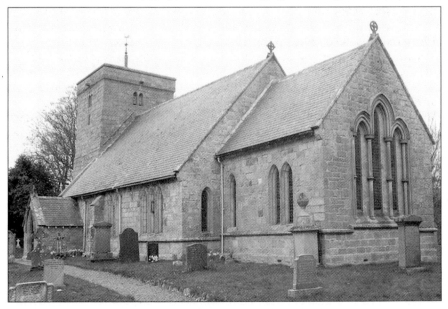

St Michael, Ingram and its rebuilt Norman tower

tower and separate nave and chancel, the former being the longer and wider of the two. Some kind of church building has stood on this site for more than 1,000 years but, in common with many ancient churches, what is now seen is the result of centuries of rebuilding and remodelling. The nave and chancel are mainly the result of a complete renovation in the 1870s, while the Norman tower was rebuilt in 1885 using the original stones in their original order.

Once you are inside the church, the existence of aisles accounts for the nave being wider than the chancel. The 13th-century arcades with sturdy octagonal columns and pointed arches are impressive. Unusually, the bays nearest to the chancel are supported by substantial rectangular stone bases. It is difficult to untangle the reasons for these, and other, architectural curiosities. They do not detract from the overall effect of solidity (and give the experts something to argue about).

The church guide describes the days of glory of the church as being around 1300, when Ingram, though held as a plurality, nevertheless "must have been something of a prize to attract the attention of such high placed ecclesiastics" such as William Reginald, who became Archbishop of Canterbury and Lord Chancellor of England. Today, St Michael's might still be seen as being prized, but now, like many similar churches, for continuing to provide a ministry to the local community and visitors.

### *Among the other features of interest are:*

❖ The font from 1662 which has a wide pedestal carved with the arms of local families.

❖ The low, wide arch between the tower and the nave; its squat supporting pillars slope outwards, presenting another curiosity.

❖ On the north wall of the sanctuary, a memorial tablet commemorating a tragic accident.

### *Information available in the church:*

❶ *St Michael's Church Ingram, The Story*, A.C. de P. Hay.

## St Michael and All Angels, Alnham

This church is near the little hamlet of Alnham, the centre of a geographically large parish consisting of a scattering of farms and cottages. Just west of the church is Alnham Tower, a former vicar's pele – a high tower constructed with thick walls. This was the vicarage for several centuries but has now been nicely converted into a private residence. It is probable that the church dates back to about 1200 but little is known of its history before the Reformation.

The building seen today is mostly the result of a major restoration carried out in 1870, which incorporated earlier work including parts of the 13th-century nave. It was in a bad state of repair after the Second World War with the roof open to the skies in several places. Over the last 50 years, the small con-

The porch at St Michael and All Angels, Alnham

gregation and local benefactors have provided funds for several repair and renewal programmes.

It is a small, simple building but is complete with a nave with bellcote, lower chancel, a south transept and porch. Unlike Ingram church, there is no tower – the vicar's pele would presumably have served as a defensive retreat in times of Border incursions. The overall simplicity is reflected inside, where there are exposed beams, stone walls and windows of plain glass in the traditional Northumbrian style. From the nave, an arch leads into the south transept and an arch on the north side indicates that there was once a north transept. Through the 12th-century chancel arch, three steps lead up to the long, narrow chancel.

St Michael and All Angels is not so much a "pretty-pretty" church, but rather a simple down-to-earth place serving the needs of a widespread parish in this lonely part of Northumberland.

### Among the other features of interest are:

❖ The small stone octagonal font dated 1664. The Percy coat of arms reflects the fact that the family have long been patrons of the church.

❖ On the north wall, the Alnham Roll of Honour, showing the names of seven who died and nineteen who served in World War I. A poignant reminder of the sacrifice made by a small community.

❖ Outside, to the east of the porch near the south wall, the grave of Gustave Adolph Renwick, who funded a major restoration in 1953, and his wife, with an affectionate dedication.

### Information available in the church:

❶ *The Church of St Michael and All Angels, Alnham.*

# The Walks

## Walk 7(a), Ingram, Prendwick and Alnham: 10 miles

Leave the church and grounds by the lych-gate **(A)** at the east end, near to the National Park information centre. Turn right and follow the road as it bears right. After about 100 metres, just beyond the bend, go through the gate on the left onto the footpath. Follow the track up the hill, with a fence on your left and go over a waymarked stile. The path bears right and then left and climbs to another stile. Go over this stile and carry on the track as it enters more open country, with a valley and hills on your left. The path eventually reaches a waymark post showing a permissive footpath to the right **(B)**.

At the permissive footpath sign, take the left-hand fork. Proceed along the well-defined track. Go over the stile and carry on in the same direction to another stile with some trees about 150 metres to your left. The path descends and runs parallel to a wood on your left. Go through the gate and follow the path to emerge, via a gate, onto a road **(C)**.

Turn right to walk through the hamlet of Prendwick. Follow the road sign to walk in the direction of Alnham for just over a mile. At Alnham take the road to the right, signposted to the church. Walk up the road for several hundred metres to arrive at the church on the right-hand side **(D)**.

After visiting the church, leave by the lych-gate, turn right and walk along the road for about 75 metres to a track on the right. There is a public bridleway sign indicating "Shank House 3, Low Bleakhope 5". Go through the gate and follow the track as it goes uphill with a stone wall on your left. Go through a waymarked gate and carry on between the stone wall and the trees. The path continues its steady and boggy climb for 800 metres or so. You go through a waymarked gate and continue ahead with trees now on your left. Where a field boundary comes in from the right, go through the gate. Turn half right and walk diagonally across the field making for a red stony vehicle track. The path you are on joins the vehicle track at a waymark sign **(E)**.

Turn left and keep to this track for the next two miles or so. The track meanders somewhat, but there are some long straight sections. You reach a metal gate with a public bridleway sign. Go through the gate and carry on in the same direction. The walk is on the level and it is almost like being on a plateau with a feeling of being on top of the world. The track passes a sheepfold over to the left and winds its way to reach a metal gate with the corner of a wood on the left. Go through the gate and keep on the path. Chesters comes into view and the path arrives at a metal gate just to the left of the farmhouse **(F)**.

Go through the gate, leave the track and walk around the farm buildings, keeping them on your right, and walk down the field to a metal gate in the corner. Go through the gate, turn left and walk straight ahead with the fence and wall on your left. At the corner of the fence/stone wall turn half right and

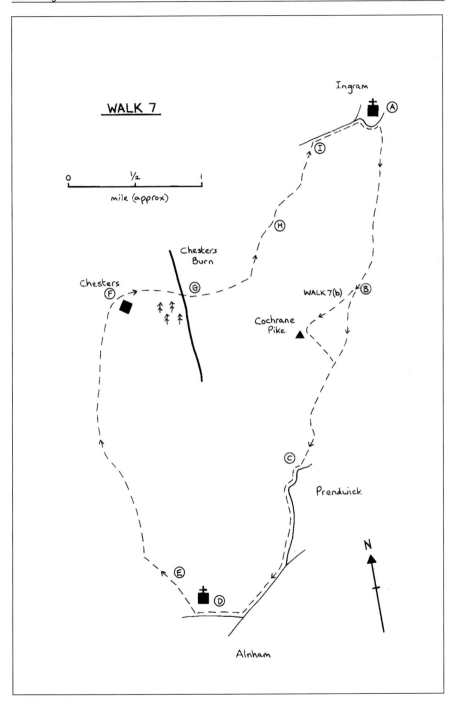

walk towards the trees ahead, aiming for the middle of the forest. Keep to the left of the drainage stream running through the field, to arrive at a small wooden gate indicating "Public bridleway only". Go through the gate into the forest and descend between the trees. Cross the Chesters Burn at a convenient point and make your way to a gate concealed behind bushes **(G)**.

Go through the gate and walk uphill for 10 metres, then turn to the right to go along the path as it runs parallel to the forest fence on your right. Follow the path as it bears left away from the forest, with a craggy hill on your left. Do not go off to the right towards the ruin of a sheepfold. In a short while, you pass a post with a waymark sign, then another post. Continue ahead, bearing slightly right, to follow a series of waymarks. Eventually a line of trees appears and you need to aim for the left-hand corner of them. Walk towards the gate to the left of the line of trees. Just before this gate there is a waymark post with blue and yellow signs. Go over the stile next to the gate and walk towards another stile and gate to the left of the stone wall ahead **(H)**.

After crossing the stile, walk straight ahead along the broad grassy bridleway. At a junction of paths continue in the same direction to follow the bridleway as it skirts the hill on your left. Look out for the ancient cultivation terraces over to the right, on the hillside above Ingram Hill farm. The path you are on follows the line of such a terrace. Just before the field boundary the track becomes more of a rutted track, swings to the left and after a short while to the right, to emerge onto a road **(I)**.

Turn right to walk through Ingram, back to the church and the end of the walk.

### Walk 7(b), Ingram only: 4 miles

Follow the directions for Walk 7(a) to **(B)**. Then, turn right and follow the permissive footpath as it climbs to the top of Cochrane Pike. You pass four waymark signs and eventually reach a fifth sign which is at the junction of a number of paths. Bear left and walk in the direction of the waymark. After about 120 metres a fence and an old wall appear ahead. You need to make for the waymark post at the left-hand corner. Now follow the fence as it descends on your right to meet a waymarked stile next to a metal gate. Turn left and walk to the point where you started i.e. at the division of the paths **(B)**. Retrace your steps back to Ingram church and the end of the walk.

# Walk 8: Edlingham and Bolton

## *King's gift, duke's case and earl's pledge*

**Location:** St John's Church (NU115091) is in Edlingham, which is 6 miles south-west of Alnwick on a minor road off the B6431.

**Distance:** Walk 8(a), Edlingham and Bolton: 9 miles. Walk 8(b), Edlingham only: 6 miles.

**Map:** OS Explorer 332: Alnwick & Amble.

**Terrain:** Mainly on quiet country roads and public footpaths with some gentle climbing and one short section on a slightly busier road.

**Churches:** St John the Baptist, Edlingham; Bolton Chapel, Bolton.

**Car parking:** Outside the church gate.

## The Churches

### St John the Baptist, Edlingham

Edlingham is one of several villages given to the monastery of Lindisfarne by the Northumbrian king, Ceolwulf, when he vacated his throne to become a monk there. It is likely that Anglo-Saxon churches were built on this site but there is little visible evidence of them. The present church is mainly Norman, described in the guidebook as "a rugged squat plain building.... used for the purposes of defence and security". This is reflected in its sturdy west tower with flat-roofed nave and chancel. It is set in a pleasant location, nestling in a green vale overlooked by moorland and, together with the

Church and castle at Edlingham

nearby ruins of Edlingham Castle (see below), presents an attractive picture. Welcoming words on the noticeboard encourage the visitor to go inside.

Entrance is through a rare, tunnel-vaulted Norman south porch, over a threshold that is a 14th-century grave cover carved with a sword and shears. Through the door, bar holes in the walls serve as a reminder of the needs of security, even in a church, in the turbulent times of its early history.

Inside, at the west end, is the oldest surviving stonework (from around 1050). Much of the Norman construction is evident; in particular, the chancel arch, of the late 11th/early 12th century. The furnishings include several memorial tablets and stone carvings. From inside, you can appreciate the sentiments of a visitor who comments on a visit, in February, on "this haven of peace (and cold!)".

### Among the other features of interest are:

❖ An octagonal stone font, dated 1701, which provides an interesting contrast with the plain stone lectern, installed in 1990, at the top of the nave.

❖ On the north wall, a First World War memorial tablet. This poignant reminder seems to include too large a number of names from such a tiny place.

❖ The communion rails from 1726.

❖ The stained-glass memorial window over the altar. It makes a colourful end-piece to the east end – but did not find favour with Pevsner (*The Buildings of England: Northumberland*) who, in the first edition, described it as "in an atrocious neo-Norman style, put in after a typical Victorian manner just to outdo the old masons".

### Information available in the church:

❶ A leaflet, *Edlingham Castle*, John Smith.

> *Edlingham Castle was originally a domestic hall/house, built in the mid-12th century and subsequently fortified. Later, as the need for defences lessened, it reverted back to a manor house and was owned by a number of notable local families. Damage from construction faults led to its abandonment by the Swinburnes in 1650. It is now in the care of English Heritage.*

### Bolton Chapel, Bolton

This chapel is in an area where border reivers held sway and where the English and Scots fought battles over several centuries. The earliest reference to a chapel at Bolton is 1135. It seems likely that there were earlier churches on the site before that date and, from 1235, there was a leper hospital nearby with its own chapel. The hospital monks were reported to have been among the earliest reivers!

The chapel sits on a mound, surrounded by its old burial ground, at the edge of the tiny village of Bolton. It is small, and has a nave, a north transept, a lower chancel and a little open bellcote. However, despite its interesting

Bolton Chapel – where armies gathered

historical associations, the present building dates mainly from a restoration carried out in the mid-19<sup>th</sup> century.

Inside, there is a definite Victorian feeling, with memorial windows in stained glass and many commemorative monuments. One typically Victorian wall plaque on the north wall is in memory of Eleanor Gray, wife of William Gray. Her father lost his case as claimant to the Dukedom of Roxburgh and had to sell his property to his Gray son-in-law. A three-arched screen divides the nave from the north transept. Looking east is the only original architectural feature: the Norman chancel arch. The chancel itself has quite an attractive, ornate ceiling.

Near to Bolton Chapel is where, in 1513, Henry VIII's army under the Earl of Surrey was encamped prior to the Battle of Flodden Field (see Walk 1, Norham). It was in an earlier chapel on the same site that Surrey and the other nobles are said to have pledged themselves to vanquish the Scots or to die on the field.

### *Among the other features of interest are:*

❖ The ornate font from 1737, given, later, by William Gray of East Bolton House.

❖ On the north wall of the nave, a painted sandstone panel displaying the arms of the Brown family of Bolton. This is the oldest of the monuments which pre-date the 19<sup>th</sup>-century restoration.

❖ The pulpit with its two decks, the upper for the preacher and the lower for the clerk.

# The Walks

## Walk 8(a), Edlingham and Bolton: 9 miles

Leave the church and grounds **(A)**. Head up the village street away from the church and take the public footpath on the right signposted "Birsley Woodside ¾". Keep to the right-hand side of the field and cross into the next field over the waymarked stile. Follow the line of trees until a farm road is crossed, and take the short metalled section towards the wood. Do not enter the wood, but instead turn left and go round the edge of the wood (with the trees on your right) and carry on via two gates to cross a waymarked stile. Walk diagonally across the field towards the house ahead. Cross a waymarked stile and walk to the gate ahead. Go through the gate onto a quiet, country road **(B)**.

Turn right and walk along the road, which runs through farmland for 2½ miles or so to Bolton. After about 800 metres pass Hillhead Farm, carry on now with views of the Cheviots to the left and (after a further 1200 metres) come to a crossroads **(C)**.

Cross the road to continue in the same direction. A high, stone wall appears on the right-hand side and the small settlement of Bridge End is reached. Follow the road, crossing the bridge over the River Aln, and continue on this road to Bolton Chapel **(D)**.

The entrance to the building is reached via a gate which is to the right as you face the chapel. After your visit, go back through the main gate (by which you entered) and continue straight ahead on the East Bolton road through the little village of Bolton. Carry on, for about 600 metres, to a crossroads where you turn right at the sign for "Abberwick 1¾". Follow this road via a copse of pine trees and over the footbridge over the River Aln, to the left of a ford. (You need to take the path on the left between the trees when the stream comes into view to reach the footbridge). Carry on to where there is a bend to the left and take the public footpath on the right-hand side to "Abberwick ¼" **(E)**.

Follow the farm track and go through the gate into an area of farm buildings, with the farmhouse on the left. Ignore the road to the left and go immediately ahead through a metal gate, down between the trees. Climb a short distance and go through a gate. Proceed up the field to the boundary and go through a waymarked gate. Continue straight ahead with trees and fence on your right. At the top of the field go through the waymarked gate on the right, turn immediately left and through a waymarked gate into another field. Keep straight ahead to descend and exit onto a narrow, quiet road. Turn right and walk to where this road joins a busier road. Turn left and walk for 300 metres to a road on the right, signposted "Lemmington Mill 1, Lemmington Hall ½" **(F)**.

Turn right and proceed along this road. Where the road divides, take the right-hand fork for "Lemmington Mill only". Walk past cottages and

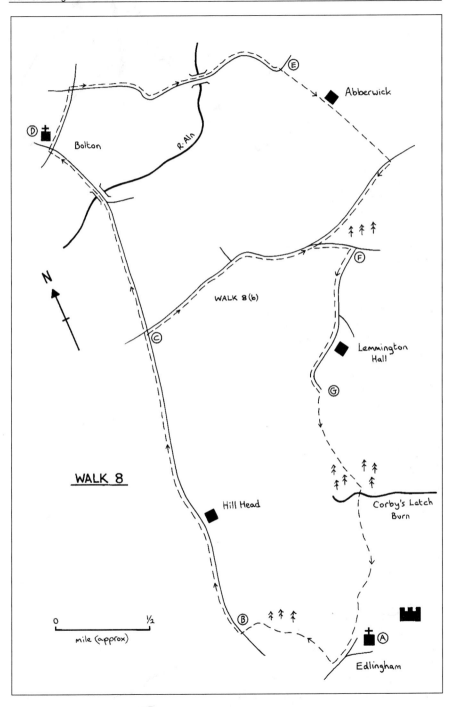

Abberwick

Bolton

R. Aln

N

WALK 8 (b)

Lemmington Hall

WALK 8

Hill Head

Corby's Letch Burn

0                    ½

mile (approx)

Edlingham

Lemmington Hall, a former convent, on your left. Over to the right, a few fields away, is a brightly coloured collection of old farm tractors and other equipment. When the road descends, follow the fingerpost on the left in the direction "Edlingham 1½ ". Keep close to the fence and trees on the left, cross the stile next to a gate and continue straight ahead with trees on your left, to a waymarked stile next to a gate with a public bridleway sign **(G)**.

Go over the stile but do not follow the farm track upward to Overthwarts, instead bear right to go diagonally across the field in the direction of the telegraph post. Continue ahead, with the telegraph post and trees on your right, until you meet a path descending from your left. Turn right, follow the path amid the trees and cross the footbridge. Turn right then go through the gate on the left. Walk towards the corner of the trees ahead on your left and continue ahead, keeping the same distance from the field boundary on the left. Make for a waymarked gate in the left-hand corner of the fence ahead. Go through the gate and continue along the perimeter of the field with the fence on your left to reach a double gate. Go through the gate and walk across the track of a former railway line. On the left is a waymarked stile with a notice "To the church". Welcome news – but this last section can be very muddy. Cross the stile, bear right to the corner of the fence, and follow the perimeter of the field with the fence on your right towards the church. Go through the gate and follow the churchyard wall, via another gate, to the front of the church and the end of the walk.

## Walk 8(b), Edlingham only: 6 miles

Follow Walk 8(a) to **(C)**. Turn right at the crossroads and walk for just over a mile to a road on the right, signposted "Lemmington Mill 1, Lemmington Hall ½". Follow the directions from **(F)** to arrive back at Edlingham Church and the end of the walk.

# Walk 9: Warkworth

## *Hotspur, harbour and hermit*

**Location:** St Lawrence's Church (NU247062) is in Warkworth on the A1068 Alnwick to Amble road, about 2 miles from Amble.

**Distance:** 6¾ miles.

**Map:** OS Explorer 332: Alnwick & Amble.

**Terrain:** The walk is mainly on the level with a section on the sands. There is a gradual climb from the river to the castle.

**Church:** St Lawrence.

**Car parking:** There is parking in the Market Square, and also beyond the church by the riverside.

## The Church

The church rests elegantly at the bottom of Castle Street within sight of Warkworth Castle and just above the River Coquet as it meanders gently around the lower part of the village. The sea, though not visible, is close at

Tower and spire at St Lawrence, Warkworth

hand. The wrought-iron gates lead into a well-tended grave-yard with a variety of interest-ing tombs and headstones.

The entrance is through a large porch where birds some-times nest and where visitors may need to be watchful! Above the porch is a room for-merly used as a schoolroom. The sturdy, very early 13th-century tower, with its narrow slits, suggests that the local inhabitants once found this a useful place of refuge from invaders from across the Scottish border and the North Sea.

There has been a church on this site for over twelve centu-ries, but the present building, according to Pevsner (*The Buildings of England: Northumberland*), is "unique in Northumberland in being a fairly complete Norman church". St Lawrence's boasts the longest Norman nave in Northumberland and its high ceiling and the single south aisle, devoid of pews, combine to create a very open and spacious effect. The walls at the west end appear to be feeling the weight of the roof, suggesting the need for some further costly restoration work to this well-loved and well-cared for building.

The long nave leads to the chancel with its fine, chiselled arch and deep-set windows. Beyond the elegantly designed 18th-century altar rails, the chancel contains an interesting collection of wall memorials to local people. However, one of the greatest treasures is above, in the form of the 12th-century vaulted ceiling which, with its zig-zag decorations, is believed to be one of the few such ceilings still to be found in England. The south aisle contains the Lady Chapel at its east end. Here you will find some of the oldest fragments of stained glass in Northumberland. Above the plain glass are some medieval pieces and among the figures, on the left, you will see St Hilda of Whitby holding a staff in her hand.

There is much to see and appreciate here in the church as well as in the village and its delightful surrounds.

### Among the other features of interest are:

❖ The stone effigy of a 14th-century knight, Hugh Morwicke, in the baptistry area in the south-west corner of the church. His origins are uncertain, but he was probably an inhabitant of the castle at one time.

❖ A useful note about the life and death of St Lawrence on the south wall, near the door. There is a modern stained-glass window near the pulpit depicting his martyrdom.

❖ The relatively modern pulpit (1929) decorated with panels portraying St Lawrence and local saints including King Ceolwulf of Northumbria who first gave this site to the monks of Holy Island in the 8th century, before becoming a monk himself.

❖ The lectern with the carved pelican, the symbol of St Lawrence, on the front. Parishioners recall the real pelican, which appeared several years ago off the coast near Warkworth. This is now stuffed and on show at the Hancock Museum, Newcastle. The parish bulletin is aptly named *The Pelican*.

### Information available in the church:

❶ *A Guide to the Church of St Lawrence, Warkworth.*

## The Walk

Leave the church grounds **(A)** through the main gate, turn immediately left and follow the lane round the churchyard walls to the main road (Bridge Street). Then turn left and proceed through the archway and over the old 14th-century bridge across the River Coquet. Proceed ahead for a short distance, before crossing the main road with care, to follow the signs to the golf course, cemetery and beach. Follow the road as it goes uphill and then bears left, and continue towards the sea, to a point where the road goes left towards the golf club and a road leads off right, to the caravan park.

Go straight ahead in the direction of the fingerpost "Warkworth beach ¼", passing the toilets on your right. Continue ahead, with the golf course on your left, and make your way through the dunes to the seashore **(B)**.

When you reach the seashore, turn right and walk along the sandy beach with Coquet Island lighthouse now clearly visible off the coast on your left. Continue as far as the breakwater and make your way through the rocks at the right-hand edge and onto the breakwater at Amble Harbour **(C)**.

Turn right and follow the track for about 100 metres to an open area. The marina comes into view opposite and just below you are the remains of the old staithes once used to load the collier boats with coal. Now follow the broad track as it bears right, along the line of the estuary that was Warkworth Harbour before becoming silted up in the 18<sup>th</sup> century. Continue along the clear track behind the dunes until, after a few hundred metres, the track converges with the path that took you to the seashore. Turn left, and make your way back to the road which you left on your outward journey near the entrance to the caravan site. Retrace your steps back along the road to the bridges at the entrance to Warkworth **(D)**.

Cross the river via the pavement over the new road-bridge. Cross over the road and, at the left of the small park on the corner, follow the sign "Public footpath to Warkworth Castle ¼ mile". (Alternatively, if you are looking for a short-cut, you can turn right at this point to return to the car park.) Proceed up the narrow snicket that climbs between walls and fences amid gardens, until eventually you arrive opposite the castle with the Sun Hotel on your left. Turn right, walk about 60 metres, then cross over the road carefully to a public footpath sign at the corner. (Again, at this point you could elect to take a short-cut and return some 200 metres down Castle Street to the church.) Follow the public footpath sign "Morwick road and riverside ¼" and when the path divides keep to the upper metalled path by the wall of Warkworth Castle **(E)**.

> *There has been a fortress of one type or another on this site for over 950 years. Early in the 14<sup>th</sup> century, the castle passed into the hands of the Percys (subsequently Earls of Northumberland). The most renowned Percy is probably Henry, son of the 1<sup>st</sup> Earl of Northumberland, whose horsemanship earned him the nickname "Harry Hotspur". He and his father later helped to remove King Richard II from the throne and both receive mention in Shakespeare's Henry IV (Part II) which opens in Warkworth Castle. The remains of the castle consist largely of the 14<sup>th</sup>-century keep. It now belongs to English Heritage and it is well worth exploring.*

Pass through the kissing gate and go diagonally across the field on the grassy path, ignoring the stony path straight ahead. Go though the kissing gate into the field marked "children's playing field", cross to the next kissing

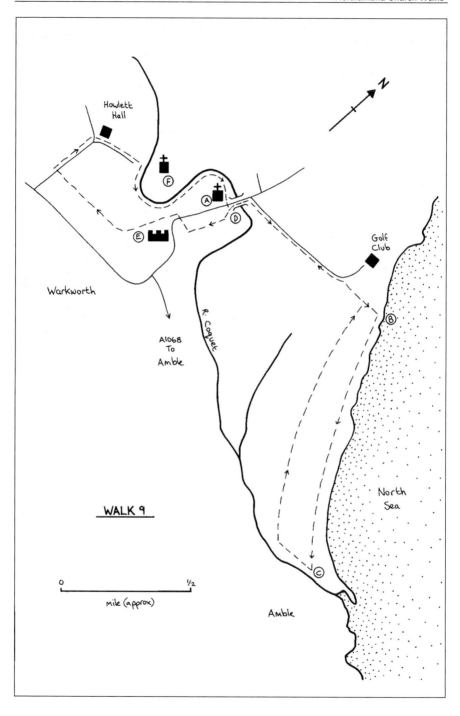

Howlett
Hall

F

A

D

E

Golf
Club

Warkworth

R. Coquet

A1068
To
Amble

B

North
Sea

**WALK 9**

0                    ½
mile (approx)

C

Amble

gate and then join the clear path as it bears behind the houses along the field edge. When this path emerges onto a road, turn immediately right and continue to the point where the road bears left to Northumbria Water at Howlett Hall farmhouse. Leave the main road at this point and go straight ahead, passing the farmhouse on your left, to follow the public footpath sign "Hermitage ¼; Warkworth ¾" through the kissing gate next to the vehicular gate. The road leads down to the riverside and a small ferry landing-stage next to an English Heritage sign with details of the Hermitage **(F)**.

*The Hermitage is believed to date from the 14th century when it was built at the behest of the Percy family as a place of prayer for their wellbeing. It is barely visible from the riverbank, being so well hidden by the ancient yew trees. It is hewn into the sandstone cliff face and comprises a number of chambers, including the remains of a chapel, sacristy and hermit's living quarters. Although the passage of time and vandalism have taken their toll, some fascinating carvings still remain and the atmosphere is worth savouring. The Hermitage is now under the care of English Heritage and you need to be taken there by a custodian in a rowing boat, all of which adds to the romance of the visit. The noticeboard gives details of opening times, generally on certain days between April and September.*

To continue the walk, turn right and proceed along the path with the river on your left towards the castle. Pass through the kissing gate and keep to the lower path, along the riverbank below the castle. The path follows the curve of the river as it gradually makes its way round the lower part of Warkworth village. Eventually you will see the walls of the churchyard. Turn right to return to the front of the church and the end of the walk.

# Walk 10: Rothbury

*Cross-shaft designs, Commission pines and cup-and-ring lines*

**Location:** All Saints Church (NY058017) is in the small town of Rothbury which is on the B6344, 30 miles north-west of Newcastle.

**Distance:** 6 miles.

**Map:** OS Outdoor Leisure 42: Kielder Water.

**Terrain:** Mainly on field paths and farm and moorland tracks over gently undulating country. There is a short, steep climb out of Rothbury and a steady climb on a quiet country road.

**Church:** All Saints, Rothbury.

**Car parking:** There is street parking in Rothbury. Alternatively, there is a large car parking area on the south bank of the River Coquet, just to the west of the road bridge.

## The Church

All Saints Church is in the pleasant mid-Northumbrian town of Rothbury which is sometimes referred to as the capital of Coquetdale. It seems likely that a church has existed here for 1,200 years. The Anglo-Saxons had a royal burgh here; surveys and dowsing have indicated the presence of a monastic building, similar to that at Jarrow, extending to the west of the present tower.

Traces of the earliest churches have long since disappeared. However, although most of what is now seen comes from a major rebuilding in 1850, All Saints retains 13th-century features in the chancel and the east walls of the transepts. It is a large, noble building with its sturdy, embattled west tower, nave and lower chancel, porch and transepts.

Inside, the church is spacious and lofty with arcades separating the north and south aisles from the nave. The 13th-century chancel arch leads into the long chancel from which a two-bay arcade gives access into a Memorial Chapel. The overall feeling here is of being in a Victorian church. Much of the furniture contributes to this: dark, rich pews and choir stalls, the fine carved pulpit, the brass eagle lectern and the chancel screen in memory of Lord Armstrong (see below) with heraldic devices of local families and institutions. The dedication to All Saints is underlined by several memorials, including the lectern carvings of Saints Aidan, Cuthbert, Hilda and Paulinus, the stained-glass windows in the chancel to Saints Aidan, Bede, Cuthbert and Oswald, as well as the west window which shows St Michael and St George.

This is a well-cared-for church, with much of interest to be seen by the welcome visitor.

### Among the other features of interest are:

❖ The font in the baptistry at the west end. The bowl is from 1664. The pedestal (the "jewel in the crown" at All Saints) is part of the shaft of an

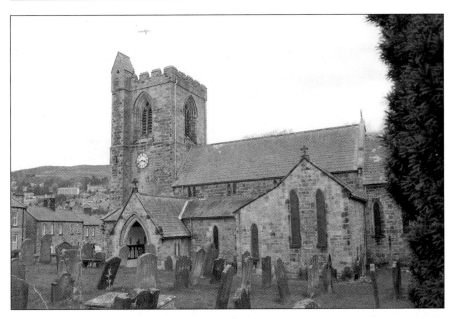

All Saints, Rothbury and its battlemented tower

Anglo-Saxon cross. It has intricate carving on all sides; that on the north is thought to be the earliest carving of the Ascension, in England. The font cover is 20th century, given in memory of Lady Armstrong.

❖ On the south wall of the baptistry, the funeral hatchment of Lord Armstrong.

❖ In the Memorial Chapel the windows by Leonard Evetts (see Walk 12, Bolam and Hartburn). They are of clear glass in the Northumbrian style and incorporate coloured regimental badges.

❖ In the Memorial Chapel, a chair with a memorial plaque, given by Lord and Lady Armstrong in memory of David Dippie Dixon, the much respected local historian.

❖ The carpet in the sanctuary with a design based on the knotwork of the font. It was worked in 1972 by the ladies of the parish.

### *Information available in the church:*

❶ A leaflet, *Welcome to All Saints Parish Church, Rothbury*, G. Burn and J. Eddershaw.

❶ Information board with details of the font pedestal.

❶ Information board with details of the Memorial Chapel.

❶ Hand-held information board with details of the heraldic devises on the chancel screen.

*Lord Armstrong (1810-1900) was born in Newcastle. He became a partner in* *a local law practice, but continued to devote much time to his engineering interests. In 1845 he was closely involved in setting up a new water company to supply Newcastle and shortly afterwards he invented the world's first efficient hydraulic crane. In 1847 he finally gave up the law and founded his engineering firm, W. G. Armstrong and Company. The company initially specialised in hydraulic machines but later in armaments – and gained a world-wide reputation. He was a noted benefactor. He built Cragside, near Rothbury, described as "the palace of a modern magician" (Grenville S. Cole, Arms and the Man) and also acquired and rebuilt Bamburgh Castle. In 1887, he was created the 1<sup>st</sup> Baron Armstrong of Cragside.*

## The Walk

Leave the church grounds **(A)** by the gate at the west end, turn right into Church Street then left into Market Place, where there is a splendid monument erected in 1902 in memory of Lord Armstrong of Cragside and his wife. Turn left round the United Reformed Church. Go down the lane and, keeping the wall on your right, come to a footbridge over the River Coquet. Cross the footbridge, turn left and walk to the exit of the car parking area and onto a road. Turn left and walk ahead. In a couple of hundred metres, just before the road bridge which goes over the river, cross the road and turn right to go up a steep, narrow road. At the top of the hill go straight ahead to a metal kissing gate. Go through the gate and turn right as indicated by the public footpath sign. (Ignore the sign to "Whitton ¼). Follow the path as it climbs diagonally through the field and goes via a waymarked kissing gate to head for a clump of trees. The path comes to a kissing gate. The building discernible ahead is Whitton Tower – a former vicar's pele which for some time served as the vicarage of Rothbury. Go through the gate and turn left to walk uphill to Whitton. At the top of the hill, on your right, opposite the main entrance to Whitton Grange, take the public bridleway to "Whitton Hillhead 1¼" **(B)**.

Go down the bridleway passing Folly House on your left and come to Sharpe's Folly on your right. This was erected by the Rev. Dr Thomas Sharpe, Rector of Rothbury; a plaque explains its interesting history. Keep on the lane. Over to the right is a caravan park. Ahead, the Simonside Hills come into view. Keep straight on, ignoring footpaths off to the left. The path passes Curlew Cottage on the right and reaches the farm of Whitton Hillhead with its two little wooden dovecotes. Follow the path as it enters and exits the farm area via waymarked gates, then turn left through a waymarked gate. Walk along the broad, grassy track, towards the Simonsides ahead. Go through a waymarked gate and arrive at another gate with blue and yellow waymarks. Go through the gate and walk to the waymark post a few metres beyond the gate, then turn left to walk down the field with the wire fence a few metres away on your left. At the bottom of the field, go through the

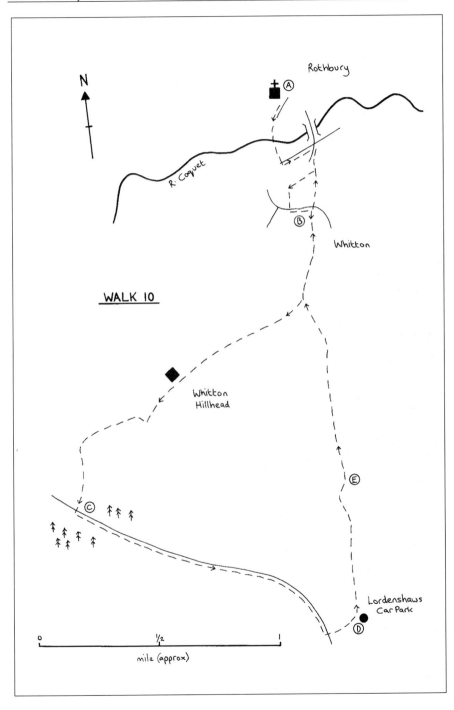

N

Rothbury

R. Coquet

WALK 10

Whitton

Whitton
Hillhead

Lordenshaws
Car Park

0          ½          1
mile (approx)

waymarked gate and follow the path as it bears right and exits onto a minor road **(C)**.

Turn left and walk up this road for about a mile. Initially, the road takes you through part of the Simonside Forest, one of several around Rothbury planted by the Forestry Commission, with pines and other species. Carry on through the open moorland area until you reach the National Park car park at Lordenshaws on your left. There is a public footpath sign for "Whittondean 1, Rothbury 2". Go into the car park to the information board, which gives interesting details concerning the ancient hill fort and rock carvings nearby **(D)**.

Leave the car park and continue ahead on the grassy track past the waymark post. In a few hundred metres, you will arrive at another waymark post. The walk takes you to the right, but by taking a detour of 100 metres or so to the left you can see an example of a cup-and-ring marked rock. After taking the detour, walk back to the waymark post. Now, follow the direction indicated and walk to the top of the hill to cross the open area occupied by the hill fort, and go down on the other side to a waymark post **(E)**.

Turn left and continue on the path via a series of waymark posts. Rothbury and Sharpe's Folly come into view in the distance. Follow the path as it descends, to go over two waymarked stiles and walk down the field towards the trees at the bottom. Bear slightly right, cross the stream and climb up the other side to cross a waymarked stile. Walk along the field edge with a fence on your right to emerge onto the lane which you used earlier. Turn right and retrace your steps via Sharpe's Folly to Whitton, opposite the entrance to Whitton Grange **(B)**.

Turn right and after a few metres, where the road bears to the right, you need to turn left at the public footpath sign indicating "Rothbury ½". Go into the car park of Whitton Farmhouse Hotel and look for the yellow waymark sign on the left-hand corner of the stable block. Cross the waymarked stile, and walk down the field to the metal kissing gate which you encountered earlier. Go through the gate and continue ahead on the road down the hill to retrace your steps to Rothbury, the church and the end of the walk.

# Walk 11: Corsenside and West Woodburn

## *Reeds, Rede and reivers*

**Location:** St Cuthbert's Church (NY890894) is at Corsenside, just off the A68, 16 miles north of Corbridge and 1½ miles north of West Woodburn.

**Distance:** 5½ miles.

**Map:** Outdoor Leisure 42: Kielder Water, Bellingham & Simonside Hills.

**Terrain:** Mainly on undulating moorland, with about a mile on a quiet country lane.

**Churches:** St Cuthbert, Corsenside; All Saints, West Woodburn.

**Car parking:** There is parking outside the church.

## The Churches
### St Cuthbert, Corsenside

This small church stands in a very isolated and commanding position over-looking the Redesdale valley, just west of the course of the Roman road, Dere Street. Its only close neighbour is a solitary farmhouse since Corsenside as a significant entity disappeared long ago, possibly due to the plague. It hardly seems to have enjoyed great material prosperity and John Hodgson (*History of Northumberland Vol.2* ) refers to a minister of 1617 living in such "sharp misery" as to appear "scandalously sordid"!

In 1750 a mission church was established 1½ miles away at West Wood-burn and by the end of the 19th century St Cuthbert's had become neglected. The growth of West Woodburn eventually resulted in the construction of a parish church there in 1906 and the practical demise of the church at Corsenside. However, the nave was repaired in 1914 and the good state of the building today is testimony to the esteem in which it is deservingly held.

There is a degree of uncertainty about its origins. It is said that St Cuthbert's coffin rested here and that the event was commemorated by the erection of a cross on the site, and hence the name "Crossensyde". The pres-ent building is basically Norman, particularly in the form of its chancel arch, and there is speculation as to whether some of the stonework came from a nearby Roman fort. Naturally, the church has been altered over the centu-ries, especially with the addition of the slightly crooked bellcote and the south porch, above the doorway of which is the date 1735. Inside, however, it retains a somewhat medieval atmosphere with its narrow nave leading to the small chancel. There are some remnants of grave and cross-slabs at the west end of the church, as well as the partial figure of a woman in stone. The only nave windows are on the south wall and they are deeply recessed. The clear glass with red motifs in the corners is thought to be Georgian and this provides an effective source of natural light.

This is a splendid spot in summer, but cold and bleak in winter. However, it always offers an opportunity for solitude and reflection and church ser-vices still take place here on occasion, during the summer months.

The isolated church of St Cuthbert, Corsenside

### *Among the other features of interest are:*

❖ The 18th-century font at the west end of the church.

❖ The finely worded plaque on the north wall of the nave, in memory of a teacher and vicar's daughter.

❖ The commandments on both sides of the wall between the nave and the chancel.

❖ The graveyard contains an interesting collection of old memorials. Against the outside of the south wall there are some to the Reeds, a prominent local family said at one time to have inhabited the adjacent farmhouse. There are also some more recent military gravestones near the boundary wall to the east of the church.

### *Information available in the church:*

❶ Hand-held information board.

## All Saints, West Woodburn

This church presents a strong contrast in every sense to its neighbour, St Cuthbert's. All Saints nestles almost hidden amid trees in a valley mid-way between West and East Woodburn, within sight and sound of the River Rede. Now the parish church of Corsenside, its history is relatively modern, having been built in 1906 to replace the mission church which had served from 1750. It appears to have remained very much intact ever since.

Externally there is little of note, except perhaps the bell-turret. Inside, however, it gives an immediate impression of cohesion. The interior is plain, simple and uniform. The long, narrow nave, with its whitewashed walls,

All Saints, West Woodburn – an early 20<sup>th</sup>-century church

leads through a slender arch into a well-proportioned chancel. Harmony is evident in the furnishings with its fine oak pews, pulpit, altar rails and stalls. Behind the altar is a wooden reredos, with carvings of St Cuthbert, on the right, and King Oswald, on the left. An overall effect of light is added to this calm and peaceful place by the opaque leaded-windows and the pine-panelled ceiling.

***Among the other features of interest are:***

❖ The notice in the porch referring to the grant of £75 from the Incorporated Church Building Society.

❖ The octagonal font with its tall, oak canopy.

❖ The dedication on the pulpit in memory of a 19-year-old who died in Singapore.

## The Walk

Leave St Cuthbert's churchyard **(A)**, turn left and go through the metal gate to take the bridleway "West Woodburn 1½". Follow the path roughly parallel to the A68 road towards farm buildings and dwellings at Coldtown. The path descends to some trees where you need to pick your way across a small stream. It then climbs gradually upwards with a burn and a wire fence on your right, until you arrive at the tiny settlement of Coldtown **(B)**.

Continue ahead through the metal gate at the right-hand corner of the wall and proceed between the buildings, noting the pretty walled garden on your right. Go straight over the gravel driveway to pass through a metal gate and then a second metal gate, before descending down the grassy path. Cross another small stream and continue ahead following the clear, green path. Over to the left the River Rede gradually comes into view.

*The River Rede: possibly a corruption of red and so named because of the blood which flowed into the water as a result of the Battle of Otterburn in 1388, in which large numbers of English and Scottish soldiers were killed or wounded. The English were led by Sir Henry Percy ("Harry Hotspur", see Walk 9, Warkworth) and Sir Ralph Percy, sons of the Earl of Northumberland, and the Scots by James, Earl of Douglas. The main conflict took place under moonlight and ended in victory for the Scottish forces, even though their leader was killed. Harry Hotspur was captured but, perhaps indicative of the chivalry of the time, he was released on ransom. The heroic deeds were subsequently embellished in ballads, one of which was Chevy Chase.*

Continue on the grassy track as it climbs to a metal gate by a fingerpost, to exit onto a metalled lane **(C)**. Proceed straight down the lane ahead as it drops towards farm buildings and dwellings. At the T-junction turn right to pass some pleasant dwellings and where there are the remains of a bastle.

> *Bastles (or fortified farmhouses) and pele towers are common in North Northumberland, showing evidence of protective measures in the light of cross-border conflicts between the English and the Scots, and as defence against the notorious families of thieves and cattle rustlers known as the "border reivers".*

As you continue along the lane, the River Rede appears close by on your left. Follow the lane as it bears left at a junction at Brae Well Close to exit onto the A68. Turn left and pass (or visit!) the Bay Horse Inn, noting the Roman milestone in the garden. Continue on the pavement across the West Woodburn Bridge over the river and after 150 metres turn left at The Old Chapel (formerly the Presbyterian Church) in the direction of East Woodburn and Monkridge. A fingerpost on the corner indicates "All Saints Church ½ mile". Proceed along this quiet road, enjoying the sight of the river on your left and the good blend of old and new dwellings, to arrive at All Saints Church **(D)**.

After visiting All Saints Church, turn right and continue up the road passing a cottage on your left with "Mission School" faintly engraved above the door lintel. After about 800 metres, you arrive at the small hamlet of East Woodburn. Follow the road as it bears left round Cross House near a junction and proceed ahead across the bridge over the Lisles Burn, a tributary of the River Rede. After a short distance, turn left after Horsley Bank Foot at the public footpath sign. Cross the cattle grid and walk down the track leading to Alder Hall. After about 40 metres leave the track, and go diagonally left down the grassy slope to a metal gate just to the right of the burn. Go through the gate and continue downstream with the burn on your left, ignoring a wooden footbridge on your left and crossing an old stile. Continue ahead, and then cross over a wall via a ladder stile on your left to go over a further stile, just before a metal footbridge which you ignore **(E)**.

Turn right and gradually climb up the grassy path with a fence on your right and the river over to the left. As the path levels out you pass through a waymarked gate to meet a metalled track almost immediately. Turn left and descend to enjoy the sound and sight of the river as the track draws closer to the bank side and makes its way through a pleasant wooded area to reach East Woodburn Bridge **(F)**.

Follow the bridleway across the bridge and climb gradually up the track to exit through a gate onto a metalled lane. Turn immediately right and you will see the public brideway sign "Corsenside 1 mile" which you passed on your outward journey **(C)**. You now need to retrace your steps back to St Cuthbert's Church. Go through the metal gate and continue on the grassy path to Coldtown, visible ahead on the hilltop. Go through the metal gates

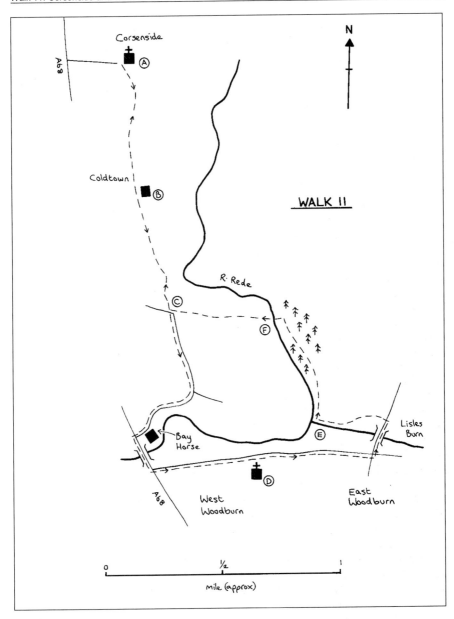

just before the farm buildings, cross the gravel drive and proceed straight ahead, between the buildings, to exit by a further metal gate. Walk straight ahead to cross the ford and climb gradually back to Corsenside church and the end of the walk.

# Walk 12: Bolam and Hartburn

*Master of design, historian fine and generous divine*

**Location:** St Andrew's Church (NZ093826) is at Bolam about 20 miles from Newcastle, north of Belsay off the A5696.

**Distance:** 7 miles.

**Map:** OS Explorer 325: Morpeth & Blyth.

**Terrain:** Half on footpaths and half on quiet country roads over gently undulating countryside.

**Churches:** St Andrew, Bolam; St Andrew, Hartburn.

**Car parking:** There is car parking outside the church at Bolam.

## The Churches

### St Andrew, Bolam

The church stands next to the former vicarage overlooking pleasant green fields and scattered dwellings. Apparently, this was once part of a substantial town of over 200 households and 900 inhabitants, adjacent to a Norman castle. However, by the beginning of the 19th century – as a result of border wars, disease and migration – Bolam had been reduced to a handful of houses.

The tall and robust west tower of late Saxon origin is an impressive sight. The rest owes much to the 13th century as, for example, in the dog-tooth decoration in the doorway in the south porch. There is, however, ample evi-

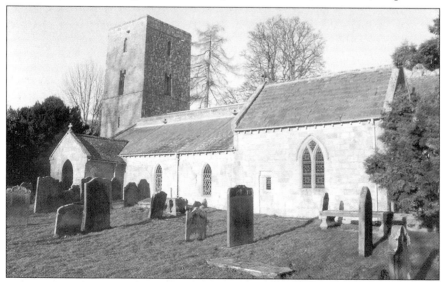

St Andrew, Bolam with its robust tower

dence of extension and renovation. Inside there is much that is Norman in style and flavour. The chancel arch leads into a choir area, beyond which there are remains of a sanctuary arch which was removed when the church was extended in the 13th century. The well-cut sandstone walls and the deeply recessed windows, filled with clear glass with leaded patterns, provide a pleasant sense of uniformity. This style of glass is a typical feature of many Northumbrian churches in the late 19th century and one of its leading exponents, F.R.Wilson of Alnwick, was originally responsible for the work at Bolam. Arcades separate the nave from a south aisle at the east end of which is the Shortflatt Chapel. Here lies an effigy said to be that of Sir Robert de Reymes, a 14th-century knight who fortified the manor house at nearby Shortflatt.

Today, although St Andrew's remains largely isolated geographically from its congregation, it is well used and well cared for and it conveys an atmosphere of peace and tranquillity.

### Among the other features of interest are:

❖ The solid and simple medieval baptismal font at the west end.

❖ Two carved heads on the north side of the chancel arch.

❖ The small oval window in the Shortflatt Chapel at the east end of the south aisle, showing what the church leaflet describes as "a joyous little angel rejoicing in the survival of the church", an early example of the work of Leonard Evetts (see below).

❖ The small window in the south aisle marked as the spot where, in 1942, a bomb fell on the church but did not explode. Leonard Evetts replaced this window and restored other damaged windows. On the window sill is a copy of an interesting account of the incident, written by the wife of the vicar at the time.

### Information available in the church:

❶ *St Andrew's Church & Bygone Bolam*, Revd Alec Macdonald (amended by Bob Carmichael).

❶ *St Andrew's Church, Bolam, Northumberland. Analysis of the fabric and archaeological assessment*, P.F.Ryder.

*Leonard Evetts (1909-1997), described in his obituary in The Times in October 1997, as "the most prolific English stained-glass artist of this century", taught at the University of Newcastle (previously King's College, Durham) from 1937 to 1974, where he became Head of the School of Design. He was particularly noted for his work in churches, which included altar frontals and furniture, as well as stained-glass windows. The outstanding contribution of his artistic work for the Church of England was recognised in 1995 when he was awarded a Lambeth Doctorate by the Archbishop of Canterbury. He also revived the Northumbrian custom of clear-glazing and was recognised for his watercolours and his calligraphy. Evetts' windows grace over 100 churches in Northumbria and 13 of them are featured in this book.*

## St Andrew, Hartburn

This church shelters among trees at the east end of the small hamlet of Hartburn, above the wooded ravine on the south through which the walk leads. It has enjoyed a long and intriguing history, details of which are expounded in the comprehensive guidebook written by Canon Fergus Donnelly referred to below. At one time it belonged to Tynemouth Abbey, later it was transferred to St Alban's and after the Dissolution of the Monasteries it passed to "lay rectors". Among the latter was the Earl of Derwentwater until his execution after the 1715 Jacobite rebellion, when the church was given to Greenwich Hospital.

The broad tower is mainly late 12<sup>th</sup>/early 13<sup>th</sup> century with some Saxon traces but, unlike its neighbour at Bolam, it is buttressed. However, just as at Bolam, the doorway within the south porch carries a strong dog-tooth motif which Pevsner (*The Buildings of England: Northumberland*) suggests may have been "the work of an over-enthusiastic Hexham mason". At the same time, the Maltese cross and the two daggers incised into the east side of the doorway have given rise to

An early example of an Evetts' window at St Andrew, Hartburn (with kind permission from the vicar)

considerable speculation about the possible involvement of the Knights Templar in the history of the church. The porch is topped by a tilted sundial.

The interior, with north and south aisles, is quite spacious as a result of the removal of chantry chapels after the Reformation. The long 13<sup>th</sup>-century chancel "squints" to the north, and the pillars in the south aisle have a marked inward inclination. Some of the capitals of the pillars carry embossed decorations of animal heads and the pillar nearest to the pulpit shows a fish. A number of interesting wall tablets, stone sculptures and military colours recall the exploits of local families.

There are several stained-glass windows of note. In the south wall, the window showing St Hilda and St Cuthbert, by Kempe (see Walk 15, Simonburn) was apparently only lightly stained to permit the pulpit and its occupant to be clearly visible. The east window and the window in the east wall of the north aisle are believed to be by Wailes (see Walk 19, Bywell). However, perhaps the most significant window is in the east wall of the south aisle. This depicts the risen Christ, and, dated 1942, it is thought to be the first of the many windows in Northumbrian churches designed by Leonard Evetts.

*Among the other features of interest are:*

❖ Facing you as you enter, the money chest which Oliver Cromwell is said to have used to transport his wealth.

❖ The two substantial 13th-century stone coffins to the west of the door.

❖ The carved oak panel of Adam and Eve, believed to be of foreign origin, hanging on the west wall.

❖ The 12th-century baptismal font with its 16th-century carved wooden cover to which a wrought-iron pulley mechanism was added during a period of major restoration in 1892.

❖ The plaque in the sedilia on the south side of the chancel in memory of the Revd John Hodgson, the famous historian of Northumberland who was vicar at Hartburn from 1833 to1845. The text tells a sad tale of family deaths.

*Information available in the church:*

❶ *The Parishes of Hartburn, Meldon and Netherwitton*, Canon A. Ferg. Donnelly.

# The Walk

Turn right on leaving the church porch at Bolam **(A)** and exit from the churchyard by the waymarked gate behind the west tower. Turn right, go through another waymarked gate and descend on the broad path to the left-hand corner of the paddock to go through a gate into a field. This next section can be marshy in parts. Go straight ahead on the faint path keeping the trees and the fence on your left and proceed through the next gate. Continue in the same direction and, at the end of the next field, go through a metal gate on the left and turn immediately right. Proceed for about 40 metres to go through another gate. Over to the left is a bungalow at Angerton Steads. Continue ahead with the fence and the hedge on your right and after some 30 metres take a stile next to a gate. Continue ahead up the side of the field until a stile takes you to a dismantled railway **(B)**.

Cross the embankment and go through the kissing gate on the other side. Bear left and make your way to a gateway diagonally opposite. Beyond the gateway, the path crosses a burn after which you turn right to walk along the field edge. At the field boundary, turn left and continue ahead with a fence on your right. Follow the field boundary as you gradually descend to exit via a gate onto a minor road. Turn right and walk along the quiet country road, passing Low Angerton Farm on your left **(C)**.

Continue ahead over a bridge that crosses the River Wansbeck. Keep on the road for about 1,200 metres as it climbs gently to pass Angerton Hall and arrive at a T-junction. Go straight ahead to leave the road by the kissing gate next to the public footpath sign "Hartburn ¾" **(D)**.

Follow the faint path to the top left-hand corner of the field and go through the gate. Continue along the field boundary with trees on your right and the sound, if not the sight, of the Hart Burn below. Pass through a gateway next to an old stile and continue up the side of the next field for about 150 metres, with a fence on your right, to go through a kissing gate that takes you onto the other side of the fence. After about 80 metres the broad path bears right to a kissing gate. Go through the gate and follow the path down between the trees and across a footbridge. Keep on the path as it bears right and ascends to a kissing gate, directly opposite St Andrew's Church, Hartburn. Cross the road with care to visit the church **(E)**.

Turn right on leaving the church porch and exit through the west gate onto the road. Walk straight ahead and follow the road to a junction at the war memorial cross, which bears the apt description "Pass Friend All is Well". Turn left for Angerton and Middleton and continue for a few hundred metres to another junction where you turn left for Angerton. Follow the road for about 800 metres to a T-junction, turn right and then immediately left to leave the road through a waymarked gate **(F)**.

Go almost immediately through another waymarked gate directly ahead and onto the fenced public bridleway. After about 200 metres go through a gate and continue in the same direction, ascending gently to pass through a waymarked gate before descending towards a wood, keeping the field boundary on your left. Just before you reach the wood, turn left through a waymarked gate **(G)**.

Continue on the public bridleway aiming for the right-hand edge of a plantation. Carry on past the plantation to exit onto the road via a gate next to a fingerpost. Turn right and follow the road as it takes you back across the River Wansbeck and past Low Angerton Farm again **(C)**. Keep on the road and ignore the footpath on the left "Bolam 1¼" (unless you wish to take a short-cut at this point and retrace your steps to Bolam Church). Walk along the quiet country road for about 800 metres to pass Angerton Station House, and then continue for about a further 400 metres (ignoring the footpath off to the right to Middleton Bank) until you reach a further public footpath sign on the right, next to a stile **(H)**.

You could follow the road back to Bolam for the next 2½ miles or so from this point. Otherwise, cross the stile and proceed across the field, in the direction of the fingerpost, to a gate at the left-hand corner of a small plantation. Go through the waymarked gate and cross the field, continuing in the

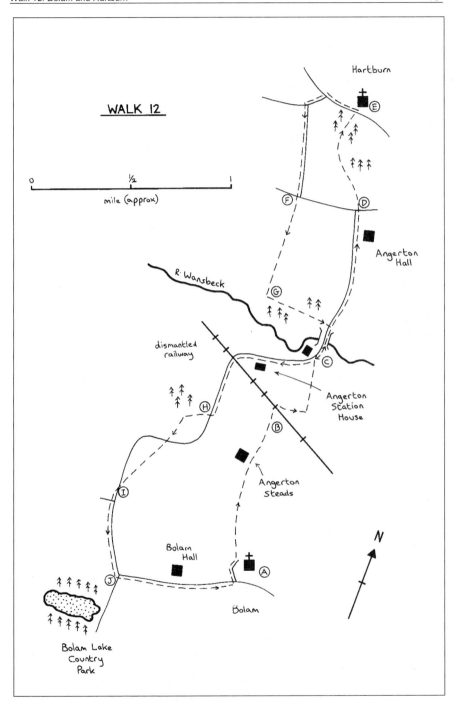

same direction, to a stile. Take the stile to exit onto the road. Cross the road and go over the waymarked stile into the field. Again continue ahead in the same direction to the diagonally opposite corner of the field to a gate, next to a fingerpost, which leads you back onto the road **(I)**.

To continue, turn left and walk along the road as it gradually climbs to pass a junction on the right to Scots Gap. At the next junction turn left at the sign "Bolam ¾", unless you have the time and energy to visit Bolam Lake Country Park **(J)**.

> *Bolam Lake Country Park can be entered via a stile on the right just beyond the road junction. The artificial lake, at one time part of the grounds of Bolam Hall, was designed by John Dobson (see Walk 14, Whalton and Meldon) in 1818, at the request of the Revd John Beresford (later to become Lord Decies and Archbishop of Armagh). The motive for this was said to be his desire to provide employment for the local poor. The hall itself had been built using some of the stones of the Norman castle which had once stood in Bolam and which in turn had occupied part of the site of a camp of the ancient Britons. Some evidence of the ditches which once surrounded the castle is still visible.*

Follow the road back to the church, past Bolam Hall, before reaching a lane on the left which takes you back, via an outhouse on which is engraved the name Decies (see above), to the church and the end of the walk.

# Walk 13: Bellingham

## Singular roof, unique wife and primary path

**Location:** St Cuthbert's Church (NY838833) is in Bellingham on the B6320 about 17 miles north-west of Hexham.

**Distance:** Walk 13(a), Bellingham and Hareshaw House: 6 miles; Walk 13(b), Bellingham only: 3 miles.

**Map:** OS Outdoor Leisure 42: Kielder Water.

**Terrain:** After an initial climb out of Bellingham the walks are mainly on the level. Walk 13(a) includes open moorland and farm fields and can be quite boggy at times. Walk 13(b) is mainly on roads and farm tracks.

**Church:** St Cuthbert.

**Car parking:** There is street parking off the main road near the church or near the Tourist Information Office.

## The Church

The church stands in its well-maintained churchyard in the small town of Bellingham. Partially hidden by nearby properties, it is by no means a picture postcard building. It is a small, low structure with a little bellcote at the end and a south transept. An unremarkable exterior conceals a remarkable feature, which can be appreciated immediately you go through the north door into the church. Here, above you in the nave, is a massive stone roof

Interior of St Cuthbert's Church, Bellingham with stone roof and arches (with kind permission from the vicar)

supported by 15 narrow semicircular stone arches; the roof of the transept is similarly constructed. Tomlinson (*Comprehensive Guide to Northumberland*), writing in 1888, was possibly the first commentator to describe it as "almost unique in England". It is thought that the church was built around 1180 and various changes to the building were made over the next 100 years or so. What is now seen is a mainly 13th-century chancel together with a nave and south transept, both of which were rebuilt with stone roofs and thick walls in the early 17th century.

Tradition has it that the church had been burnt down twice by marauding Scots in the border wars, which could account for the incorporation of fire-proof stone roofs. Strong walls, roofs, and narrow windows were important defensive features of ecclesiastical and domestic buildings in vulnerable places such as Bellingham in the turbulent times of the border wars and the border reivers.

Another local tradition holds that Bellingham was one of the resting places during the flight of monks from Lindisfarne with St Cuthbert's body during the 9th century – which could account for the church's dedication to the saint. Just outside the south wall of the church grounds is St Cuthbert's (or "Cuddy's") well, with a long held reputation for miraculous healing powers.

There are several memorial plaques including some to members of well known local families, such as the Charltons and Robsons. All respectable now but with "interesting" histories in the times of the reivers. The stone roofs, white plastered walls, attractive stained glass and sturdy pews contribute to the overall feeling of solid simplicity in this ancient church. Visitors are made to feel welcome here, not least by the timed light switch near the entrance door.

### Among the other features of interest are:

❖ The octagonal stone font at the west end of the nave near the entrance door. The cover, which has a carving of the Madonna and Child, is the war memorial for World War II with the names of the fallen inscribed on its metal rim.

❖ To the left of the chancel arch, a glass case containing three cannon balls found in the roof in 1861, which are thought to have been fired during a raid in 1597 by the Duke of Buccleugh's men.

❖ The 13th-century chancel arch.

❖ In the south wall of the sanctuary, a memorial plaque to a local physician and surgeon and the adjacent stained-glass window and its apposite depiction of St Luke the healer.

❖ In the north part of the graveyard, the "Long Pack" tombstone, a reminder of a legend of an attempted felony with a tragic ending when a prospective robber, concealed inside a peddler's pack, was shot when he moved. Subsequently, four of his companions met a similar fate when they arrived at the call of a whistle found in the pack.

### Information available in the church:

❶ Hand-held information board.

❶ Plan of the church on a pillar in the south transept.

# The Walks

## Walk 13(a), Bellingham and Hareshaw House: 6 miles

Leave the church and grounds **(A)** and turn right. Walk to the road on the right, signposted "West Woodburn". Go along this road and follow it as it leaves the town and bears left to go up a steep hill. At the top, the road bears sharply to the right but straight ahead there is a Pennine Way sign. Go through the gate to join the Pennine Way and walk along the farm track to arrive at a junction of paths at Blakelaw Farm **(B)**.

At the farm turn left, as indicated by another Pennine Way sign. As you pass the farmhouse on your left, notice the interesting warning notice. Go through the gate ahead, into a field. There is a series of waymark posts to follow. Bear slightly right to follow these, aiming for the right-hand edge of the copse of trees on the hill ahead. Keep to the right of the rocky outcrop until you arrive at a gate in a stone wall **(C)**.

Up until this point, there have been wide views over cultivated country but ahead is a stretch of rugged moorland. Go through the gate and head for the next waymark post. At this post, there are two signs, one pointing to the right indicating "Pennine Way" and the other pointing to the left indicating "Alternative Pennine Way". Take the right-hand path and follow this as it crosses the moorland with crags over to the right. The trees on the skyline ahead surround the property at Hareshaw House, the direction you need to follow. Pass a sheepfold on the left and cross a little plank bridge near a large drainage pipe. You are now in a fairly remote, austere area which allows you to have (albeit for only a short while) an experience of the Pennine Way, the first – and possibly the best – long distance walk in England. Carry on in the same direction to arrive at a noticeboard with a map giving details of local permissive paths. Continue on the broad path and, after 200 metres, leave the path and bear right, aiming for the right-hand edge of the small copse ahead. Cross the small burn, making use of the little plank-bridge, and walk past the copse to a waymarked ladder stile. Go over the stile, bear right, and descend to cross the burn. Proceed ahead on the raised path. Aim for the waymarked stile just to the left-hand edge of the plantation ahead. Exit onto a farm road just below Hareshaw House **(D)**.

Turn left to walk along the road for 450 metres and, just before a metal gate, leave the road and turn left to walk, with a wall on your right, to a wooden gate. Go through the gate and proceed the short distance to a finger-post near a ladder stile **(E)**.

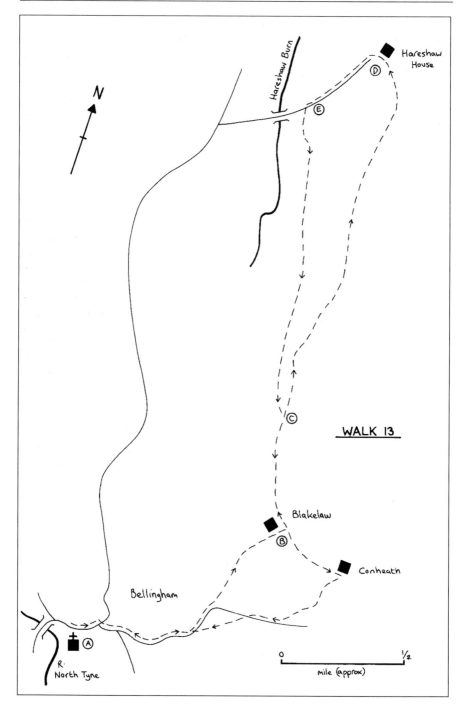

N

Hareshaw Burn

Hareshaw House

Ⓓ

Ⓔ

WALK 13

Ⓒ

Blakelaw

Ⓑ

Conheath

Bellingham

Ⓐ

R.
North Tyne

0                                    ½
mile (approx)

Take the direction indicated for "Alternative Pennine Way" and walk to a ladder stile which is slightly to the left about 100 metres ahead. Cross the stile and bear right to take the faint path which runs roughly parallel to the wall over to your right. Follow the path for 450 metres or so. Keep on the path as it bears left for a short distance and then bears right, again paralleling the wall, now about 100 metres over to your right. Follow the path, now with a fence over to your right, to arrive at a fingerpost (showing "Pennine Way" and "Alternative Pennine Way") which was passed earlier. Follow the direction indicated for "Pennine Way" to walk up the broad grassy track to reach a fingerpost and the gate in a stone wall at **(C)**.

Walk in the direction indicated and retrace your steps, past the house at Blakelaw Farm, to **(B)**.

Walk ahead on the farm track for 600 metres to reach Conheath. Immediately after the house, opposite a waymark post on the left, turn right onto the pasture land (you might have to go under a strand of electric fence wire). Walk straight up the grassy slope and continue in the same direction to go through the waymarked gate which appears ahead. Walk up the slope bearing slightly right and then proceed downhill, with a fence over to your right, to a waymarked stile. Cross the stile and follow the waymark direction to walk diagonally left to a fingerpost in the field corner. Cross the stile to exit onto a road and turn right to walk to a public footpath sign on your left for "Noble Street ¼". Cross the stile and walk in the direction indicated to exit via a stile onto a lane near houses. Turn right and walk the short distance to a junction with a road. Turn left and walk through Bellingham, back to the church and the end of the walk.

## Walk 13(b), Bellingham only: 3 miles

Follow the directions for Walk 13(a) to **(B)** in the first paragraph. Turn right to walk 600 metres to Conheath. Then follow the directions in the last paragraph to the church and the end of the walk.

# Walk 14: Whalton and Meldon

*Clever collage, compelling cycle and canine comforts*

**Location:** St Mary Magdalene's Church (NZ131813) is in Whalton, 18 miles north of Newcastle and 5 miles from Morpeth on the B6524.

**Distance:** Walk 14(a), Whalton, Meldon and Dyke Neuk: 8 miles; Walk 14(b), Whalton and Meldon only: 4 miles.

**Map:** OS Explorer 325: Morpeth & Blyth.

**Terrain:** On quiet country lanes and footpaths over gently undulating countryside.

**Churches:** St Mary Magdalene, Whalton; St John the Baptist, Meldon.

**Car parking:** The parking area near Whalton Parish Church is used by the school during school hours, but there is plenty of space on the road through the village.

## The Churches

### St Mary Magdalene, Whalton

The church, standing at the south of the delightful village of Whalton, occupies a commanding position over the rolling Northumbrian countryside. Its dominant external feature is the substantial west tower. It is believed to date from the 11$^{th}$ century, but it has been subject to several alterations. A clock with a single pointer was added to the east face towards the end of the 18$^{th}$ century and restored in 1982. Well below the top of the tower stands the lightly coloured stone core of the building under a low, pitched roof. Entrance is through the south porch, added in 1908.

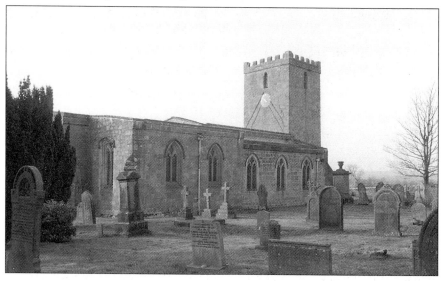

The notable clock tower of St Mary Magdalene, Whalton

Once inside, you need to imagine the church without the 18th-century carved oak screen and the elaborate wall tablets to appreciate what is predominately a 13th-century structure. The short, almost square nave with arcades on both sides leads to the chancel which, in turn, opens on the north to a chantry, referred to as the Ogle Chapel.

Before entering the chapel, you find one of the most striking features of the church in the form of the moulding on the pillar supporting the dividing archway. This is a particularly good example of the dog-tooth decoration that was used extensively in the 13th century. There are also some interesting small faces on the corners of the pillar, as well as various crude heads in other parts of the building, for example on the south-aisle arcades.

The Ogle Chapel itself is a memorial to the family who once lived close-by in what is now the small hamlet of Ogle. Several tablets and monuments depict their careers and travels and their coat of arms is found incised in the floor.

### *Among the other features of interest are:*

❖ The "Whalton Christ", a collage of nearly 3,000 photographs taken in the village to mark the millennium celebrations and assembled by Ian Johnson to produce a montage of the face of Christ.

❖ The small 15th-century font.

❖ The benefactors' board of 1720, on the north wall.

❖ The coat of arms of George III, on the east wall of the south aisle.

❖ The well-cared-for graveyard where you will find several indications of high rates of infant mortality in the 18th and 19th centuries. Of more recent interest, behind the west wall of the church, is the grave of Lyall Wilkes, a former MP, circuit judge, local historian and biographer.

### *Information available in the church:*

❶ *The Parish Church of St Mary Magdalene Whalton.*

### St John the Baptist, Meldon

This is an early 13th-century church that was restored in 1849 by the Newcastle architect, John Dobson (see below). It stands, set into a mound rising from the road within a fine walled churchyard, amid a small gathering of farms and dwellings. The exterior is small and modest, with its low roof relieved by the addition of a bellcote at the time of its restoration. Entrance is now generally by the second of the two finely hinged doors and involves stepping down directly into the chancel end of the church.

The interior is a fascinating blend of the old and the relatively new. It is not difficult to imagine this as a medieval place of worship. The simplicity of the neat and narrow single-chamber, with its low arched doorways, its slender lancet windows and the arching of the east window, provide an echo of bygone centuries. At the same time, the wooden chancel screen, the Minton

The simplicity of St John the Baptist, Meldon

floor tiles and the painted and panelled chancel ceiling recall the mid-19th-century renovations. The east windows now contain splendid modern stained glass, with appropriate rural images of the plough, the sun, the sheaf and the grain of harvest, designed by Leonard Evetts (see Walk 12, Bolam and Hartburn).

## *Among the other features of interest are:*

❖ The stone effigy, at the west end of the church near the font, of Sir William Fenwicke, a royalist executed in London in 1652. His wife is said to have been Meg of Meldon whose ghost is reputed to be compelled to wander these parts, guarding her treasures, in seven year cycles.

❖ The coats of arms, in the windows, of various owners of Meldon including that of the Radcliffes whose ownership came to an untimely end with the execution in 1716 of the, by then titled, Earl of Derwentwater.

❖ The recessed tablet in the north chancel wall in memory of Isaac Cookson, for whom John Dobson designed nearby Meldon Hall in 1832. The family is also recalled on wall tablets inside the church and the gravestones of several members of the family are in the south-east corner of the grave-yard.

❖ Two unusual late 17th/early 18th-century headstones, slotted in stone posts, outside the entrance door to the church. Just behind them is a well worn 13th-century cross-slab.

## Information available in the church:

**ⓘ** At the time of writing there was no information in Meldon Church; however, *The Parishes of Hartburn, Meldon, and Netherwitton*, by Canon Fergus Donnelly, is available at Hartburn Church (see Walk 12).

*John Dobson (1787-1865), born in North Shields and resident in Newcastle for most of his life, is generally recognised as Northumbria's most outstanding architect. He undertook hundreds of commissions and played a major role in executing much of Richard Grainger's "modernisation" plans for the centre of Newcastle. About a quarter of his work involved designing, restoring or altering church buildings and, according to Thomas Faulkner and Andrew Gregg (John Dobson: Architect of the North East), he was regarded as "an ecclesiastical architect par excellence". However, these authors also point out that this work often involved almost complete reconstruction, an approach which would now be viewed as "insensitive". Users of this book might like to make up their own minds on the issue.*

# The Walks

## Walk 14(a), Whalton, Meldon and Dyke Neuk: 8 miles

Leave Whalton Church **(A)** and turn left. Just beyond the church gate you will see what looks like a mounting block, but which in fact was once the base of a footbridge over to the old rectory. Proceed up to the T-junction with the main road through the village. Turn left, walk along the main street with what is almost a village green on the right-hand side. Just past the Beresford Arms, turn right at the road sign "Meldon 2 Bolam 3¼". Follow the road as it climbs gradually away from the village, past some newer housing. After it levels out you will pass the entrance to North Farm **(B)**.

About a mile from Whalton, at a bend, just after the road crosses the Molesden Burn, take a stile on your left next to a gate at a public footpath sign **(C)**. The walk continues across the field, but in muddy conditions you may prefer to walk on the road to point **(D)**. The right of way is diagonally across the field in the direction of the fingerpost and you need to make for a telegraph pole, the top of which is just visible mid-way between the two electricity pylons. This will bring you to a gateway next to a public footpath sign, where you exit onto the road at a T-junction **(D)**.

From the field exit, continue straight down the road in the direction "Meldon ½" over the dismantled railway line to reach the small hamlet of Meldon with its stone walls, well-kept grass verges, pleasant dwellings, farm buildings and its church **(E)**.

On leaving the churchyard turn right. Follow the road a short distance, ignoring the footpath sign to Howlett Hall, and just beyond the telephone box and post box on your left, look out for a sign "North Side 1¼", just inside Meldon farm gateway. Proceed across the farmyard in the direction of the fingerpost to the field boundary, turn left and walk a few metres to go over a waymarked ladder stile. Go through the gate ahead and continue along the side of the field, with trees on your left, through a gate into another field. Go through a further gate and carry on straight ahead keeping to the high level with the field boundary on your left. The path passes an old gatepost and descends past a collection of old tree trunks and branches to join a broader track coming via a gate from the left. Keep on this track as it bears slightly right, and away from the field boundary, to descend to the corner of the field. A cottage appears over to the right as you make your way down to the right of the buildings of Mill House farm, to exit through a waymarked gate onto a metalled lane opposite the renovated old deerhunters' lodge **(F)**.

Turn left in the direction of the public footpath sign "North Side ½m" and, after a few metres, leave the lane to follow the track on the right which descends past the old mill and crosses a bridge over the River Wansbeck. Follow the farm track as it climbs up from the river, with the wood on your left, until it ends at a waymarked gate. Go through the gate, walk up the field and cross a waymarked stile to exit onto the Mitford-Hartburn road at the cottages of North Side **(G)**.

Turn right and walk down this slightly busier road, which offers a generous grass verge if necessary, for about 400 metres to The Dyke Neuk bar and restaurant. Whether or not you are lured by the sign "Quality food always available", you need to follow the direction of the sign "Meldon 1 Whalton 3" at the road junction just beyond the hostelry **(H)**.

Proceed down this road, crossing the River Wansbeck again, for about 1,200 metres to the next road junction and as the road bears right continue straight ahead in the direction "Molesden 1¾" **(I)**.

Continue along the quiet lane, in the direction of Molesden, for about 400 metres to the Rivergreen Kennels and just opposite the last cottage leave the metalled lane, to take a waymarked stile on your right next to a gate. Follow the track across a field, cross a waymarked stile next to a gate and continue in the same direction through an old gateway and across the dismantled railway. Pass through a waymarked gate and go up the field with a plantation on your left. You may come across "Beware of the bull" signs in this area! At the field boundary there are two gates, go through the right-hand gate and follow the slightly raised track towards the farm buildings ahead. Go over the waymarked ladder stile next to a metal gate just before Penny Hill **(J)**.

Aim for the right-hand corner of the line of trees a short distance ahead and pass through the little wooden door-like gate. This next section may be boggy. Proceed straight ahead with a fence on your right and trees on your left as far as the gorse bushes. Turn left and descend about 100 metres to find a wooden footbridge over the burn. Cross the bridge and turn right. Walk round the perimeter of the field until you reach an open gateway just before a telegraph pole. Go through the gateway, turn left and continue up the side of the next field, following the vehicle tracks towards the buildings of North

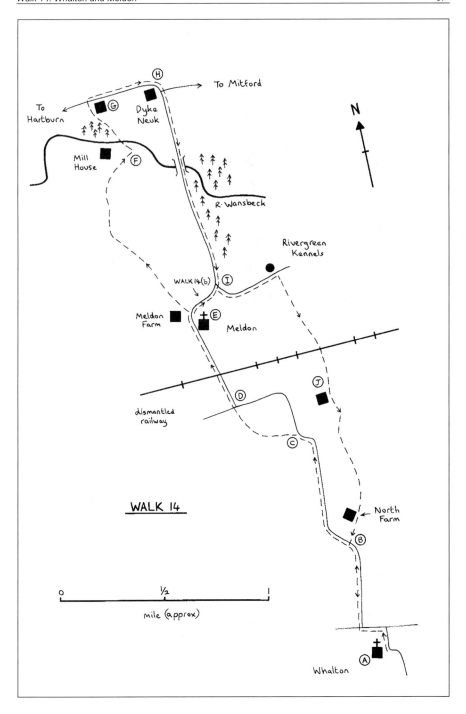

Farm. Proceed through the farm gates, past the barns, and walk down the track to exit back onto the Whalton-Meldon road again **(B)**.

Turn left and follow the road for about 500 metres back to Whalton and the end of the walk.

## Walk 14(b), Whalton and Meldon only: 4 miles

Follow Walk 14(a) as far as Meldon Church **(E)**. On leaving the church turn right and continue along the road to the junction with the road to Molesden **(I)**.

Continue from this point as indicated above in Walk 14(a) back to Whalton Church and the end of the walk.

# Walk 15: Simonburn

## *Mainly Kentigern, some of Kempe and bits of keep*

**Location:** St Mungo's Church (NY 871736) is in the small hamlet of Simonburn, 28 miles north-west of Newcastle and 9 miles from Hexham off the B6320.

**Distance:** Walk 15(a), Simonburn and Latterford: 6½ miles: Walk 15(b), Simonburn only: 4¾ miles.

**Map:** OS Outdoor Leisure 43: Hadrian's Wall.

**Terrain:** A fairly steep climb in the early stages, but otherwise a gently undulating route on footpaths across open country and fields, with some sections on very quiet country lanes.

**Church:** St Mungo.

**Car parking:** There is a car park to the left of the church.

## The Church

The church is in the quiet village of Simonburn on the corner of the village green which is surrounded by pleasant cottages and houses. Mungo is the familiar name given to St Kentigern, meaning "beloved". This Celtic missionary (believed to have lived about 518-603), the patron saint of Glasgow, is generally associated with the west coast although it is believed that his travels may have taken him to Simonburn in the 6th century. This is the only church in Northumbria that bears this dedication and an account of his life can be found in the showcase in the south aisle of the church.

The remains of a 7th-century cross-shaft in the church porch, and other fragments built into the east wall of the porch, suggest that the Angles may have been the first to build a church on this site. The present building, however, can be traced back more accurately to the Normans in the 13th century. Until the early 19th century it served a huge area of 260 square miles and was said to be the largest parish in England, earning for itself the epithet "The Great Parish". The attractive external appearance of the building, with its substantial buttresses and imposing bellcote, certainly suggests that this is too great a church for, what is nowadays, such a small hamlet.

There is a lot to see and appreciate within these walls. However, even without closer inspection, the evocative nature of its intrinsic charm is evident. From the rear of the nave, the eye is carried down the slight (yet obvious) slope past the slender columns, towards a chancel of almost equal proportions, to be led up the steps of the choir and the altar, finally to rest on the fine stained-glass of the east window.

The inscription above the lych-gate in memory of Lancelot Allgood of Nunwick, is just the first memorial to one of the important patron-families of this church. There are a significant number of plaques, in the north aisle and in the chancel, which recall the travels and travails of this family. Their family motto, which with humorous effect translates, "Do all good", is enshrined in the hatchment on the south wall of the chancel.

St Mungo, Simonburn with its imposing bellcote

The south aisle is more the domain of the Ridley family of Park End, and some of their exploits can be discerned in the monuments and plaques in that area of the church. Four stone figures in the east corner represent the Revd Cuthbert Ridley and members of his family. He was rector here for some 32 years, during the reigns of James I and Charles I, and was responsible for restoring the somewhat neglected church to its former glory. When religious practices swung to more puritan tendencies, the family figures were discarded and the Lady Chapel was destroyed. Happily the effigies in their Jacobean costumes were later discovered in the churchyard and restored to their present position.

Although the passage of time has brought several extensions and renovations, St Mungo's undoubtedly preserves a sense of history and an atmosphere of spirituality. As the church guidebook states, "One senses immediately that this church has been prayed in for many centuries".

### *Among the other features of interest are:*

❖ The existence of two baptismal fonts: the decorated Victorian font, currently in use and appropriately positioned near the entrance to the church; and the plain Georgian font near the organ.

❖ The stone head carvings on the capitals of the chancel arch representing, on the left column, St Mungo and on the right, St Catherine.

❖ The gravestone in the floor to the south of the altar which tells of the first English bishop to marry and whose four sisters-in-law were also married to Bishops!

❖ The unusual double piscina of the 13th century on the south wall of the sanctuary and which is still used to wash the communion vessels.

❖ The seven windows by Kempe (see below) which are located as follows: north aisle-centre, north aisle-east, chancel-east, chancel-south, chancel-south-west of priest's door, south aisle-east and south aisle-west most.

*Charles Eamer Kempe (1837-1907), having worked with the noted stained glass designers Clayton and Bell, established his own studio in London in 1869. This became one of the most significant establishments producing stained-glass windows during the Victorian period, and one which carried on in similar style (after his death) until 1934. Northumbria possesses many fine examples of Kempe windows, as evidenced in this volume. Church visitors may like to try to discover one of the trademark wheatsheaf logos, often – but not always – used. For example, in St Mungo's, the three-light window at the east end of the south aisle has the single wheatsheaf at the bottom right-hand side of St John, and the western-most window in the south aisle has a wheatsheaf with a superimposed tower in the bottom left-hand corner.*

### Information available in the church:

❶ *The Great Parish of Simonburn from Hadrian's Wall to Carter Bar,* Revd Canon C.D. Ward Davis.

## The Walks

### Walk 15(a), Simonburn and Latterford: 6½ miles

Leave the church by the lych-gate **(A)** and turn left. Walk in front of the cottages and at the end of the village green, bear left up the metalled Castle Lane, ignoring the lane on the right that leads to the Simonburn Post Office and Tea Rooms (unless you want to begin with refreshments!). Follow the lane until it crosses a bridge and turn left in the direction of the public footpath sign "Fenwickfield 1". The track climbs quite steeply through the wood, and you pass the ruins of Simonburn Castle on your right.

*Little remains of Simonburn Castle today apart from some overgrown masonry, some evidence of well-dressed stone walls and a couple of sturdy archways. A castle has stood on this rise between the Hopeshield and Castle Burns since the early 12^{th} century. For over 400 years, it served as a defence against the Scots in this frequently fought-over border area. It passed into the hands of the Heron family, owners of neighbouring Chipchase Castle, and then it was sold to the Allgoods in 1718. As the usefulness of the castle diminished, it fell into disrepair and the local inhabitants more or less dismantled it in the mistaken belief that it contained buried treasure.*

After about 1,600 metres, the track reaches the farm buildings of Fenwickfield **(B)**. Continue straight ahead in the direction of the public footpath sign, passing the farm on your right, to go through a waymarked gate. About 50 metres beyond the gate, bear right to a waymark on the corner of the fence bordering the plantation. At the fence turn left and walk for a few hundred metres in the direction of the waymark, across the grazing land, to a waymark post on the line of the old boundary wall **(C)**.

Go through the gap in the ruined wall and turn right to follow the line of the old wall as it descends to arrive at a gate. Go through the gate and continue in the same direction as the path climbs to the top of the rise. Stop here to catch your breath and admire the fine views on all sides. Descend in the same direction, crossing a dyke, to reach a grassy track. Turn left and proceed along the grassy track to pass a plantation on your right. Follow the track as it skirts round the plantation and passes through a metal gate onto a metalled lane. Turn right and walk up the lane to exit through a gate, opposite the sign "High Moralee", onto Ward Lane **(D)**.

Go over the lane and continue straight ahead to descend past the entrance to High Moralee. Follow the narrow road as it descends steeply to cross the bridge over the Gofton Burn and then rises again to contour high above the burn on your right. After passing the farm buildings of Low Moralee on your left, the lane cuts through the edge of a plantation. Just before the farm buildings of Latterford, take the right fork down another lane, which crosses the burn. An old footbridge stands on your left **(E)**.

Continue up the lane and, about 50 metres past The Croft on your left, leave the lane just before two further dwellings at a public footpath sign on the right, "Conshield ½".

Cross the stone and wooden stiles and walk up the side of the field. Take the waymarked stone stile. Here you should be able to see Chipchase Castle on your left. Continue ahead in the same direction and go over two stiles in quick succession. Follow the track for about 20 metres with a stone wall on your right, then bear right up the track to the farm buildings of Conshield **(F)**.

Go through the first metal gate on your left, turn right, and leave the farm via the farmyard. Follow the farm road for about 50 metres but, as it bears left, leave it and go straight ahead through a metal gate. Take the left-hand fork to ascend a track that bears left. As the track levels off, go diagonally right across the field and make for a gate in the top left-hand corner of the field boundary. Go though the gate and continue climbing with a fence and a plantation on your left. The path now descends to return via a gate onto the tree-lined Ward Lane **(G)**.

Turn left and walk down the metalled lane for about a mile. About 100 metres beyond the public footpath sign, "Castle Lane ½", leave the road to take the public footpath "Simonburn ½" on the right **(H)**.

Walk down the side of the field, cross the small footbridge, and a waymarked stile. Continue in the same direction keeping to the left of the fence ahead to cross a gated footbridge. Keep the fence on your left and, after two waymarked gates in quick succession, you arrive at Simonburn Post Office (and refreshments!). Proceed by the village green to the church and the end of the walk.

## Walk 15(b), Simonburn only: 4¾ miles

Follow Walk 15(a) as far as **(D)**. Turn right and walk down Ward Lane for about 1¾ miles as far as the public footpath on the right "Simonburn ½". Complete the walk as from **(H)**.

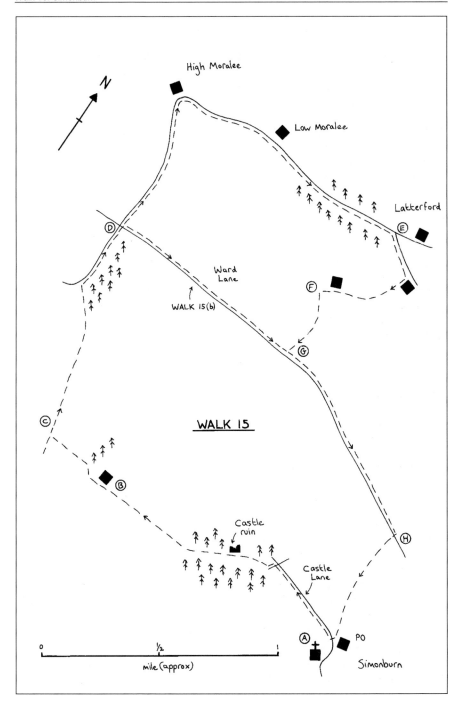

# Walk 16: Heavenfield and Wall

## *Victory, views and villages*

**Location:** St Oswald's Church (NY937696) is on the B6318, 1 mile east of Chollerford and 4 miles west of the crossing of the B6318 with the A68.

**Distance:** Walk 16(a), Heavenfield, Acomb and Wall: 7 miles. Walk 16(b), Heavenfield and Wall: 4 miles.

**Map:** OS Outdoor Leisure 43: Hadrian's Wall.

**Terrain:** Mainly on field paths and quiet country lanes in undulating country, with one steep descent and one short steep ascent.

**Churches** St Oswald, Heavenfield; St George, Wall.

**Car parking:** In a lay-by outside the church grounds.

## The Churches

### St Oswald, Heavenfield

From the roadside, this small church is visible at the top of a gentle rise. It is a simple, low, single-chamber building with a porch on the south wall and a bellcote sitting on the roof above the porch. Surrounded by its graveyard in a walled enclosure, its position is both isolated and exposed, but this is compensated for by the splendid views over the Roman Wall country to the north and over the Tyne valley to the south. Its location is in a place of great historical significance being where Oswald, King of Northumbria, (see below) defeated the British King Cadwalla in 635. For many years following, in those ancient times, this was a place of pilgrimage and for centuries its position was marked by a cross, set upon a Roman altar. Today, a large wooden cross, erected in 1935 at the side of the road, identifies its location and the story of the battle is summarised in a display panel alongside.

The present church, which is probably the third on the site, dates from 1737 and there is a sundial on the south wall from that date. The previous church was a simple, two-cell building, which had been restored during the reign of the first Elizabeth (its foundations have been identified by dowsing). Some relics from this earlier church are displayed in the porch. It served as the parish church for Wall village and the immediate area until St George's Church in Wall was consecrated in 1897. W.S. Hicks (see Walk 17, Corbridge and Halton), the architect of St George's, carried out a Gothic renovation of St Oswald's at the same time.

The external simplicity of this place is matched by its simple, undecorated interior which, with gas lamps and candles on the wall, somehow seems appropriate for a church in this sparsely populated part of the county. A small room behind the west wall contains an exhibition on the Battle of Heavenfield and St Oswald.

The church is still used for services on festivals and some other occasions.

## Among the other features of interest are:

❖ Opposite the entrance, the Roman altar, later used as the base of a Christian cross.

❖ On the west wall, the hatchment bearing the Andrewe coat of arms.

❖ A drawing of a plan of the original two-cell church, located behind the organ.

❖ Masons' marks and an inverted cross on the east wall.

❖ Painted figures of St Aidan and St Oswald behind the altar.

This wooden cross marks the spot where King Oswald defeated King Cadwalla in 635

## Information available in the church:

ℹ Hand-held information board.

*St Oswald (c.604-642) returned from exile in Iona, where he had become a Christian, to regain the family kingship of Northumbria by defeating the tyrannical, heathen king Cadwalla at Heavenfield in 635. Oswald wished for the conversion of the kingdom. To that end, Aidan (see Walk 4, Bamburgh) came from Iona as missionary bishop, and Oswald granted him the island of Lindisfarne for the development of a monastery. Oswald was a well-respected monarch who sometimes took an active part in missionary work by accompanying Aidan and acting as his translator. He was killed in battle against the pagan king Penda of Mercia in 642.*

### St George, Wall

This is a small, stone church which, along with neighbouring houses, forms the centre piece of the large green in the charming village of Wall. It is a rectangular, single-chamber church with quite a large bellcote at the west end. Unusually, it has a north – south orientation. St George's was built in 1896, thus saving the villagers the 1½ mile walk to St Oswald's, Heavenfield, which it replaced.

The interior presents an interesting comparison with the simple plainness of St Oswald's. Here, there is a definite Victorian "feel" but, overall, the effect is cosy rather than cluttered. There is a high wooden ceiling and attractive, plain stone walls with low-level dark wooden panelling. The nave has chairs rather than pews and, except for two wall tablets, no adornment. Light comes mainly from the large plain-glass south window and six similar, but smaller, windows on the east wall and one on the west, as well as from the stained-glass north window.

From the nave, before you climb the three steps to the chancel, you are presented with an almost startling contrast. The chancel is divided from the

The late 19th-century church of St George, Wall

plain nave by a low carved rail, which incorporates a pulpit and lectern with carved priests' stalls behind. Above is a magnificently carved screen and cross.

### *Among the other features of interest are:*

❖ The stone font which has a fluted pedestal and an octagonal basin with carvings of flowers.

❖ The tablet on the north wall in memory of a long-serving churchwarden.

❖ The splendid five-light north window by Kempe (see Walk 15, Simonburn), with Christ in the centre and including depictions of St George, St Oswald and St Aidan.

## The Walks

### Walk 16(a), Heavenfield, Acomb and Wall: 7 miles

Leave the church **(A)** and grounds and cross the B6318, with great care, to take the minor road opposite. Walk past St Oswald's Cottage on your right and follow the road as it swings to the right and climbs to arrive at a gate, beyond which is a post with two public footpath signs. Go through the gate and take the path indicated towards Fallowfield, going across the field aiming for the right-hand corner of the long plantation in the distance. Near the corner of the plantation turn right, and follow the overgrown vehicle track to a gate beyond which is a small post with waymark signs **(B)**.

Go through the gate and turn left on the public bridleway and walk to a gate. Go through the gate and bear left at the fork to continue on the track, in line with the plantation over to your left, to a gate in a wall. Go through the gate, bear right to walk, with the wall on your right, to follow the field edge to the wood at the bottom of the slope. Some disused mine buildings are over to the right, part of the remains of the once prosperous mining activity, which provided much local employment, centred on the village of Acomb. Go through the waymarked gate into the woods and follow the path until a junction with another woodland path is reached at a waymarked post. Turn right and walk along this path to emerge from the woods near to a large house on your right **(C)**.

Walk past the house and proceed along the track to arrive at a junction at Fallowfield Dene Camping and Caravan Site. Bear left, cross the bridge and follow the road for about 800 metres, passing the Mariners Cottage Hotel on your left. The road comes out at a junction where you turn right towards Acomb. When you reach the village keep to the main street, passing the Miners Arms Inn (1750) on the left, until you see the Sun Inn on the right-hand side and, just before the inn, look for a public footpath sign to Halfway House on your right **(D)**.

Take this path and keep to the right to go below the gardens of houses to your right. The path comes out at a gate. Go through the gate and descend to a footbridge. Cross the bridge, go up the steps and over the stile. Turn right and climb up the bank to enter the next field. Now follow the waymark and head up the field with the field boundary on your left. Carry on in the same direction until you reach a waymarked ladder stile on your left. Cross the stile and turn right to walk uphill, keeping to the right of the house ahead. Beyond the building (the aptly named Low Engine Cottage, which incorporates part of the engine house of the former Acomb pit) turn left and walk up the field, keeping to the left of the small copse, and go over the ladder stile onto a farm track. Turn left and walk a few metres to a junction with another road. Halfway House Farm is on the other side of this road **(E)**.

Turn right and walk uphill for about 1,500 metres to Fallowfield. At Fallowfield House, look out for the public footpath sign to "Wall" on your left **(F)**.

Go along the road indicated until you reach the last house on the right. The public footpath goes up the drive of this property for a few metres, until you reach a stile going over the wall on your left. Go over the wall and walk between the trees to exit the wood, via another stile, over a wall into a field. Head slightly to the right to make for the left-hand edge of the long plantation in the distance. Go over a stone stile, just beyond a waymark, into the wood. The path winds between the trees and bracken and eventually exits into a field via a waymarked stile. Walk towards the left-hand edge of the gorse bushes in the field ahead. Beyond the bushes go over a waymarked stile into a grassy area between two walls. Bear left, then right, to skirt a small copse. Continue ahead with the wall on your right and go over a waymarked stone stile. Bear left and walk the short distance to go through an open gateway

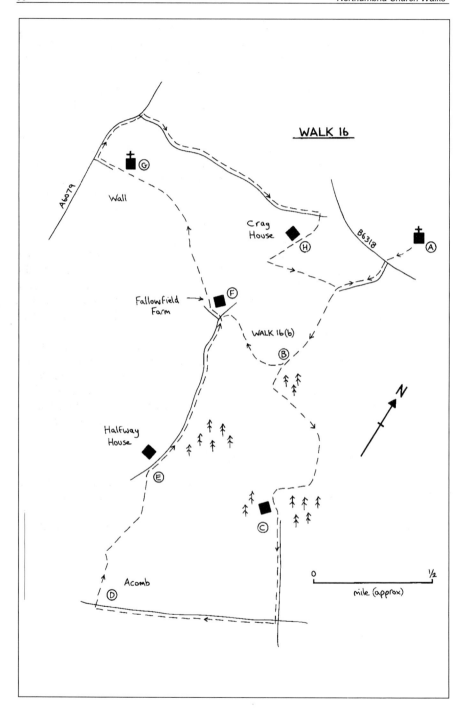

WALK 16

between two metal posts. Cross the rough ground, which contains vestiges of an ancient settlement. Turn slightly right to arrive at the top of a hill with Wall below. Proceed downhill towards the village. The slope is steep and can be very muddy. As you approach the bottom, go through the gate and down steps to another gate. Go through this gate and a kissing gate and across the small field, to enter Wall village at another St Oswald's Cottage. St George's Church is ahead on the left **(G)**.

Coming out of the church, turn right and right again, past the south end of the building and proceed ahead over a minor road, past the village green to reach a main road at a T-junction. At the junction, if a refreshment stop is needed, the Hadrian Hotel is a few metres down to the left on the other side of the road. For the continuation of the walk you need to turn right and walk uphill to the end of the village. At a junction after the speed de-restriction sign, turn right and take the left-hand fork. This road is not signposted. Follow the road, which climbs uphill for about 1,500 metres, passing Chesterwood on your left. The grounds of the aptly named Crag House appear on the right. At a point where there are public footpath signs to the left and right, go over the stone stile on your right to take the path "Fallowfield ¾". Go straight up the steep bank to come to a waymark post. Follow the direction indicated, which is slightly to the right, to arrive at a gate leading onto a farm track. Crag House is over to your right **(H)**.

Go through the gate and turn left. Follow the farm track past the plantation on your left to arrive at a metalled road. Turn left with trees on your left and keep to the road, going through a gate, to arrive at a gate near a fingerpost. This is the gate near to the start of the walk which you came through earlier. Go through the gate to retrace your steps back to the B6318, the Military Road. Cross the road, with care, to the lay-by near St Oswald's Church and the end of the walk.

## Walk 16(b), Heavenfield and Wall: 4 miles

Follow Walk 16(a) as far as **(B)**. Go through the gate and turn right to follow the track as it passes through gates at Fallowfield to join a minor road. Turn left and after about 50 metres turn right past a barn. Now follow the directions from **(F)** to Wall and back to Heavenfield and the end of the walk.

# Walk 17: Corbridge and Halton

*Roman remains, social reformer and towering ruins*

**Location:** St Andrew's Church (NY988644) is in Corbridge on the B6530 off the A69 about 7 miles from Hexham and 20 miles from Newcastle.

**Distance:** 7½ miles.

**Maps:** OS Outdoor Leisure 43 Hadrian's Wall, Haltwhistle and Hexham, and OS Explorer 316: Newcastle upon Tyne.

**Terrain:** The walk is on minor roads for the first 3 miles then on public footpaths across waymarked fields and through woodlands.

**Churches:** St Andrew, Corbridge: St Oswald, Halton.

**Car parking:** There is a public parking area down the road by the side of the Abbeyfield home, opposite the west end of St Andrew's Church, Corbridge.

## The Churches

### St Andrew, Corbridge

St Andrew, Corbridge – an important Saxon monument

The church is located within a fine, walled churchyard overlooking the village square with its iron market cross, dated 1814, which bears the crescent and lion symbols of the Percys, Dukes of Northumberland. The remains of a 14th-century pele tower, home and refuge of the vicars of Corbridge against marauding invaders for over 300 years, stands within the church grounds. The original stone market cross has been placed near the entrance to the pele tower.

St Andrew's is described by Pevsner (*The Buildings of England: Northumberland*) as "the most important surviving Saxon monument in Northumberland, except for Hexham crypt". Although the first historical reference to the church was in 786, it is believed to have been founded towards the end of the 7th century by St Wilfrid (see Walk 21, St John Lee and Hexham).

The entrance to the grounds is by a lych-gate, a memorial to the large number of local men who fell in the 1914-18 War. The church itself is entered through a 20th-century porch that serves to protect a splendid 12th-century Norman arched doorway with its characteristic zig-zag mouldings. The major remaining Saxon section is at the west end of the church under the tower. A massive arch, said to be a re-assembled gateway from the Roman camp at Corstopitum, the original Corbridge, marks the original entrance from the porch into the nave. The archway now leads into the baptistry where, behind the font, are traces of the old Saxon doorway. Although there is evidence of early stonework in other parts of the building, the remaining structure is largely 13th century, with 19th- and 20th-century furnishings.

The nave has aisles on each side, as well as both north and south transepts. The slender columns and arches, together with the high ceiling, produce a sense of spaciousness, as the eye is carried forward to the tall and delicate 13th-century chancel arch and beyond to the fine lancet windows. The three east windows were given by the family of John and Hannah Grey, one of whom was Josephine Butler (see below). These windows, together with several others – notably the small rounded window in the baptistry showing St Andrew – are believed to be the work of William Wailes (see Walk 19, Bywell).

St Andrew's clearly contains a great deal of interest for the visitor, much of which is detailed in the good selection of literature available in the church.

***Among the other features of interest are:***

❖ The modern stained-glass window of St Christopher in the north aisle opposite the entrance to the church, by Leonard Evetts (see Walk 12, Bolam and Hartburn).

❖ The coat of arms of George III on the north wall. A poignant reminder to local people of where their loyalty should lie, particularly in view of the proximity of Dilston, a former residence of the Earls of Derwentwater, famous for their allegiance to the Jacobite cause.

❖ The millennium window in the east wall of the north transept, given by Corbridge Parish Council.

❖ The memorial on the east wall of the north transept to a missionary who was buried in Jerusalem at an early age.

❖ The portable altar in the south transept used by local Roman Catholics for their weekly Mass, an encouraging sign of inter-denominational co-operation.

***Information available in the church:***

❶ Information sheets in various languages.

❶ *A Guide around St. Andrew's Church, Corbridge*, M.G. Malden.

❶ *St Andrew's Church Corbridge, The Stained Glass,* Lesley Milner.

❶ *Josephine Butler,* JT.

> *Josephine Butler (1828-1906) was one of the daughters of John and Hannah Grey, a noted Northumbrian family who lived a short distance from Corbridge at Dilston Hall. Josephine is renowned for the important role she played in campaigning for social reform and women's rights. She based her work on her strong commitment to Christian values and she is given special recognition by the Church of England, which has dedicated May 30 to her memory. It is interesting, in the context of her work, to see that the two outer lights of the east window represent a female figure carrying out works of mercy. The central light represents scenes from the creed.*

### St Oswald, Halton

The full dedication of this church is to St Oswald, St Cuthbert and King Alfwald. This title relates to the theory that the original church was built here on the site of the murder of King Alfwald of Northumbria in 788. It stands in a magnificent setting, within a tidy graveyard containing two imposing chest-tombs, and next to a well preserved 14th-century tower and a 17th-century house. A path leads to the entrance at the south-west end of the church.

While there is uncertainty as to the exact historical development of the

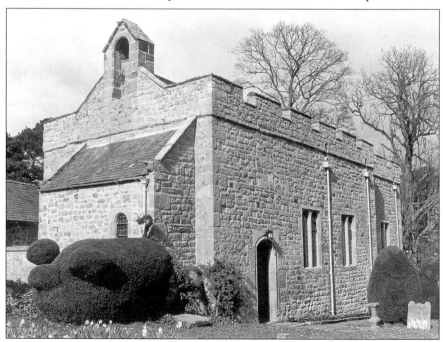

St Oswald, Halton and its topiary pig

present building, it appears likely that some of the external stonework reflects the re-use of stones taken from the nearby Roman Wall area. A further connection with the Roman period can be seen in the Roman altar that stands in the churchyard about 10 metres south of the door. Lesley Milner, in the church leaflet, makes the point that the thickness of the walls matches that of Escomb church (see Walk 27), suggesting therefore that Halton owes its origins to the Anglo-Saxons. The 18th century saw the addition of the embattled parapet, which mirrors that of the tower next door, and also the present bellcote. A 20th-century addition is clearly marked with the date 1938 and a fine topiary-pig stands at the west end!

Once inside, the most distinguished historical feature that remains is the chancel arch, believed to be 12th-century Norman. However, little appears to have been done by way of improvement after the 13th century and the church is said to have gradually fallen into disrepair. In the 16th century some attempt at reconstruction was made by Cuthbert Carnaby, a member of a noted local family, whose initials, together with those of his wife Margaret, are set in the stone arching above the east window. The white washed walls are unadorned, apart from an interesting memorial behind the pulpit to a former minister and the commemoration behind the lectern of a parishioner killed in World War I. This is one of those places that, thankfully perhaps, was not subject to 19/20th-century restorations. Instead, it is now lovingly maintained by a faithful congregation, to whom we have reason to be grateful for the opportunity to experience an atmosphere of simplicity and peace.

*Information available in the church:*

**❶** *Halton Church: an historical guide,* Lesley Milner.

## The Walk

Leave St Andrew's, Corbridge by the lych-gate **(A)**, turn right and follow around the walls of the churchyard to take the first road opposite on your left by the side of the Abbeyfield residence. Go down the lane past the car park and take the footpath on the right "Stagshaw Road ¼". Follow the path past Trough End House, and turn left immediately after Barn Close down the easily missed narrow lane. Proceed up the path, with the stone wall on the right and the fence on the left, to meet a road. Cross over the road and turn left, and walk up Roman Way which then becomes Colchester Lane. After passing Colchester Towers on the right, Beaufront Castle appears ahead amid the trees and then on your left you pass the English Heritage Corstopitum museum. Just prior to passing under the A69 Newcastle–Hexham road you will see the medieval cultivation terraces on the hillside opposite. There is a generous grass verge along the roadside as you follow Colchester Lane for about a mile to a junction where you turn right for "Sandhoe 1; Stagshaw 2½" **(B)**.

Now follow the quiet country lane for 800 metres to the crossroads and turn left for "Sandhoe ½". The lane passes through an old plantation and then climbs more steeply towards the houses ahead. As the road levels out, stop, take a breath, and admire the fine views of the Tyne Valley before leaving the road to go over the stile on the right and onto the public footpath "Mount Pleasant ¼". Climb up the side of the field and exit onto a minor road **(C)**.

Turn right and keep on the road until you reach the church of St Aidan built in 1885 by W.S.Hicks.

> *W.S.Hicks built St Aidan's in the grounds of Stagshaw House as a private chapel for the Straker family. It is generally closed except for occasional services, although you can at least catch a glimpse of its splendid spire which contrasts with the sturdy towers of most of the Tyne Valley churches. A leading exponent of the revival of the Gothic style, Hicks was responsible for numerous ecclesiastical buildings, restorations and furnishings in Northumbria. As Thomas Faulkner ("Architecture in Newcastle", Newcastle upon Tyne: A Modern History) points out there is almost a line of succession in local architects on a pupil/partner basis which links Dobson (1787-1865), Austin (1822-67), Johnson (1832-92) and Hicks (1849-1902). Hicks' own practice survived as Hicks & Charlewood until the 1940s.*

Continue up the road, which eventually levels off for the last time. Thankfully, it is all downhill from now on! At the T-junction, carefully cross over the busier road which runs along the route of the old Roman Dere Street, and bear left on the public footpath signposted "Halton 1; Military Rd 1". The path, which follows the line of the wall on your right, is initially overgrown and boggy. At the metalled road by Low Houses take the left fork for "Halton ½" **(D)**.

Follow the metalled road towards the white house visible through the trees ahead. Just before a right-hand bend where the road crosses a burn, take the almost hidden public footpath signposted "Halton", off to the right. Make your way on the faint path through the bracken. Listen for the dogs barking from the nearby kennels as the path takes you through an old wood with a stone wall on the right. At the end of the wood, cross over a broken wall about 15 metres from the right-hand corner. Bear right and proceed along the narrow path with a fence on your right and a small pond ahead. Follow the burn downstream to the footbridge. Cross the burn, proceed along the other bank and ascend in the direction of the remains of the 14th-century Halton Tower to go through a waymarked gate on the left. The path has been legally diverted for a short distance from here, but you might find some "Bull in field" notices. Hopefully you won't be intimidated. Walk round the perimeter of the field on your right for about 140 metres to take a waymarked stile ahead. Turn right and walk along the field boundary to leave by a waymarked ladder stile and join a metalled lane. Turn right and go through the small gate to the left of the cattle grid. Follow the metalled lane as it bears left and descends for about 150 metres to Halton Church **(E)**.

After pausing at Halton, continue in the same direction down the lane and after 400 metres take the left fork "Aydon Castle ¾". Follow the road to the

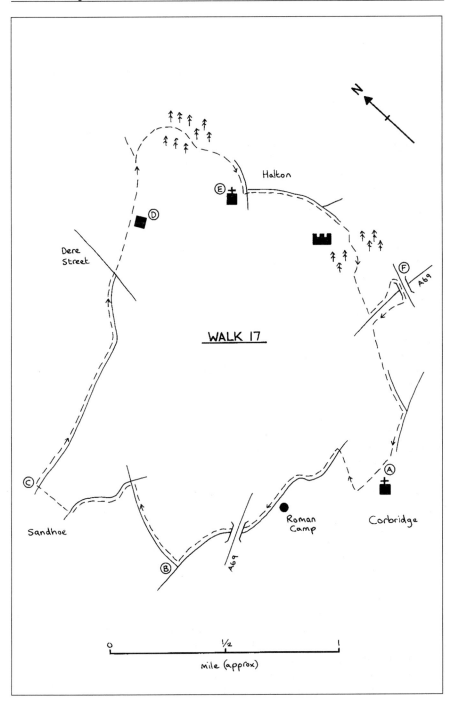

Halton

E

Dere
Street

D

WALK 17

F
A69

C

Sandhoe

Roman
Camp

Corbridge

A

B

A69

0                    ½                    1

mile (approx)

castle car park and then join the public bridleway "Corbridge 2" leading to the ruins of Aydon Castle, a towering 13th-century manor house, now in the hands of English Heritage. Just before the entrance to the castle, pass through two waymarked gates in quick succession and follow the narrow path that descends to cross a footbridge over the burn. Climb up the path on the other side of the burn, and continue ahead as the path skirts the edge of the wood. Leave the wood by the waymarked gate and contour across the field along the faint path to go through a further gate. Watch out for horses in this area. Turn left in the direction of the blue arrow and proceed, with a wall on your left, to pass through the gate ahead. Follow the narrow (and often muddy) path as it leads along the side of the A69 to take you onto a bridge over the main road **(F)**.

Cross the bridge and turn right to follow the bridleway "Deadridge Lane ¼". The path leads onto a metalled track and meets the Aydon Road at Riversdale. Turn right and follow the road into the centre of the town. Turn right at the Tourist Information Office on Hill Street to return to the church and the end of the walk.

# Walk 18: Beltingham

## Royalty, Ridley and riverbank

**Location:** St Cuthbert's Church (NY790640) is in Beltingham, which is about 10 miles west of Hexham on a minor road going south off the A69.

**Distance:** 6 miles.

**Map:** OS Outdoor Leisure 43: Hadrian's Wall.

**Terrain:** Mainly on quiet country lanes and footpaths, with one steep descent through woodland. There is a section on a riverside path with a steep ascent away from the riverbank.

**Church:** St Cuthbert.

**Car parking:** Parking is available outside the church for one car. This space could be used for the church visit. For longer parking, take the road to the left of the church for 300 metres or so and park in a convenient place.

## The Church

This is a charming old church set in the delightful hamlet of Beltingham. Beltingham's stone houses nestle round a miniscule green and the church, which itself is set above the quite steep ravine of the Beltingham Burn to the east. The dedication to St Cuthbert fits in with the claim that this was one of the places where the saint's remains rested on the journey from Lindisfarne to Bewcastle in the 9th century.

The present building dates from about 1500 but there is evidence of earlier churches on the site, from Saxon times. It was built as a chapel-of-ease

Attractive arched windows at St Cuthbert, Beltingham

for Haltwhistle and is thought that the Ridley family (see below) used it as their domestic chapel. By 1650 it was in a ruinous state; subsequent renovations were carried out, culminating in an extensive restoration in 1884. It is a fairly small, single-chamber building with attractive arched windows.

Inside are dark wooden pews and furnishings. The high ceiling, and lack of division between nave and chancel, helps to give an impression of spaciousness which is enhanced by the light from the splendid stained glass. There are a number of memorial tablets displayed – particularly on the north and south walls – possibly too many for some people's tastes. Nevertheless, on the whole they seem to be in keeping and, at the very least, provide an introduction to the interesting personages who have had connections with St Cuthbert's. There is a strong association with the family of the late Queen Mother, the Bowes-Lyons. Several of the stained-glass windows are in memory of family members and the family has a separate plot in the graveyard, provided in 1904 by the Hon Francis Bowes-Lyon who lived at nearby Ridley Hall at that time.

Visitors are made welcome in this peaceful old church. A leaflet with appropriate verses is provided to help those who wish to spend a little time here in quiet contemplation.

### *Among the other features of interest are:*

❖ On the north wall of the chancel, a stained-glass window by Kempe (see Walk 15, Simonburn).

❖ On the north wall of the chancel, a grill set over a lepers' "squint". An accompanying notice gives further information.

❖ On the south wall of the chancel, a stained-glass window by Leonard Evetts (see Walk 12, Bolam and Hartburn). The modern design provides an interesting contrast with the other stained glass in the church. An adjacent information board provides an explanation.

❖ The imposing east five-light window by Kempe, showing Christ Crucified in the centre with the Virgin Mary and St Peter on His right and St John and St Paul on His left. Two local saints are shown in the lower level: St Cuthbert on the left and St Aidan on the right.

❖ Outside the north side of the church, an ancient yew tree, supported by metal bands.

### *Information available in the church:*

❶ *The Church of St Cuthbert, Beltingham,* Rev C.W. Herring.

# The Walk

Leave the church grounds **(A)**, turn right and follow the road as it descends out of the village. Carry on along this road, initially parallel to the River South Tyne, for about 900 metres. Pass the nature reserve on the right, before coming to a footbridge over the river leading to Bardon Mill. Keep on the road and carry on in the same direction for a further 1,200 metres, passing the entrance to Partridge Nest on your left. Keep on the road to arrive at the farm of Willimoteswick, once the home of the Ridleys **(B)**.

*The Ridleys were a famous Tynedale family whose name was feared in the times of Border raiding. Willimoteswick Castle (the curious name is thought to be derived from either "guillemot" or "William") was their principal residence but they were also associated with nearby Ridley Hall, which derives its name from them. Willimoteswick is now a farm with extensive buildings which incorporate the former castle gatehouse. It is claimed that Nicholas Ridley, who became Bishop of London, was born at Willimoteswick in about 1500 (a similar claim is made for Unthank Hall a few miles away). Nicholas Ridley was burnt at the stake at Oxford, in 1555, for his opposition to papal supremacy. The Ridley family forfeited their estates in 1652 following Musgrave Ridley's backing for the Royalist cause during the civil war.*

Opposite the entrance to the farm, turn left to follow the road through a gate. The road climbs and passes the woods of Willimoteswick Dene on your right. The way ahead, now a track, goes through a number of gateways and after about a mile comes to a gate leading onto a minor road **(C)**.

Turn left and proceed along the road as it climbs to reach a T-junction. Turn left and follow the road 800 metres, to where it meets a road going off to the right. Keep walking in the same direction as the road continues to descend for a further 900 metres. Just before the road bears left, look for the sign to Briarwood on your right **(D)**.

Take the broad farm track and follow it as it turns right to head for the farm buildings. Do not go into the farm area but pass the barn on your left and go straight ahead to cross a stile next to a gate. Walk a short distance across the field to arrive at a kissing gate next to a sign "Briarwood Banks Nature Reserve". Go through the gate and descend between the trees, quite steeply at times, ignoring minor paths off to the left and right. At a major junction bear left and continue down to a junction of paths near a footbridge over a tributary of the River Allen, with the Allen itself in front of you **(E)**.

Turn left and walk through the woods with the River Allen on your right. In a few hundred metres, you pass a sign indicating that this area is Allen Banks and belongs to the National Trust. A little further on the path ascends to cross another tributary by a plank bridge, and after 150 metres there is a fork. Take the right-hand path to continue along the riverside. Carry on, until eventually a waymark directs you to the right and the path descends closer to the river and reaches a suspension bridge. After a further 400 metres you reach a footpath which goes off to the left and almost doubles back as it ascends between the trees by a series of steps. At the top, emerge into a clearing with a public footpath sign and a stile in the fence ahead **(F)**.

Go over the stile. Over to the right is Ridley Hall. Follow the line of trees and the boundary wall/fence on your left to pass through a clump of trees and reach a waymarked stile next to a metal gate. Cross the stile and proceed along the track to the road. Turn right and walk for 500 metres or so, passing Ridley Bastle on your right, to a public footpath sign on your left showing "Beltingham ¼" **(G)**.

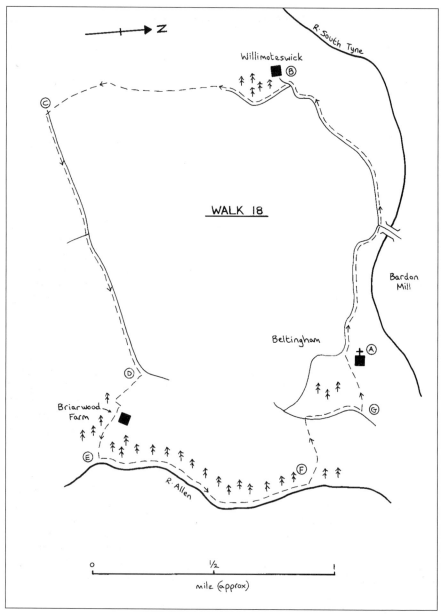

Cross the stile to take the footpath. Follow the track, with a wire fence on your left, then go through a kissing gate and proceed in the same direction, with a wire fence now on your right. Keep on the track as it enters a wood and crosses a burn to arrive at Beltingham, the church and the end of the walk.

# Walk 19: Bywell

## *Medieval monks, marvellous mosaics and major manufacturer*

**Location:** St Andrew's and St Peter's Churches (NZ048615) are at Bywell just off the B6309, a short distance from the A69, about 18 miles from Newcastle and 7 miles from Hexham.

**Distance:** 6 miles.

**Map:** OS Explorer 316: Newcastle upon Tyne.

**Terrain:** Mainly on pleasant country lanes, with two gentle climbs through fields.

**Churches:** St Andrew and St Peter, both at Bywell.

**Car parking:** Parking is available close to the two churches.

## The Churches

Here are two splendid churches standing virtually side by side, separated only by a hedge, a driveway and a medieval cross. The two churches of St Andrew and St Peter were established at the dividing point of the territories of two different baronies, with the assistance of two religious orders: the White Canons of Blanchland (see Walk 22); and the black-robed Benedictines, whose distinct robes gave rise to the local epithets of the "white church" (St Andrew's) and the "black church" (St Peter's).

### St Andrew

Bywell was once a thriving village of over 500 inhabitants, but as its industries, based on iron, declined in the 18$^{th}$ and 19$^{th}$ centuries, so did the population to the extent that it now consists only of a handful of elegant residences. Clearly it became more and more of a struggle to maintain one – let alone two – churches, and so it was that St Andrew's, the smaller of the two, was declared a redundant church in 1973. However, thankfully under the Churches Conservation Trust, it has been repaired and well-maintained for visitors to enjoy.

The church stands in an almost circular graveyard, indicative of its original foundation – possibly as early as the 7$^{th}$ century – by St Wilfrid of nearby Hexham Abbey (see Walk 21). Externally, attention is drawn to the splendid tower with its fine belfry and window openings, described by Pevsner (*The Buildings of England: Northumberland*) as "a first rate Saxon west tower, the best in the county". The base is believed to date from the 9$^{th}$ century and the upper parts from the 10$^{th}$ century. The large well-cut stones, like so much stonework in the Tyne valley, are probably of Roman origin from nearby Hadrian's Wall.

The small and intimate interior was subject to alterations in the first half of the 19$^{th}$ century by John Dobson (see Walk 14, Whalton and Meldon) and in the second half of the century to major restoration and additions by other architects and designers. Today you find a nave and chancel of almost equal lengths with transepts on either side and, to the north of the chancel, a chapel area linked with the north transept and devoid of furnishings other than pews. However, St Andrew's is still evocative of earlier times. One of its most important features is its remarkable collection of mainly 12<sup>th</sup>-and 13<sup>th</sup>-century grave covers. These bear symbols, such as shields, swords, horns and shears, to represent the trade, rank or gender of the deceased. Some were set in the external side of the north wall, one forms the lintel over the south door and several have been transferred to the north and south transepts for preservation.

The Churches Conservation Trust certainly welcomes visitors to St Andrew's with a guidebook and courtesy light, both of which help to facilitate a greater insight into this historic and peaceful building.

St Andrew, Bywell – the white church

***Among the other features of interest are:***

❖ The stone baptismal font of the early 14<sup>th</sup> century with a 17<sup>th</sup>-century cover.

❖ Several memorials to the Fenwick family, including, in the entrance floor, the gravestone of William Fenwick, the first owner of the adjacent Bywell Hall (now the property of the Allendale family).

❖ The stained-glass window in the north wall of the nave by the local manufacturer William Wailes (see below) whose name, unusually in his case, is inscribed (in Latin) at the bottom of the window.

❖ The ornate stone lectern and pulpit of 1871.

❖ The splendid mosaic sanctuary floor, the mosaic reredos showing St Andrew and St Peter and the fine triple-lancet east window, all of which were added in the 1880s.

***Information available in the church:***

❶ *St Andrew's Church: Bywell, Northumberland,* The Churches Conservation Trust.

## St Peter

The "black church" stands beyond the medieval market cross of Bywell, literally a stone's throw from St Andrew's. It is beautifully positioned in an extensive graveyard, amid the ivy-covered trees which usually serve to conceal the River Tyne, as it flows by on the south side. It is believed that there was a church here as early as 802. However, although the aisles and porch contain remnants of Saxon grave slabs and crosses, the present building is mainly early Norman and 13th century. It has a squatter and more elongated structure than its neighbour and, viewed from the outside, the additions over the centuries are more apparent. As with the "white church", St Peter's has been subject to considerable restoration with some of the 19th-century work being "overdone", according to some authorities.

The initial impression within the church itself is of an active place of worship, with hymn books, banners and noticeboards, in contrast to its redundant neighbour. Simon Jenkins (*England's Thousand Best Churches*) aptly calls it "friendly and domestic". The nave, short in length, but high and wide, leads to a rather long, narrow chancel with its opulent oak choir stalls covered with cushions bearing the emblems of St Peter: keys and fishes. The elegant chancel arch is believed to be a mid-19th-century replica of the 13th-century version. Behind the high altar, the tall lancet windows, so popular in Northumberland, cast a welcoming light.

Beyond the north aisle is a 14th-century chapel built as a chantry for the Neville family. The chantry chapel practice of offering masses for the dead ended with the Reformation and this area of the church later acted as the village school room until 1849. Nowadays its significance lies in its fine collec-

St Peter, Bywell – the black church

tion of Victorian stained-glass windows which are dedicated to various members of the local Wailes family and which are presumed to be the work of William Wailes (see below).

**Among the other features of interest are:**

❖ The notice from 1849, over the doorway in the west wall, about free as opposed to rented pews.

❖ The medieval baptismal font and its elaborately carved 18th-century wooden cover with pulley.

❖ The carved head of King Edward I above the capital of one of the pillars on the south side of the nave. The King is believed to have halted here in the 13th century on his way to attack the Scots.

❖ The window showing St Peter in the south wall of the chancel, in memory of a curate who died tragically.

**Information available in the church:**

❶ *A Short Guide to Bywell, St Peter's Church.*

❶ Hand-held information board.

> *William Wailes (1801-1881), born and bred on Tyneside, became an interna-tionally renowned manufacturer of stained glass, employing at one time about 100 men with a prolific production of nearly 400 windows a year. How-ever, some controversy exists as to the extent of his work as a designer and/or manufacturer. While Pevsner (The Buildings of England: Northumberland) describes him as "one of the most successful artists in stained glass", Mar-shall Hall (The Artists of Northumbria) questions "that he actively involved himself in the designing of his windows", and suggests rather that his talent lay in selecting good artists to help him. Whatever the case might be, it is clear that he was very much associated with John Dobson's church restoration work and that "Wailes" windows grace many Northumbrian churches.*

# The Walk

Leave the churches **(A)** and walk back down the road to the entrance to the remains of the 15th-century castle built by the Neville family of Raby Castle (see Walk 29, Staindrop) and now incorporated into the adjacent private dwellings. Turn right through a gate to take the public footpath "Bywell Bridge ¼". Then after a kissing gate, cross the road and, without crossing the bridge over the River Tyne (although a detour to admire the river view is rec-ommended), continue along the road in the direction "Ovington, Ovingham, Wylam". Walk parallel to the river for some 700 metres, then leave the road to take a ladder stile on the left onto the public footpath signposted "Ovington 1" **(B)**.

Go diagonally right over the field, as indicated by the fingerpost, and leave by the waymarked ladder stile almost concealed in the largest clump of haw-thorn bushes in the field boundary. Continue across the next field in the

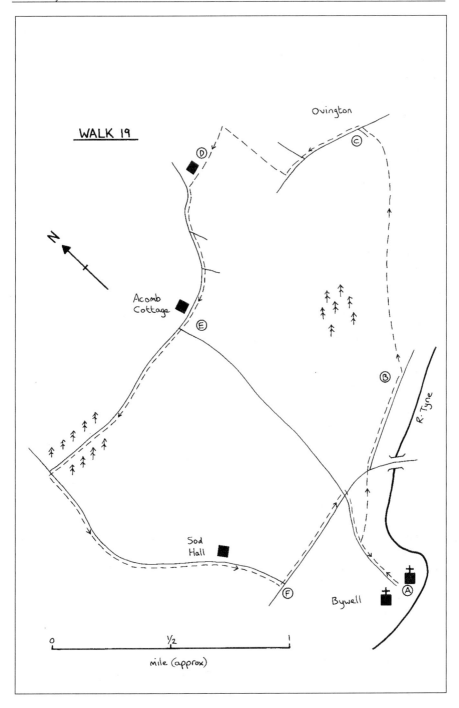

WALK 19

Ovington

© D

Acomb Cottage

© E

© C

© B

R. Tyne

Sod Hall

© F

© A

Bywell

N

0                    ½                    1

mile (approx)

direction of the waymark to a waymarked stile, near a gate to the left of a break in the hedge. Cross the stile and follow the faint path straight ahead, to a further waymarked stile near a gate. Ascend the field in the direction of the waymark sign and, at the top of the rise, as you bear right to cross the waymarked stile in the fence, the small village of Ovington comes into view. Now keep straight on, keeping to the high ground for about 300 metres, as the slightly larger village of Ovingham comes into view by the river below, with Prudhoe Castle ahead to the south-east. Gradually descend to the left as the next waymarked stile appears in the bottom left-hand corner. Cross the stile and the footbridge and turn left to follow the generous path that takes you around the perimeter of the field, with a hedge on your left, to a stone stile in a fence, some 30 metres before the end of the field. Cross the stile and climb towards the right of the house which appears at the top of the field. Leave the field by the gated stile into a cul-de-sac. Walk to the main road ahead **(C)**.

Turn left (unless you are in search of refreshments, in which case you could take a detour to the shop and tea room a few hundred metres to the right) and continue straight ahead for some 300 metres, ignoring the right turn to Corbridge and Heddon, to pass some pleasant dwellings and reach a public footpath signed "Bearl ¾". Turn right and go through the gap next to the gate marked "private road" to follow the footpath as it climbs, via stiles, through some paddocks to a stile in a field corner. Cross the stile and turn right to follow the path around the perimeter of the field. Carry on to a stone stile in a short section of wall and onto a track, which leads to the farm buildings of Bearl **(D)**.

Pass the farm buildings, the cottages and the veterinary clinic to meet the road at a corner. Proceed straight ahead along the road past Acomb Cottage, with its shield above the doorway, and as the main road turns left, carry straight on along the country lane (you could, of course, elect to follow the main road back to Bywell if you wanted to shorten the walk) **(E)**.

To continue with the walk, carry on along the tree-lined lane for about 1,200 metres as it descends gradually to a T-junction. Turn left and follow the road, on the generous grass verge if so wished, as it descends past Sod Hall to a further T-junction **(F)**.

With the tower of St Andrew's now clearly in sight, turn left and follow the road for 800 metres or so to the crossroads at Bywell. Turn right and follow the road back to the churches and the end of the walk.

# Walk 20: Ovingham

## *Tall tower, illustrious illustrator and canny cabins*

**Location:** St Mary the Virgin's Church (NZ 085637) is in Ovingham, off the A69, 15 miles from Newcastle and 8 miles from Hexham.

**Distance:** Walk 20(a), Ovingham and Ovington: 4½ miles; Walk 20(b), Ovingham only: 2 miles.

**Map:** OS Explorer 316: Newcastle upon Tyne.

**Terrain:** Through pleasant woodland, across fields with some gradual ascents but no steep climbs. Walk 20(a) includes a short section on a minor road.

**Church:** St Mary the Virgin.

**Car parking:** There is limited car parking behind the church, otherwise in the village.

## The Church

The church stands on the main road through the village, opposite the finely restored former vicarage. Across the lane behind the church lies the footpath that led worshippers to the church from the northern part of a much larger ancient parish. It is thought that the name of the village is derived from that of a Saxon chief, Offa, who probably settled here at the beginning of the 7th century. The west tower shows signs of stonework of Saxon origin, and is said to be the tallest in the Tyne valley. It stood not only as a testimony to the Christian faith of the local inhabitants but also more pragmatically as their place of refuge during numerous Scottish wars and border conflicts. However, the basic framework of the church is mainly 13th century, with nave, chancel and transepts in cruciform style. It owes much to the D'Umfravilles, the Norman family who were responsible for building the castle at Prudhoe, a short distance away on the other side of the Tyne.

Entrance is by the south porch, above which stands a statue of the Virgin and Child placed there in 1987 as a result of a competition won by Daniel Oates. The porch, protecting a fine Norman arch within, contains fragments of ancient crosses, as well as the memorial stone that previously stood behind the west tower beside the grave of Thomas Bewick (see below).

The interior of the church is largely Victorian as a result of major restorations during the 19th century and, perhaps not surprisingly, there are numerous memorials to prominent benefactors, particularly the Blackett and the Bigge families. Imposing arcades separate aisles on the north and south sides and also extend into the transepts. However, it is the beautiful windows that create the greatest impact. Simon Jenkins (*England's Thousand Best Churches*) states that "Northumberland is truly the county of the lancet light"; the twenty-one elegant lancets of St Mary's, housing some fine examples of 19th-century stained glass, definitely show this feature to wonderful effect.

In recent times the building has been very well looked after and redecorated.

The tall Saxon tower of St Mary the Virgin, Ovingham

St Mary's is clearly a living church and one where visitors are welcome to reflect on the past and ponder on the future.

### Among the other features of interest are:

❖ A plaque behind the pulpit in memory of a vicar who died while preaching.

❖ The central lancet in the north wall of the chancel, depicting King Oswald at the battle of Heavenfield by Kempe (see Walk 15, Simonburn).

❖ The beautiful east window, *The vision of God*, by William Wailes (see Walk 19, Bywell).

❖ The modern window in the south wall of the nave, by Leonard Evetts (see Walk 12, Bolam and Hartburn) to commemorate the millennium of the tower in 1990 and to mark the occasion of his marriage to his second wife Phyl in this church in 1987.

### Information available in the church:

❶ *Offa's Church*, David Goodacre.

> *Thomas Bewick (1753-1828) a naturalist, painter and wood-engraver, whose engravings and book illustrations have earned him an international reputation, is said by Marshall Hall (The Artists of Northumbria) to be "the most celebrated artist ever produced by Northumbria". He worshipped at St Mary's from an early age and is even said to have practised his artistic skills as a child by drawing in chalk on the gravestones! Thomas Bewick was born at Cherryburn, south of the Tyne from Ovingham, where a cottage, museum and*

*printing house owned by the National Trust provide fascinating insights into his life and work. In St Mary's, in addition to the headstone in the porch referred to above, he is recalled in a tablet on the south wall of the chancel and in a tapestry on the north wall of the nave.*

# The Walks

## Walk 20(a), Ovingham and Ovington: 4½ miles

Leave the church grounds **(A)** by the rear gate on the north side, cross the lane and go over a stone stile to take the public footpath "Whittle Mill, Whittle Dene and Nafferton". Follow the track to cross a waymarked stile and continue straight ahead, keeping a stone wall then a hedge on your right. Cross two stiles in quick succession and continue on the path as it descends to go through a kissing gate where the Whittle Burn comes into view. Proceed along the well-defined path and climb gradually to a kissing gate at the edge of the wood ahead. Go through the gate and follow the path through the wood as it continues to climb slightly and then passes some quaint cabins, before reaching the ruins of a flour mill near a Woodland Trust information board. Proceed ahead for a further 350 metres between the trees, with the burn on your left, until you reach a major fork **(B)**.

Take the left fork and continue on the path with the burn to your left. As you pass a low wall round an old well, take care to keep on the path as it bears slightly right and the bankside drops steeply towards the burn. Continue ahead until you reach a footbridge on your left over the Whittle Burn **(C)**.

Cross the footbridge to a Woodland Trust information board. Climb the stone steps and (ignoring paths off to the right) climb to a junction at the edge of the wood, to a welcoming message on a further Woodland Trust noticeboard. Do not cross the stile ahead to leave the wood, but instead turn left and follow the track at the edge of the wood, with trees and hedge on your right. Continue until this path leads you out of the wood at yet another Woodland Trust sign. Walk down the clear track by the side of the field until eventually you arrive at a T-junction at the corner of a field boundary. Ahead to the left you may see the tower of Ovingham Church **(D)**.

Turn right and walk along what is known as St Andrew's Lane until you arrive at the village of Ovington.

*Ovington, like Ovingham, also proudly traces its history from the time of the Saxon Chief, Offa. Its inhabitants have long made their way on the footpaths and the road to the parish church at Ovingham, although there was a Methodist chapel in Ovington from 1861 to 1981. A book about the village can be obtained at the shop and tea room (opened in 2002 as a result of a local community initiative) in the former Ship Inn, about 100 metres beyond the Social Club. Walkers will be most welcome here.*

Turn left immediately after the Social Club to meet the Ovington to Ovingham road. Proceed down this road, ignoring the right fork to Bywell, until

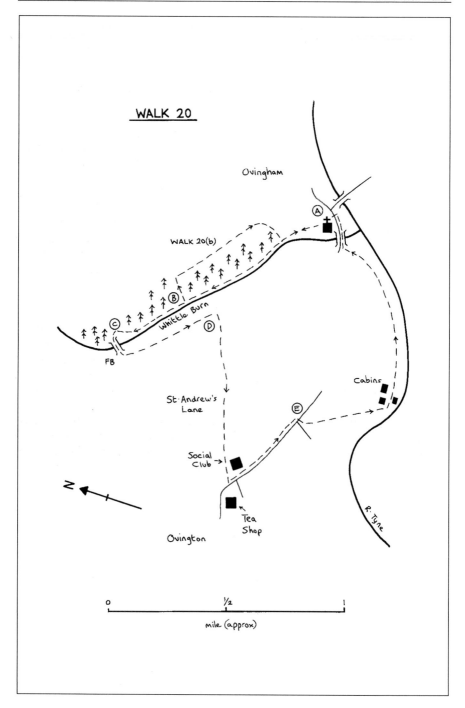

WALK 20

Ovingham

WALK 20(b)

A

B

C

Whittle Burn

D

FB

St·Andrew's
Lane

Cabins

E

Social
Club

R. Tyne

N

Tea
Shop

Ovington

0                    ½                    1

mile (approx)

after about 800 metres you arrive at a junction with a road off to the right to Bywell and Stocksfield **(E)**.

Leave the road and take the public footpath "River Tyne ¼" onto a metalled access road across a field, to pass a further collection of somewhat quaint and unusual holiday cabins. Follow the road as it bears left, and then take the right fork to walk parallel to the river with the Newcastle to Carlisle railway on the opposite bank. As the road bends up to the left at the edge of the settlement, take the footbridge with the white railings by the side of the last cabin ahead. Now continue straight ahead along the path by the river, ignoring the waymarked path off to the left. Gradually, Ovingham Bridge, the church tower of St Mary's, Prudhoe Castle and a factory building come into view. The path widens to a track that bears left, away from the river, at a point where the Whittle Burn flows into the River Tyne. You eventually cross an open green to a public footpath sign at the end of the Pack Horse Bridge. Cross the pedestrian bridge, go straight ahead with the Bridge End Inn on your left, turn left between the buildings and then right onto the pavement by the main road. Now proceed some 100 metres ahead to return to the church and the end of the walk.

## Walk 20(b) Ovingham only: 2 miles.

Follow Walk 20(a) as far as **(B)**. Take the right fork, cross over some duck boarding and climb some stone steps to the path that now bears right and heads back towards Ovingham. Continue on the path as it climbs gradually to go over a ladder stile at the edge of the wood. Turn right and go through a gate some 20 metres ahead. Turn right and go down the side of the field. At the end of the line of trees on your right, and just before field boundary makes a right angle, cross a ladder stile. Continue straight ahead, cross another ladder stile and bear right down the side of the field towards the houses. At the bottom of the field, cross a waymarked ladder stile and turn left onto the path that leads back over the stiles to the church and the end of the walk.

# Walk 21: St John Lee and Hexham
## *Rat, road and rail*

**Location:** The Church of St John of Beverley (NY933657) is at St John Lee, just north of the A69 at the Bridge End roundabout entrance to Hexham.
**Distance:** 5½ miles.
**Map:** OS Outdoor Leisure 43: Hadrian's Wall, Haltwhisle & Hexham.
**Terrain:** Almost entirely on quiet country lanes with one gradual ascent.
**Churches:** St John of Beverley, St John Lee; Hexham Abbey.
**Car parking:** There is parking just beyond the church.

## The Churches
### St John of Beverley, St John Lee

This church lies half-hidden in a quiet and secluded location, despite the proximity nowadays of the busy A69. What you find here is an ancient site, but not an ancient building. "Lee" means clearing in the wood, and it is

thought that John of Beverley frequented the area before briefly becoming Bishop of Hexham in 685. Not too far away is The Hermitage, where he is believed to have exercised a healing ministry. However, the first historical record of a church on the current site is in 1311 when, according to the list of clergy displayed in the baptistry, John del Clay became vicar. Later, it appears that St John's suffered very badly at the hands of the Scots during the border wars of the 17th century, and by the beginning of the 19th century it required major surgery. Hence the church of today is largely a result of the rebuild in 1819 by John Dobson (see Walk 14, Whalton and Meldon) and the major alterations carried out in 1886 by W.S.Hicks (see Walk 17, Corbridge and Halton).

An elegant spire rises above
*The elegant spire of St John of Beverley*    its towered west end and over its

sturdy, but otherwise undistinguished, exterior nave and extended chancel. On entering through the north-west door you immediately find yourself in the baptistry, a veritable store of treasures in itself. On the right is a cup-and-ring stone known as the "Oakwood Stone", said to date from 1600 BC; on the left is a Roman altar converted into a sundial; in front is the font; beyond, on the wall, is the carved head of a bishop, some fragments of 13th-century gravestones, and a funeral hatchment.

Once inside the main body of the church, the eye is drawn towards the beautiful, interlaced fretwork screen of vine branches. This, together with the magnificent wooden ceiling was designed by W.S. Hicks. Above the screen is a modern crucifixion scene made by Robert Craggs of Allendale to a design by Leonard Evetts (see Walk 12, Bolam and Hartburn). The eye is then led beyond the screen to the bold east window. This window is in memory of two daughters of John Hunter, one of whom was the wife of Robert Lancelot Allgood of Nunwick (see Walk 15, Simonburn). The remaining stained-glass windows in the nave, with their generous collection of northern saints, present an invitation to ponder on Northumbria's Christian heritage.

### *Among the other features of interest are:*

❖ In the north-east corner, the effigy of a young man, killed in action in 1916, with his head resting evocatively on his saddle.

❖ Wall tablets recalling exploits of local families. Numerous but not intrusive.

❖ The funeral hatchments on the south wall.

### *Information available in the church:*

❶ *A Leaflet on the Church of St John Lee,* Canon S.E. Pritchard.

❶ Explanatory notes, *The hatchments at St John Lee.*

### The Priory and Parish Church of St Andrew (Hexham Abbey)

The abbey stands rather like a spiritual oasis in the centre of the market town of Hexham, surrounded by pleasant grounds, busy streets and a market place. It has had a long and chequered history since its original foundation in about 674 as a monastery, under Benedictine rule by St Wilfrid (see below). It was laid waste by the Vikings in the 9th century and it was not until the beginning of the 12th century that it was refounded, this time as an Augustinian priory. It then prospered for nearly 200 years until it was gutted in 1296 by the Scots who, for good measure, returned the following year to destroy anything of value that remained. Nevertheless, the resolute monks set about its restoration and, although the nave area was abandoned, the priory rose again in the 14th century to survive further incursions and enjoy some two centuries of comparative prosperity – until the Reformation.

The monastic significance of Hexham was brought to an end by the dissolution of the monastery in 1537. Nevertheless, it continued to function as a parish church and, while the building in general fell into disrepair, worship

Hexham Abbey, the priory and parish church of St Andrew

took place in the surviving chancel and transept areas. Over the ensuing years, ownership of the property and the living passed through the hands of several noted Northumbrian families, including the Hattons, the Fenwicks, the Blacketts, the Wentworths and the Beaumonts. Today the church's patronage is in the hands of their successor Viscount Allendale, and the Mercers' Company.

What you find now is a very substantial and elegant parish church, containing a fascinating blend of the ancient and the modern. This is, to a large extent, the result of the major reconstruction that took place between 1898 and 1917 and, in particular, to the work of Temple Moore, who was responsible for reconstructing the nave to the same dimensions as the medieval priory nave.

The tall building consists of nave, chancel and transepts, with a relatively low and capped central bell and clock tower. You enter by a surprisingly small south door and proceed along a narrow passageway, known as the slype, into the south transept. Here, you may be even more surprised: on both sides, tiered arcades; to the right, a 7th-century cross; to the left, a Roman memorial; ahead in the north transept magnificent stained-glass windows in their slender lancets; and then behind you, the dramatic Night Stairs. You certainly need to pause awhile to absorb the splendour of it all.

The Night Stairs, "one of the finest monastic relics in an English church", according to Simon Jenkins (*England's Thousand Best Churches*), were originally used by the canons to descend from the dormitory into the abbey church to pray and sing their nocturnal offices. Nowadays, you may have the good fortune to see the church choir proceeding down those same thirty-five steps from the Song School which is housed above.

Advance a few metres and you are at the crossing where you can admire the full extent of the nave, the transepts and the screen. The splendidly carved screen, used in pre-Reformation times to separate the lay parishioners from the clergy, is referred to as Prior Smythson's, as he was responsible for its construction around the beginning of the 16<sup>th</sup> century. The statues that once occupied the many niches did not survive the zeal of the reformers, but several somewhat faded paintings did. On the lower part of the screen, local saints and bishops are depicted; while within the entrance through to the choir you find, on the north side, the Annunciation of the Archangel Gabriel to the Virgin Mary; and, on the south side, the Visitation of Mary to her cousin Elizabeth. Beyond the screen are the choir stalls, with their early 15<sup>th</sup>-century misericords, and the elegant sanctuary.

However, perhaps the most evocative of all Hexham's treasures is in the centre of the nave itself. The curious wooden stall in the centre of the aisle is, in fact, the entrance to the 7th-century crypt. It was here that Wilfrid stored some of the treasures that he brought back from Rome, including possibly some relics of St Andrew, the patron saint of the abbey. This became a place of pilgrimage until the dissolution of the abbey, after which it lay empty and hidden until its accidental rediscovery in 1725. Now, with the assistance of the stewards, you can savour the atmosphere of this special place and appreciate the Saxon use of Roman stones in its construction.

Although Hexham Abbey contains a wealth of heritage, which the excellent literature and the attentive stewards can help the visitor to enjoy, it is very much a living church – proud to uphold its traditions, yet prepared to welcome innovation.

### *Among the other features of interest are:*

❖ The 7<sup>th</sup>-century stool in the centre of the choir. This low seat was carved out of a single block of stone and used as St Wilfrid's throne. It is known as the Frith Stool, or Chair of Peace, as it symbolised the right to sanctuary offered by the abbey (see also Walk 25, Durham Cathedral).

❖ The late 15<sup>th</sup>-century chantry chapel of Prior Leschman, between the right-hand end of the north choir aisle and the sanctuary. It has a stone base with crudely carved grotesque heads, animals and foliage and an intricately carved wooden cover. Barely visible behind, lies a stone effigy of the Prior.

❖ St Wilfrid's Chapel at the end of the north choir aisle. A place for quiet prayer and reflection, with a stained-glass window by Kempe (see Walk 15, Simonburn) showing St Wilfrid.

❖ The Dance of Death, the four lower panels on the screen on the north side of the sanctuary, depicting death dancing with eminent personages to represent the inevitability of death for all. This is said to be the best surviving version of this medieval allegory in England.

❖ The Ogle Chantry at the left-hand end of the south choir aisle. This contains an early 15th-century painting with an unusual history, as related in an adjacent notice.

❖ The tiny 7th-century chalice in a showcase in the south choir aisle.

❖ The millennium banner on the south wall of the nave. A magnificent piece of work by members of Hexham Embroiderers' Guild, showing scenes from local life and history, to commemorate the advent of the third Christian millennium.

### Information available in the church:

❶ A plaque on the west wall giving details of the early 20th-century reconstruction work.

❶ *Hexham Abbey,* Colin N. Dallison.

❶ A series of leaflets by Tom Corfe, Shelia and Tom Corfe, Colin Dallison.

> *St Wilfrid (c.633-709) was seemingly of noble parentage and, after a formative period on Lindisfarne, he pursued his education in Rome for six years. During this period he gained a deep appreciation of the forms of worship and the style of church buildings that he found there. So much so, that he became the principal advocate for this cause at the Synod of Whitby in 664, when he successfully argued in favour of the Roman (as opposed to the Celtic) tradition of Christianity. Thereafter, he played a significant role in the Church, becoming a Bishop as well as establishing many monasteries and churches including, of course, Hexham in 674. He is sometimes portrayed as being arrogant and abrasive, as, for example, in Melvyn Bragg's "Credo". Is this perhaps a reflection of the Northumbrian regard for the more simple Celtic tradition?*

## The Walk

Leave the church **(A)** and turn right. Walk down the lane, bear right at the T-junction, and then take the lane to Oakwood to the left of Peaslaw Gates cottage. Climb steadily, and after the road levels off you can rest for a moment on a bench and view Hexham on your right – where you should be able to identify the clock on the Abbey tower. Continue along the narrow, tree-lined lane and shortly after passing Lark Rise you arrive at a junction. Bear left in the direction signposted to Oakwood and Anick. At the next junction bear right as you follow the indications towards a noted hostelry, The Rat. Walk past some of the fine properties of Oakwood and continue until you reach The Rat where, if time allows, you may wish to stop to partake of refreshments or to admire the garden gnomes **(B)**.

Continue down the road as it now drops sharply towards the busy A69 Newcastle to Carlisle road. As the road levels out you arrive at a T-junction. Turn right and follow the road as it carries you over the A69. The road into Hexham is now busier and you may need to use the grass verge from time to time. After walking parallel to the A69 for a short while the road winds to the

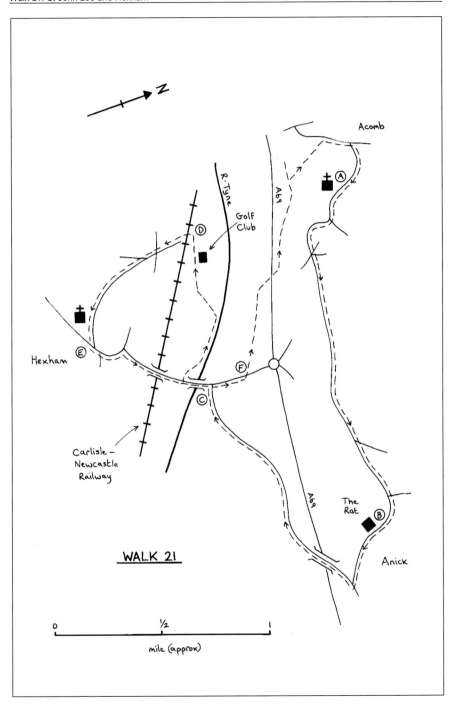

Acomb

R. Tyne

A69

Golf
Club

Ⓓ

Ⓐ

Hexham

Ⓔ

Ⓒ

Ⓕ

Carlisle —
Newcastle
Railway

A69

The
Rat

Ⓑ

Anick

**WALK 21**

0 ½ 1

mile (approx)

left, and extra care needs to be taken as the grass verge disappears. After a few hundred metres you pass through an industrial estate and the entrance to the Egger chipboard factory, which you couldn't help but notice earlier on the walk! You can now follow the pavement to arrive at the main road into Hexham **(C)**.

At the junction, bear left and cross the bridge over the River Tyne. Cross over to the other side of the road at the bollard before the roundabout, and turn right to follow the second pavement as it bears left towards the river. Continue on the metalled surface for about 100 metres to a noticeboard "Welcome to Tyne Green Country Park" and make your way around the Tyne Green Café to join the riverside path. Turn left and follow the path for a few hundred metres, until you draw level with a children's play park on your left and a stream goes under the pathway. Turn left to leave the path and walk a few metres, to cross a footbridge leading towards the play area. Bear right and proceed across the grass, past the picnic area, for about 120 metres until you reach the access road. Join the road and continue in the same direction to pass Tynedale Golf Club. Just beyond the clubhouse, ignoring the railway-crossing gates ahead, bear right and follow the clear path to go over a footbridge. Bear left to the gate and stop, look and listen carefully before crossing the busy Newcastle to Carlisle railway line **(D)**.

Now continue straight up the road ahead while noting the old mill and the burn on the left, behind the low wall, in an area once noted for its leather goods. The cap of the tower of Hexham Abbey comes into view and you soon reach a main road at Eilansgate. Cross over with care and continue ahead, in the direction of the swimming pool. As you pass the water fountain (1858) on your right, look just beyond it for Holy Island House (1657) with its attractive doorway and the crest of the noted local Kirksopp family (recalled in the north transept of the abbey). The former industry here is then called to mind as you pass The Old Tannery (formerly The Skinners Arms). On your right, about 40 metres past the swimming pool and just beyond the gates of Hexham House, you arrive at The Priory Gate-House (St Wilfrid's Gateway). Go through the gateway and then appreciate your first clear view of the abbey. Continue straight ahead, walk through the private car park, past the west end of the abbey and under the archway. Turn left, proceed through a further archway, and walk round the green of the former cloister. Go through a small memorial gate in the wall ahead (on the other side of which is a memorial to the Royal Northumberland Fusiliers), and turn left to pass the Abbey Gift Shop to arrive at the entrance to the abbey **(E)**.

After visiting the abbey, turn left, and walk to the east end of the building to the information board with details of the history of Hexham. Cross the road into the Market Place and turn left at The Gatehouse. Follow the road signposted to Chollerford and descend on the pavement down Hallstile Bank. At the junction bear right and after a few metres take the pedestrian crossing to the other side. Now continue ahead along the pavement for about 800 metres towards the A69, crossing over both the railway and the river bridges. Immediately before the signpost to Kielder Water, leave the pavement to turn left along the public bridleway to Acomb and St John Lee Bridge **(F)**.

Walk along the pleasant tree-lined lane and, just before you cross the bridge back over the A69, you will see a private road on your left which leads into the grounds of The Hermitage, possibly one time abode of St John of Beverley. Once over the bridge, turn left to continue along the public bridleway which runs parallel to the A69 for a short while. Later, as the lane widens and bears left, look out for a public footpath on the right "Alnmouth Terrace ¼". Go through the kissing gate and continue straight across the field. A hedge appears on your right as you proceed ahead to go through a kissing gate and then cross a small footbridge that leads to a metalled lane. Turn right, walk up the lane for about 100 metres, and then turn right at a junction of roads. Continue up the narrow lane as it climbs quite steeply, pausing where appropriate to admire the views westward up the Tyne Valley and back across to the village of Acomb. As the lane levels off, the steeple of the church of St John Lee comes into view and you need to take the first turn on the right to return to the church and the end of the walk.

# Walk 22: Blanchland

## *Canons, Crewe and cattlemen*

**Location:** St Mary's Church (NY966504) is in Blanchland. Blanchland lies south-west of the Derwent Reservoir about 12 miles south-west of Corbridge, on a road off the A68.

**Distance:** Walk 22(a), Blanchland and Pennypie House: 5 miles; Walk 22(b), Blanchland only: 3 miles.

**Map:** OS Outdoor Leisure 43: Hadrian's Wall and OS Explorer 307: Consett & Derwent Reservoir.

**Terrain:** On riverside and field paths, farm roads and forest tracks. There are several gradual ascents and descents and a short steep uphill section on a busier road.

**Church:** St Mary.

**Car parking:** There is a car park 300 metres north of the church.

## The Church

The sturdy tower of St Mary, Blanchland

The church is in the charming, planned village of Blanchland which lies in the upper reaches of the Derwent Valley just inside Northumberland. In about 1165, followers of St Norbert, who had founded an abbey at Premontre in northern France in the first half of the 12th century, established an abbey at Blanchland. Because of their white habits, the Premonstratensian monks were referred to as "white canons". It seems likely that Blanchland, meaning "white land", was named after them. The abbey was dissolved in 1539. In 1721, the buildings and estates were taken over by the Lord Crewe Trustees (see below).

When the abbey and its lands were taken over by the Crewe Trustees, much of the abbey itself was in a ruinous state. In 1752, the Trustees built the present church using the surviving parts of the abbey – tower, north transept, crossing and sanctuary – and by filling in the gaps with new walls. Today, from the entrance to the church grounds, you see the result – the sturdy tower joined to the former north transept which leads to the reconstructed sanctuary area.

The north-west entrance leads into the tower and, to your right, into the original north transept, now used as a welcoming lobby area where information and literature can be obtained. The siting of the tower at the end of the transept is an unusual arrangement – although not for Premonstratensian abbeys. Turning to your left and looking up, you can appreciate the impressive tower arch. In the lobby area, there are medieval grave slabs on the floor and behind these, the chapel of St Gabriel. This was formed in 1953 to provide a warm place for winter worship. The transept arch to your right, at the south end, leads into the nave of the present church.

The nave and chancel have a fine carved wooden ceiling The west wall of the nave was built in 1753, to fill in one of the gaps when the present church was formed from the surviving abbey ruins. The east end was rebuilt in the 1880s when the choir stalls, screen and reredos were installed.

So what we have here is an L-shaped building, with the church being the tail of the L, joined at right angles to the former abbey's tower and north transept. A fascinating, if unusual, configuration.

Carved ceiling and screen at St Mary, Blanchland (with kind permission from the vicar)

*Among the other features of interest are:*

❖ In the peaceful St Gabriel's Chapel, the window behind the altar filled with traditional Northumbrian glazing.

❖ At the west end, windows in the plain glass Northumbrian style (two in the lobby and two in the nave) by Leonard Evetts (see Walk 12, Bolam and Hartburn).

❖ Fragments of 13th-century stained glass in the chancel windows, including an abbot and a white canon at prayer.

❖ In the south wall of the chancel, a sedilia with sculptured heads of King Edward III and Queen Philippa. Edward stayed at Blanchland in 1327 during the Border wars.

*Information available in the church:*

❶ *Blanchland: a short history*, G.W.O.Addleshaw.

❶ *A walk round Blanchland Abbey.*

❶ *Look at Blanchland.*

> The Lord Crewe Trustees inherited both Blanchland and Bamburgh estates on the death of Lord Crewe, a Bishop of Durham, in 1721. Following the dissolution of Blanchland Abbey, its lands and properties had passed to the Radcliffes and then to the Forsters of Bamburgh. Both estates became impoverished and were sold to Lord Crewe. His second wife, Dorothy, was a Forster and had jointly owned the two estates. In 1752, the Trustees rebuilt most of Blanchland's houses from the ruins of the abbey as well as constructing the new parish church. Apart from their association with Blanchland, the Trustees administer the distribution of income to specified educational and ecclesiastical charitable objects.

# The Walks

## Walk 22(a) Blanchland and Pennypie House: 5 miles

Leave the church and grounds **(A)** and turn left. Walk straight ahead through the village passing the Lord Crewe Arms, built on the site of the abbot's lodge and guest house, on your left, to come to the river. Just before the bridge take the public footpath "Carrick 1¾" on your left leading to the River Derwent and walk along the riverside, with the river on your right, for about a mile. When you reach a junction of paths, take the broad path to the left signposted "Public Bridleway Blanchland ¾". Follow this as it goes straight ahead and then takes a ninety degree turn to the left, until it joins a road which is one of the main roads into Blanchland and can be quite busy. Turn right and walk up the steep hill. At the top, the climb seems worthwhile as the Derwent Reservoir comes into the picture, ahead on the right. Look for the public footpath sign "Shildon 1" on the left, just before Cowbyers farm, and go over the stile into the field **(B)**.

Walk across the field to the stone wall opposite and then walk up the field,

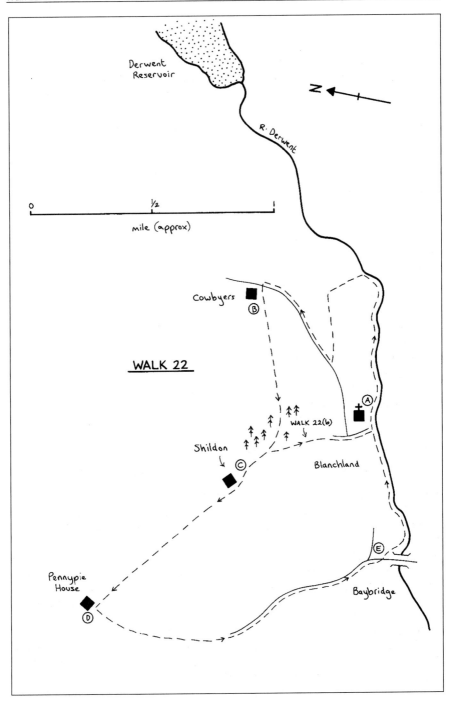

Derwent
Reservoir

R. Derwent

N

0 ½ 1
mile (approx)

Cowbyers ■ Ⓑ

**WALK 22**

Ⓐ †■

↑↑
↑↑↑ WALK 22(b)
Shildon ↑↑↑↑↑ →
↓ ◆ Ⓒ
Blanchland

Ⓔ

Pennypie
House
◆ Ⓓ
Baybridge

with the wall on your right. Go over a stile into a newly planted area, and over another stile as you come out of this area. Carry on to where the wall meets a fence and go over the stile in the fence. Continue in the same direction passing two waymark posts to reach a waymarked ladder stile. Cross the stile and walk through the wood. Turn right at a waymarked post, to go through a waymarked gate. Continue ahead with the fence on your left. Go through a waymarked gate into the farm area, and skirt the farm buildings and farmhouse to go through another waymarked gate. Turn left and descend to a metalled lane **(C)**.

Turn right and proceed up the stony lane as it heads uphill towards Pennypie House. Its unusual name is said to date from the times when cattle drovers were able to stop here and buy a pie for a penny. Near Pennypie House, look for the sign to Baybridge on the left **(D)**.

Take the path indicated, crossing the little burn by a footbridge. Follow the path, with a stone wall on your left, for about 1200 metres until you meet a metalled road. Bear left down the road to go through the gate and follow the road as it descends quite steeply. At the bottom of the hill, you come to the little hamlet of Baybridge. Walk ahead, past the picnic area on your right, to the bridge. Turn left onto the public footpath for "Blanchland ¾, Carrick 2½" **(E)**.

Go over the duck boarding and walk along the path with the River Derwent on your right. Nearing the village, the path passes a children's playground. Go across a small footbridge. Beyond the footbridge, exit the field to join the main road. Turn left and walk back to the church and the end of the walk.

### Walk 22(b) Blanchland only: 3 miles

Follow the directions for Walk 22(a) to **(C)**. Turn left, and walk down the metalled lane back to the church and the end of the walk.

# Walk 23: Roker and Whitburn

*Priestman's Morrismen, Parson's Rock and pastor's long service*

**Location:** St Andrew's Church (NZ404594) is in Roker, a northern suburb of Sunderland. It is in a residential area, 400 metres from the coast road running from Sunderland to South Shields. (The church is open for visitors between 9am and 1pm Monday to Friday).

**Distance:** 4 miles.

**Map:** OS Explorer 308: Durham & Sunderland and OS Explorer 316: Newcastle upon Tyne.

**Terrain:** On the level, mainly along the sea front and field paths.

**Churches:** St Andrew, Roker; Whitburn Parish Church.

**Car parking:** Outside the church.

## The Churches

### St Andrew, Roker

The church, built in 1906-1907, is in Roker, a seaside suburb of Sunderland. Roker was developed at the turn of the 20th century, during the urban growth which followed improvements to the docks and prosperity in shipbuilding. Fittingly, the principal benefactor was Mr (later Sir) John Priestman, who started life as a shipyard labourer and became a millionaire. Mr Priestman was a man of progressive tastes who commissioned as his architect E.S.Prior, who had been associated with the early development of the Arts and Crafts Movement (see below).

St Andrew's is set in well tended, tree-lined grounds surrounded by stone walls. Adjacent to it at the west end is the Priestman Hall, housing the church hall and offices, and built in a similar style in 1928. From the outside, this huge church has an almost fortress-like appearance and the stonework, locally quarried at Marsden, of rough, grey magnesium limestone adds to this effect. From the sea, its 24-metres-high east tower sitting astride two short transepts, provides a well known landmark for sailors approaching the River Wear. Entrance is gained via the Priestman Hall. (Ring the bell on the door near the south–west porch of the church).

The boldness of the exterior is matched inside. The long, wide nave has a roof supported by a series of elliptical arches of reinforced concrete faced with stone, starting from almost ground level. A sense of strength and solidity is provided here. The arches rest on unusual, internal buttresses which have been tunnelled through to form narrow side passages. To many observers, the overall impression is that of an upturned boat – which seems apt given the church's history and location. From the west end the eye is drawn to the highly coloured chancel ceiling and the magnificent stained-glass east window.

The fortress-like St Andrew, Roker

Most of the decorative work and furnishings are from some of the best-known practitioners of the Arts and Crafts Movement, including Burne-Jones, Eric and Macdonald Gill, Gimson, Payne and Wells. The contributions made by these artists and craftsmen explain why the church is known as "the cathedral of the Arts and Crafts Movement". Simon Jenkins (*England's Thousand Best Churches*) describes it as "a rich gallery of ecclesiastical art". There is certainly a great deal to see here. However, as the guidebook points out, St Andrew's is not only a treasure house but also remains a living place of worship.

### Among the other features of interest are:

❖ The font, by Randall Wells, and the later wooden cover by Thompson of Kilburn (the "Mouse-man"), with the mouse trademark carved on the rim.

❖ At the rear of the pews near the south-west door, a memorial table with a marble top engraved by Eric Gill, one of several examples of his work in the church.

❖ The plain-glass nave windows with simple "stick like" tracery allowing in plenty of light.

❖ The lectern by Ernest Gimson with its splendid inlays of ivory, mother of pearl and silver.

❖ At the north-east end of the nave, the small wooden font recording a tragic accident in the sea nearby.

❖ The chancel mural of the Creation, painted by Macdonald Gill in 1927 and restored in 1967 by local artist Maurice Partland.

❖ The reredos, a tapestry depicting the Adoration of the Magi, woven by Morris and Co. from a painting by Burne-Jones.

❖ The main east window, designed by H.A.Payne of Birmingham. It depicts the Ascension, and is best seen in the morning when the sun lights up the blues, reds and golds of the stained glass.

❖ In the fine Lady Chapel, two splendid stained-glass windows. That on the south wall is by Payne and is based on the text "Come unto me all who are heavy laden and I will give you rest". The design of the smaller round window on the east wall, showing the symbols of the evangelists, is attributed to Burne-Jones.

### Information available in the church:

❶ *Guidebook St Andrew's Church.*

❶ Information sheet, *The Organ.*

❶ Information sheet, *The Sanctuary Mural.*

❶ Information sheet, *Short history of the Church.*

> *The Arts and Crafts Movement started about 1875 as a counter to contemporary Victorian decoration and furnishings. It was a revival of English decorative arts, which produced very different styles from what had gone before. Similar developments took place in Europe and America. Early influential figures included the poet and craftsman William Morris (1834-96), the painter Edward Burne-Jones (1833-98), and the painter and poet Dante Gabriel Rossetti (1828-1882). Morris and others looked not only to the quality of design but also to the quality, for the craftsmen, of the working process. Examples of the combining of art and craft were seen in the products of the factory of Morris and Co. whose output included wallpapers, fabrics, tapestries, carpets, furniture and stained-glass windows.*

#### Whitburn Parish Church

Whitburn Parish Church is not usually open except for services but its beautiful setting and attractive stone exterior make it worth visiting. A local mansion, Whitburn Hall (which was demolished in 1980), stood to the east of the church beyond the existing buildings. It was formerly the home of Sir Hedworth Williamson, whose wife was a second cousin of Alice Liddell, the model for Lewis Carroll's *Alice in Wonderland.* She often visited the Hall and was probably familiar with the church.

The church has a sturdy west tower with very high buttresses. The upper half of the tower is 15$^{th}$ century and there is 13$^{th}$-century work in the nave and chancel, but what is now seen comes mainly from a restoration in 1865-68. You can peep through windows on the north side to gain an impression of the interior. Outside, there are two carved heads on the entrance arch of the south-west porch and a number of interesting tombstones and memorials. Among these is that of the Revd Thomas Baker, at the south west corner near the foot of the tower; he was rector here for almost 56 years. Opposite the entrance of the porch are the gravestones of the Barnes family, including Thomas Barnes (see below).

# The Walk

Leave the church **(A)** and grounds by the lych-gate near the east end. Cross the main road and turn right to walk 300 metres or so along the pavement, to reach the ornamental metal gates at the entrance to Roker Park on your left. Go into the park and proceed ahead, with the miniature railway on your left and the bowling green on your right. A little further on, at a crossing of paths, go straight ahead to come to the bandstand on your right. Near the bandstand is a memorial erected on the centenary of the founding of the Sunday School movement and also a dedication to Sir Hedworth Williamson of Whitburn Hall, who gave part of the land occupied by the park. Continue and soon arrive at a notice board on the right which indicates that you are at the" Roker Park Ravine Conservation Site" and gives an explanation of the rarity of this type of landscape. Here you can see outcrops of magnesium limestone, the material from which the church was built. Continue ahead until you reach the sea front and climb the steps immediately on your right. Turn right and walk along the pavement, with the sea on your right, for about 100 metres to come to a tall stone cross of Celtic design. This was erected in 1904 as a memorial to the Venerable Bede (see below). Its finely sculptured stonework depicts scenes from Bede's life as well as quotations from his *Ecclesiastical History of the English People*. It is in a very good state of repair – possibly partly because it was removed for safety reasons during both world wars **(B)**.

> *The Venerable Bede (c.673-735) was born near present day Sunderland. He was sent to the monastery at Monkwearmouth at the age of seven, and was educated there and subsequently at the twin monastery at Jarrow. He became a monk and spent his life at Jarrow, fulfilling his monastic duties and writing. His many and varied works include scriptural commentaries, lives of saints and, perhaps most famously, the "Ecclesiastical History of the English People" from which comes most of our knowledge of St Cuthbert. He was working on a biblical translation when he died. A much respected writer, often referred to as the "first English historian", he is buried in Durham Cathedral.*

The walk follows the sea front for just over a mile. Carry on in the same direction, then leave the main pavement and follow the white railings as they bear right. At low tide Parson's Rock can be seen below. You pass a small lighthouse. This was taken from its original position on Sunderland south pier and reassembled here in 1983, to allow for harbour improvements. Just beyond the roundabout near the Marriott Hotel, go down the steps to the lower promenade, with its black painted metal seats, and continue in the same direction. At the end of the promenade, walk past the cream-coloured shelter and climb the steps, then walk along the flagged path towards the houses ahead. Carry on with the sea on your right, to pass behind the terrace of some interesting properties. Exit onto a main road **(C)**.

Cross the road and take the public footpath to Whitburn. This is a metalled track running alongside a park on the right and fields on the left. Whit-

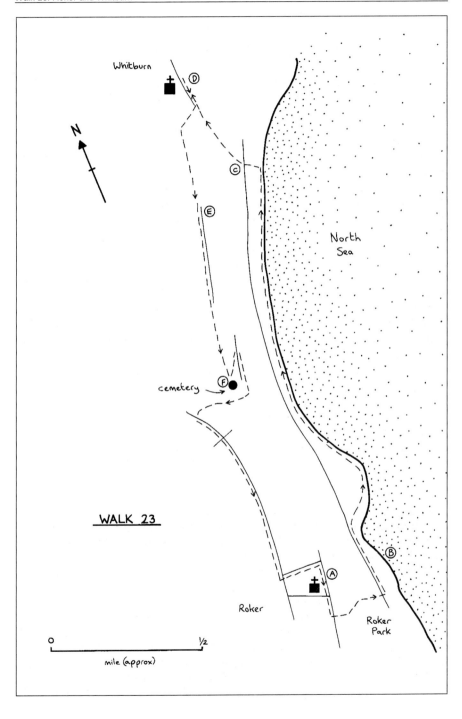

Whitburn

Ⓓ

N

Ⓒ

North
Sea

Ⓔ

cemetery Ⓕ ●

WALK 23

Ⓑ

Ⓐ

Roker

Roker
Park

0 ½

mile (approx)

burn church can be seen through the trees ahead. Emerge via wooden barriers onto a metalled road. Proceed ahead, passing the Red Cottage on your left. It was built by Thomas Barnes.

*Thomas Barnes was a prominent Victorian businessman who owned a local brickworks. In building the ornate Red Cottage in 1842-43, he took the opportunity to incorporate a wealth of decorative brickwork into its construction. Local tradition has it that he subsequently used the property to demonstrate the possibilities of ornamental brickwork to potential customers (no doubt drawing attention to its similarities to Hampton Court). A subsequent owner, a cricketer, added his own embellishment with a cricket stump and a cricket ball on the two columns at the front of the roof.*

Walk ahead and go through the lych-gate on your left, into the graveyard of Whitburn Church **(D)**. After viewing the church, walk back to the lych-gate to exit from the church grounds. You need to turn right to follow the walk, but you might like to see something of Whitburn – and possibly enjoy some refreshments – before you return. In which case, turn left and walk past houses to emerge onto a main road with large greens on both sides. You need to turn right to visit the main street. To continue the walk, return to the gate leading to the church grounds and carry straight on past The Red Cottage, now on your right, to reach the end of the footpath by which you arrived. Do not go onto that path; instead, take the narrow path on the right and walk between the wall on your left and a fence on your right. Go through the kissing gate and follow the path, which soon bears left, to go straight across the middle of the field towards the houses ahead. Exit onto a metalled path and follow this to come out into a pleasant housing estate **(E)**.

Bear left and walk down the road, passing a Rosedale Avenue sign on the right. Carry straight on and eventually reach a T-junction at Cleveland View. Take the footpath between the houses, just to the right of the street sign. Follow this as it bears right then left, then runs alongside a playing field on your right. Beyond a brick building turn right and follow the path to turn left between a pergola-like structure. Walk straight ahead and at a junction of paths turn right and walk the short distance to exit onto a road **(F)**.

Cross the road and turn left, to walk 50 metres to a footpath going off to your right. Take the path, with a dyke (sometimes dried up) on your left, and after passing a metal barrier come to a footbridge. Cross the bridge and go straight ahead for 15 metres, then bear left to walk the short distance to join a metalled road. Turn left and follow this cemetery road to come to one of the main entrances to Mere Knolls Cemetery. Leave the cemetery grounds, cross the busy road, and take the road opposite with a T.A. Centre on the left. Walk up the road to arrive at another busy road. Cross over to take the road opposite (Mere Knolls Road/Garcia Terrace). Carry straight ahead for 400 metres or so and turn left into Claremont Road. At the end of this street, on the right-hand side, is the church and the end of the walk.

# Walk 24: Edmundbyers and Muggleswick

*Legendary Saxon, last sorceress and local sculptor*

**Location:** St Edmund's Church, Edmundbyers (NZ015499) is about 3 miles west of the A68 on the B6278 Shotley Bridge to Stanhope road.

**Distance:** Walk 24(a), Edmundbyers and Muggleswick: 7½ miles; Walk 24(b), Edmundbyers only: 2½ miles.

**Map:** OS Explorer 307: Consett & Derwent Reservoir.

**Terrain:** Walk 24(a) has a few steady climbs and is mainly along footpaths and across moorland. Walk 24(b) is on the level on a footpath, returning on a quiet road.

**Churches:** St Edmund, Edmundbyers; All Saints, Muggleswick.

**Car parking:** On the roadside by the church.

## The Churches

### St Edmund, Edmundbyers

This small Norman church, with its neat graveyard, nestles among trees at the western edge of the village on Church Lane. No one is too sure of the connection with the legendary 9th-century St Edmund, the martyred King of East Anglia, but whether he was ever here or not, it is certainly believed that a wooden Saxon building once stood on this site. However, the present church dates from the mid-12th century and is basically Norman in style.

Externally, there is little of note apart from the bellcote and the strange,

St Edmund, Edmundbyers – a compact church

carved heads on the side of the porch and the gable ends. Inside it is small and intimate, the carefully restored stonework giving the interior a neat and harmonious appearance. The compact nave is separated from the small chancel by a quaint triple arch. This was introduced in the late 1850s when, according to the church information leaflet, major restoration work was "quite ruthlessly" undertaken, as box pews, gallery and triple-decker pulpit were removed. The only significant vestiges of the original church to catch the eye are probably the deeply set, narrow windows in the south wall of the chancel and in the north wall of the nave. These, with the few later windows, permit a little natural light to enter, but this is one of those cases where a torch would be useful.

However, it is the woodwork which is perhaps most remarkable. St Edmund's, never a wealthy parish in its own right, appears to have inherited a substantial amount of its furnishings from other places. The heavily carved, dark oak panelling, which once served as the vestry at the west end of the church, was assembled in the late 19th century seemingly from various sources, including Auckland Castle and Durham Cathedral. There is evidence of a splendid door, some pew ends and a shield and bosses – all acquired for £3!

St Edmund's clearly welcomes visitors, in the words on the noticeboard at the gates: "to enjoy the peace and tranquillity to be found within these ancient walls".

### Among the other features of interest are:

❖ In the west wall of the porch, the gravestone of a priest showing his chalice.

❖ On the west wall of the church, the memorial tablet to members of the Lee family which includes Elizabeth Lee, said to be one of the last of the witches for which the area was apparently notorious.

❖ The stone altar which had been removed in accordance with a Reformation edict, but which was found buried under the chancel during the restoration work in the 1850s. It now sits in its original place, supported by stone arches believed to have been recovered from the churchyard.

### Information available in the church:

❶ Information board on the west wall.

❶ An information leaflet, *St Edmund's Edmundbyers*.

## All Saints, Muggleswick

Muggleswick is a tiny hamlet consisting of a few houses and the aptly named Priory and Grange farms. There has been a church presence on this site since at least the 13th century when the monks of Durham Cathedral built a monastic grange here. However, the grange fell into disrepair after the dissolution of the monastery in 1539, and all that remains today is the impressive wall that can be seen from the north-east corner of the churchyard.

The present church dates from the beginning of the 19th century but it has been subject to various restorations and modifications, notably in the 19th century. It stands half- hidden by the churchyard trees, distinguished only by its bellcote and the south-west porch. Inside, the single-chamber church is light and attractive, despite the evidence of decaying plasterwork, and the eye is drawn to the raised altar and the bold lettering behind it on the east wall. Two plaques on the chancel walls attribute most of the internal furnishings to the generosity of the Ritson family.

Although the church is normally only open during summer weekends, the noticeboard in the porch contains details of how to gain access at other times, together with some interesting information about the history of Muggleswick. Come what may, it is clear that a small but enthusiastic group of people struggle to preserve this peaceful haven against the odds.

### Among the other features of interest are:

❖ The roll of honour on the north wall to those who served and fell in World War I. The total number of those who enlisted is high in relation to the population of the area.

❖ The plaque on the south wall in memory of the Ritsons, who fell in World War II.

❖ The lych-gate in memory of Utrick Ritson and his wife Annie, made from teak from the battleship *HMS Powerful.*

❖ The Mayor memorial (details of which are on the notice in the porch) near the lych-gate. This modest headstone is said to be the first commission carried out by the distinguished sculptor John Graham Lough (see below). His name can just be seen on the north edge of the memorial.

### Information available in the church:

❶ In the porch there are notices giving information about Muggleswick Grange, the lych-gate and the Mayor memorial.

❶ *Muggleswick Parish and Church: a brief history,* Muriel E. Sobo.

*John Graham Lough (1798-1876), born close to*

Mayor memorial, All Saints, Muggleswick

*Muggleswick, rose from humble origins to become a highly regarded Victorian sculptor. Nancy Ridley (Northumbrian Heritage) ranks this "poor boy of genius who made good" as a great Northumbrian. At about the age of 27 he moved from Newcastle to London where he was based until his death. He exhibited at the Royal Academy and carried out commissions for wealthy patrons and members of the nobility throughout the country. Two of his most famous works in the North East are the memorial statues of Lord Collingwood at Tynemouth, and George Stephenson near Newcastle Central Station.*

# The Walks

## Walk 24(a), Edmundbyers and Muggleswick: 7½ miles

Leave St Edmund's Church **(A)** by the lych-gate and turn right. Walk a few metres down to the junction with the Edmundbyers to Stanhope road and turn right. Follow the road for about 175 metres, and then leave the road to take the public footpath "Lead Mining Trail" on your right. Follow the clear, stony track as it gently climbs for about 150 metres and, just before a metal farm gate, take the track off to the left. Now continue ahead along the foot of Edmundbyers Common. Over to the left beyond the road is Muggleswick Common, over which you will soon be walking. Soon you reach a stile by a waymarked gate. Cross the stile and proceed straight ahead, ignoring a subsequent track off to the right. The track passes through gorse bushes and below to your left you may catch a glimpse of the Burnhope Burn. The burn flows from a dam which soon comes into sight and which is part of the Derwent Reservoir system. After a few hundred metres, cross another stile next to a waymarked gate. Then a few hundred metres later you arrive at a junction with a surfaced track. Bear left on this track as it passes an old cottage on your right and then bears past some waste from a disused mine. The track crosses a bridge over the burn and leads to a metal gate. Go through the gate and continue along the track as it climbs gently for a few hundred metres, to go through another metal gate and emerge onto the B6278 **(B)**.

Turn right and walk a few metres to a public footpath sign on the left-hand side of the road. Follow the faint path diagonally left, in the direction of the footpath sign. The path for the next 1,200 metres is somewhat vague in parts, and there are many sheep trods across the bracken and heather of Muggleswick Common. You need to climb gently, while keeping more or less parallel to the road below. Aim to pass two fenced-off inspection covers, and then keep the high ridge 200 metres or so to your right. You should pass well above some farm vehicles and materials on your left. Ignore the vehicular track that goes off right towards the disused quarry. Eventually a wall appears ahead and you need to make for the bottom left-hand corner of this wall. Hopefully if you have been contouring round the Common at about the right level you should pick up a broad green track a short distance before the wall. Continue past the corner of the wall along the green track, with the wall

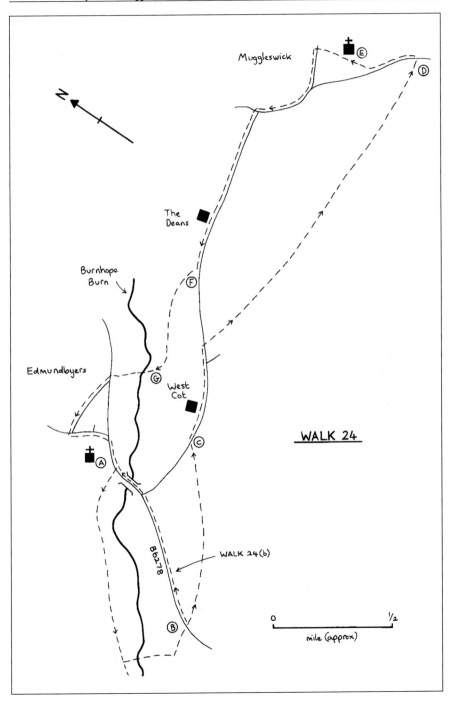

on your right, for a few hundred metres as the track descends to join a minor road **(C)**.

Turn right and walk along the road, past West Cot Farm. Ignore public footpaths off to left and right and then, about 100 metres beyond the private road to Lambshield, leave the road to take the public footpath off to the right. Climb the clear green track through the heather and, after a few hundred metres, ignore a vehicular track which goes off right to a grouse shooting area. The track soon bears right and ahead in the distance is the town of Consett. The path becomes fainter for a while as it levels off though the bracken and heather. Continue in the same direction until a small reassuring cairn is reached. The track becomes broader as it goes via a number of cairns and shows evidence of the passage of vehicles along it. On top of the ridge, over to the right, you will see three stone cairns known as the "Three Curricks". The track brings you to some well-constructed grouse butts. Continue along the clear track, which soon begins to bear left, and descend past the corner of a wall to join the Waskerley to Edmundbyers road **(D)**.

Turn left and walk along the road to the second public footpath sign on the right. Go through the small gate and walk down the side of the field with the fence/trees on your right. Cross a stile, go over the drive, cross another stile and continue in the same direction for a short distance, to go through a small gate. Now continue to Muggleswick church ahead **(E)**.

After visiting the church, walk behind the west wall of the church down a grassy path and through two small gates onto a farm road, opposite Priory Farm. Turn left and walk up the road to a metal gate. Go through the gate and past the telephone box to join a road. Bear right up the road and follow it for about a mile. It climbs quite steeply at first, and then when it levels off you can see the Derwent Reservoir again. Ignore the road going off right to Shotley Bridge. About 250 metres past The Deans take the public footpath on the right **(F)**.

After a few metres, go over the stile next to a gate and follow the track straight ahead. This can be quite muddy. Ignore a track off to the right through a gateway, and continue ahead with a wire fence on your left. As the track bears left, go through a gate in a wall. Continue straight ahead, still with a wire fence on the left, as the track becomes fainter. After a further 150 metres or so, bear right and descend to pass a solitary tree just before the corner of a plantation. At last you come to a waymark on a fence post by the plantation. Continue to descend on the faint path to a waymarked metal gate. Go through the gate and walk along the side of the field with the woods on your right for about 150 metres, to cross a waymarked stile over a fence. The path begins its descent a little to the right of the stile, and drops quite steeply to meet a fence as another path joins from the right. Continue downhill through the bracken for about 40 metres and look out for a stile, at the beginning of a wall, on your right. Cross the stile and continue downhill on the narrow path as it wends its way through the bracken to the Burnhope Burn.

Bear left and cross a small stream and proceed with the burn on your right, to cross the burn by a waymarked footbridge **(G)**.

Now bear left and climb up the bankside bearing left, quite steeply at first, aiming for a caravan in the top left-hand corner. There are several paths which lead over a series of ridges. Just before the caravan bear right and follow the line of the wire fence to ascend steeply past further caravans. Eventually go through a kissing gate and after a short distance, exit onto the road at the entrance to Edmundbyers. Turn left and walk into the village past the YHA and then at the junction cross over the road and take the road on the right, signposted to Blanchland. Pass the Punchbowl Inn to arrive at the village green on your right. Continue by the side of the road for a few hundred metres to pass Heatherlea Cottage. Then take a sharp left turn down a minor road (in fact, Church Lane) back to the church and the end of the walk.

## Walk 24(b), Edmundbyers only: 2½ miles

Follow Walk 24(a) as far as **(B)**, then turn left and walk back along the road for about 1,000 metres to the bottom of Church Lane. Turn left and return to the church and the end of the walk.

# Walk 25: Durham

## *Carey, cathedral and composer*

**Location:** St Nicholas's Church (NZ274426) is in Market Place in Durham City.
**Distance:** 5 miles.
**Map:** OS Explorer 308: Durham & Sunderland.
**Terrain:** Mainly on the level along riverside paths.
**Churches:** St Nicholas; Durham Cathedral; St Oswald.
**Car parking:** In one of the city's pay and display or pay on exit car parks.

## The Churches

### St Nicholas, Durham

There has been a church on this site from at least 994. The building you see today, with its noble spire, dates from 1858 when the previous church was replaced. Externally, there has been little change since then. There was, however, a major restoration of the interior in 1980-81. This was carried out during the incumbency of the Revd George Carey, Vicar from 1975-1982, and subsequently Archbishop of Canterbury. His vision was that the rede-signed building would be "a natural bridge between the Christian church and the outside world".

This bridging is partly achieved by the expanse of glass which encourages you to go inside through the porch, where you enter direct from the Market Place. Another "bridge" is provided by the alternative entrance – which is through a shop! The Gateway World Shop is a Christian organisation which campaigns for fair trade and also markets products for which the producers have received a fair price.

In contrast to its Victorian exterior, inside, as the church guidebook says, "it's rather different … no pews and the platform and holy table are posi-tioned along the side". Overall, there is a feeling of openness which allows for services and other activities integral to the evangelical tradition of this church. The original short chancel has been divided off by a glass screen to form "a quiet chapel". Otherwise, the "Handsomely simple, spacious inte-rior" recognised by Pevsner (*The Buildings of England: County Durham*) remains, including the north arcade with four bays and the two bays of the south aisle.

There is much of interest here, both in the architecture of the 1858 build-ing and in the symbolism of the modern furnishings, and visitors are made most welcome.

### *Among the other features of interest are:*

❖ Two windows by Leonard Evetts (see Walk12, Bolam and Hartburn). They
   are adjacent; one in the shop, the other at the foot of the stairs. The church

guidebook gives a detailed description of the symbolism used in their design.

❖ The two fonts, providing a complete contrast in style. Near the entrance, the older (possibly the oldest object in the building), a traditional stone font. At the north-east end to the left of the chancel arch, the modern font has a dramatic flame-like representation of the descent of the Holy Spirit.

❖ The Fish Window, on the left as you enter, set in the glass window behind the Communion Table. The outline shape of a fish is an ancient Christian symbol.

❖ At the top of the pillars supporting the arches, intricate carvings of foliage, animals and birds.

❖ At the east end, perhaps best seen from inside the quiet chapel, an attractive stained-glass window with brilliant reds and yellows.

The welcoming statue of the patron saint outside St Nicholas, Durham

## Information available in the church:

🛈 *St Nicholas, Durham - A Guide for Visitors.*

### The Cathedral Church of Christ and Blessed Mary the Virgin (Durham Cathedral)

The cathedral and the castle at Durham are on a high rock almost surrounded by a narrow loop in the River Wear – a superb defensive position for the original builders. Durham Cathedral presents an imposing, magnificent sight from whichever direction you look at it and several different aspects will be seen on the walk. For their first close-up view most visitors will make their way up through the town to arrive at Palace Green in front of the north side of the Cathedral. Worshippers, pilgrims and visitors have been coming to this place for more than 900 years and many people recognise an aura of sanctity here.

Across Palace Green you see a palatial building with a massive central tower, to the left of which are the choir and the pinnacles of a large chapel at the east end, while to the right are the nave and the two towers at the west end. A path leads to the north door which is the main entrance for visitors. Here you are confronted with an interesting piece of the cathedral's history. On the door is a replica of the Sanctuary Knocker (the original is in "The Treasures of St Cuthbert Exhibition" inside). In the Middle Ages, until 1634, those outside the law could obtain sanctuary here, as explained on the adjacent panel. However, the cathedral's origins go back much further than this.

Durham Cathedral has always been associated with St Cuthbert (see Walk 2, Holy Island). Monks from Lindisfarne, seeking a final resting place for the saint's body, reached Durham in 995 and by 1017 had completed a stone church to house a shrine. Later, in 1083, the Norman Bishop, William of St Carileph, introduced Benedictine (or "black") monks to carry on the monastic tradition and take over from the Anglo-Saxon monks as guardians of Cuthbert's relics. In 1093 he demolished the old church and laid the foundations of the present building. The nave, transepts and choir were completed by 1133. For the next 450 years or so the church and monastery were linked together as Durham Priory. During most of this time important additions were constructed, culminating, between 1465 – 1490, with the rebuilding of an earlier bell tower. From the 11th century the Bishops of Durham were known as the "Prince Bishops" (see below). Some 50 years after the completion of the bell tower, Henry VIII reconstituted the church and monastery as the Cathedral Church of Christ and Blessed Mary the Virgin.

Symbol of sanctuary at Durham Cathedral

Going inside, at the west end of the nave is the information area and, nearby, the impressive font with its splendid carved cover, both from about 1670. Standing at the rear of the nave and looking east, you can begin to appreciate the magnificent architecture of this superb building. High above you is the vaulting of the nave ceiling and ahead stretches the long nave to the tower crossing. Beyond is the vaulted choir and beyond that the screen and high altar with the rose window above, drawing the eye to the east end. Behind you is the Galilee

Chapel, the cathedral's Lady Chapel, built 1175-1189. This houses the tomb of the Venerable Bede (see Walk 23, Roker) whose body was brought from Jarrow to Durham in 1022. From the south wall, doors lead into the cloisters and other buildings from the times of the Benedictine monks. These include the monks' dormitory, the kitchen (now the bookshop) and the well-named Undercroft Restaurant. There is much to see in Durham Cathedral and you need to look up as well as around you to enjoy the soaring columns and arches, the wonderful roof structures and the glorious stained glass.

### Among the other features of interest are:

❖ In the peaceful Galilee Chapel, Bede's tomb. Also two interesting modern works: from 1991, the wooden carving, representing the Annunciation, by the Polish sculptor, Joseph Pyrz and, from 1993, in the north-west corner, a stained-glass window by Leonard Evetts (see Walk 12, Bolam and Hartburn). An interesting contrast in styles of stained glass is provided by the eastern-most window on the north side. This is by Kempe (see Walk 15, Simonburn).

❖ On the south wall, beyond the door to the cloisters, the poignant Miners' Memorial with its miner's lamp and the Durham Miners' Book of Remembrance to the many men who perished in the pits of Durham.

❖ In the south transept, the Durham Light Infantry Memorial Chapel. This was converted in 1923, from two medieval Lady Chapels, in memory of those members of the Regiment killed during the First World War. Remembrance has subsequently been extended to all fallen members of the Durham Light Infantry.

❖ On the south wall, to the east of the south transept, the Millennium Window by Joseph Nuttgens of High Wycombe.

❖ At the east end behind the high altar, the Shrine of St Cuthbert.

❖ Beyond the shrine, on the east wall, the Chapel of Nine Altars, built 1242-1280. The short, black columns are made from local Frosterley marble, characterised by visible coral fossils. The delicately coloured embroidered panels behind the altar and the bold altar frontal, designed by Leonard Childs, include representations of St Cuthbert, St Aidan (see Walk 4, Bamburgh) and St Bede.

❖ The cloisters, reminiscent of the solitude and serenity of the Priory monks.

### Information available in the cathedral:

❶ Details of guided tours and a great deal of literature.

❶ *A walk round Durham Cathedral.*

❶ *Durham Cathedral, The Authorised Cathedral Guide.*

> *The Prince Bishops were the king's representatives in their area – known as the County Palatine – which stretched from the Tees to the Tweed. Proximity to the Scottish border and the importance of St Cuthbert's shrine caused Wil-*

*liam I to grant extensive temporal authority to the Bishop of Durham – much more so than elsewhere. Hence, as well as their ecclesiastical powers and being significant landowners, the bishops had their own parliament, their own coinage and the right to build castles. They reigned from Durham Castle (see below) and, from the 12th century, they also had a residence at Bishop Auckland. Their powers did decline, but it was not until the death of the last Prince Bishop, William Van Mildert, in 1836 that their secular powers were ceded to the Crown.*

### St Oswald, Durham

The church may be open between 11am and 1pm, otherwise it is not usually open except at service times. It is a large building with an impressive west tower, a long nave and chancel, and north and south aisles. It has a long history, possibly pre-Conquest. Much of it was rebuilt in a major restoration in 1834 by Ignatius Bonomi, probably Durham's most noted architect of the first half of the 19th century. Further restoration work was needed after a disastrous fire in 1984. Inside, there are windows by Morris & Co., Clayton & Bell and Kempe. Outside, there are some interesting gravestones, including

one, at the north-east corner near the path, for "A Singing Man". Another association with singing arises from the fact that one of the most famous English composers of hymn tunes, J.B.Dykes, was the rector here. Two windows in the church are in memory of him. A new organ was installed in 1988, to keep up the tradition for good music inspired by Dykes.

*John Bacchus Dykes (1823-1876) was a precentor at Durham Cathedral and then rector of St Oswald's from 1862 until his death in 1876. He was a prolific composer of hymn tunes, many of which have been associated with a particular hymn; for example, the tune for the hymn "Holy, Holy, Holy" sung on Trinity Sunday. This, and many others, have retained their popularity. He also wrote other music forms and was a noted theologian. Dykes is buried at St Oswald's.*

St Oswald, Durham – of musical fame

# The Walk

Leave St Nicholas's church **(A)** by the porch into Market Place and walk straight ahead, up to the collection of signposts near the statue of Neptune. Follow the signs to the cathedral. To do this, you need to take the street to the left. After a few metres a sign on the right shows that you are on Saddler Street. Continue along Saddler Street until you reach Owen-gate. Turn right to walk up this narrow, steep road to emerge at Palace Green and the cathedral. Keep to the path and walk to the right, past the entrance to Durham Castle.

> *Durham Castle, dating from 1072, was built by William I as a stronghold for the Prince Bishops of Durham, most of whom took the opportunity to add to or restore much of the building. It is generally recognised as England's best example of a Norman castle. In 1832 it was granted to the newly founded Durham University and it is now occupied by University College, the university's founding college. Guided tours are available for visitors.*

Proceed round the square, passing the University Library on your right, to arrive at the north door of the cathedral **(B)**.

After visiting the cathedral you leave by the north door. Retrace your steps towards the University Library. Take the passageway, signposted "Museum of Archaeology", immediately before the library and walk down to meet a path. Turn left and walk along the path which runs above the river and passes close to the walls of the cathedral on your left. Ignore the path on the right to the museum. Keep to the main path which descends to meet the river at Prebends Bridge. Turn right to cross the bridge and keep to the right–hand side. About half-way across look below to the right to see, by the riverside, the *Kathedra,* a sculpture by Colin Milbourne representing the judgement seat of a bishop. Go to the end of the bridge where there is a quotation from Sir Walter Scott which captures some of the magic of this place. Proceed to the end of the metalled section. On the path on the right, is the *Revealed,* a sculpture by Richard Cole, constructed from redundant stone made available when a cathedral pinnacle was replaced. The light coming through the aperture at different times of day is a reminder of the changing light coming into the cathedral. Now cross the road to the left-hand side to continue the walk in the same direction as before, but now with the river on your left. Follow the main path, ignoring paths off to the right, and after about 300 metres take the path which forks right uphill.

As you ascend you see that the path runs alongside a little gully on the left. Look out for an unfenced stone footbridge on the left and cross this to a wooden gateway (which is rather like a kissing gate without the gate). Carry on, now fairly high above the river, keeping to the main path, and go through a similar gateway. A wall appears over to your right and you soon arrive at steps leading into a graveyard. Go up the steps and follow the path to arrive at the tower of St Oswald's Church **(C)**.

Follow the path to the left of the tower and walk down the side of the church to meet a road. The walk continues by turning left.

If, before doing so, you wish to visit Dyke's grave, you need to turn right and walk 100 metres to cross the road at the zebra crossing and go into the park and play area (converted from the former graveyard extension). The grave is 50 metres down the path on the right-hand side. Retrace your steps back to the church gate.

To continue the walk, carry on along the pavement, with the church grounds on your left, and continue until you reach a set of traffic lights. Here, you need to turn immediately left onto the wide, paved area and walk ahead to Kingsgate Foot Bridge. Walk across this footbridge and up the steps at the far end,then turn sharp left to descend steep steps down to the river **(D)**.

Turn left to go under Kingsgate Bridge and proceed along the riverside path, with the river on your right. Walk under old Elvet Bridge and straight ahead to pass the boat-hire building on your right. Continue on, going under the concrete bridge and in a short while come to a lower, concrete, pedestrian bridge **(E)**.

Do not cross the bridge but keep on the metalled riverside path, now with more open aspects on the opposite side of the river. The path goes over a waymarked bridge and the metalled section comes to an end. Carry on for 600 metres to reach a waymarked post after which there is a division of paths. Take the middle path and walk straight across the clearing to the trees ahead. Continue between the trees and soon a fort-like boundary wall appears over to your left. Bear right to go between the walls of a former railway bridge, and walk 100 metres or so to cross a footbridge ahead. Bear left to go through the gap in the hedge onto a sports field. Although the right of way is over to the left, custom and practice (and a wish not to become involved in a game of soccer or rugby!) indicates that you need to walk straight across the field, to the large metal footbridge ahead **(F)**.

Cross the bridge and bear right to walk 30 metres to a kissing gate at the corner of the wood. Go through the gate and turn left to walk along the edge of the woodland, with a fence/hedge on your left. After 200 metres or so take the right-hand fork and climb, quite steeply, straight ahead to come to a stile. Cross the stile into the clearing and walk ahead, with a hedge on your right. At the end of the clearing go through the gap to reach a somewhat rickety stile. Cross the stile, proceed through the wooded area and pass a school on your left. Carry on with the fence and hedge on your left until you see a brick wall on the right. This is just before a Home Office prison sign **(G)**.

(If you wish to take a short-cut at this point, you need to walk to the end of the path to exit onto a busy road. Turn right and walk for about 200 metres and bear left onto Old Elvet. Walk to the crossroads and go over Elvet Bridge into Market Place, St Nicholas's Church and the end of the walk).

To continue on the main walk, turn right before the brick wall and walk down the path, with the fence on your left. At the end of the fence turn left down the stepped path and follow the steps as they bear right. Carry on along

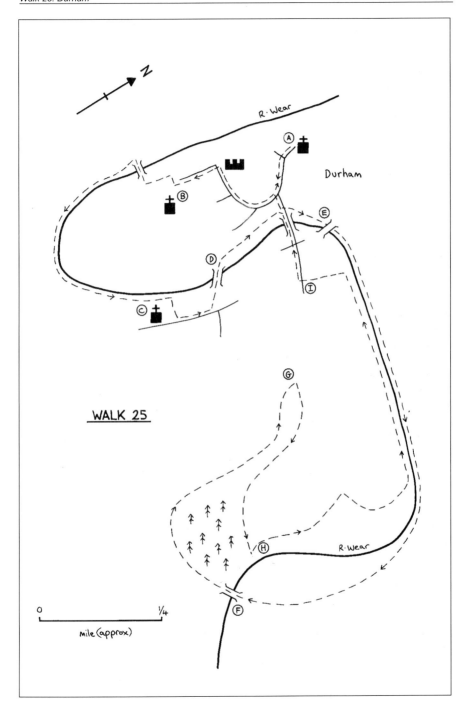

WALK 25

the main path. Ignore two paths to the left leading to the playing fields. Continue in the same direction, with playing fields behind the fence on your left and woods on your right. The path joins the main riverside path **(H)**.

Turn left and follow the path, with the river on your right, for 250 metres or so until it bears left and, after a few metres, turns right at a junction of paths. The path exits onto a metalled lane. Cross the lane, go through the gap in the fence and bear right to walk towards the building ahead. Keep to the path which goes to the left of the building and joins the wide grassy area alongside the river. Follow the path past the bandstand and the *Durham Cow*, a sculpture by Andrew Burton. This sculpture draws inspiration – specifically – from the legend that a woman, looking for her cow, directed the monks of Lindisfarne to the place where they found St Cuthbert's final resting place; and – more generally – from the many ways in which the cow features in folklore and religion. Walk past the low-level concrete bridge you saw on the outward journey. Take the lane to the left of the swimming baths, then go up the narrow passage to emerge via a tunnel onto a road **(I)**.

Turn right and walk to the crossroads, passing the finely spired Elvet Methodist Church on your left. Cross over and walk to Elvet Bridge. Go across the bridge into Market Place, St Nicholas's Church and the end of the walk.

# Walk 26: Trimdon

## *PMs' rivalry, quiet reminder and recycled railway*

**Location:** St Mary Magdalene's Church (NZ371342) is in Trimdon Village east of the B1278 about 3 miles from Sedgefield, midway between Durham and Darlington.

**Distance:** Walk 26(a), Trimdon Village and Trimdon Colliery: 7 miles; Walk 26(b) Trimdon Village and Trimdon Grange: 2½ miles.

**Map:** OS Explorer 305: Bishop Auckland and OS Explorer 306: Middlesbrough & Hartlepool.

**Terrain:** Both walks are largely on the level. Walk 26(a) begins with just under a mile of road walking then continues across farmland and farm tracks, with a short section on an old railway. Walk 26(b) is mainly on well-defined paths across fields.

**Church:** St Mary Magdalene, Trimdon Village.

**Car parking:** There is parking near the church on the side roads beyond the village greens.

## The Church

This is a beautifully located church on one of the several long greens in the centre of Trimdon Village. It stands in an elevated position, enclosed on three sides within its own walls and open on the east to the landscaped replacement of part of the former graveyard.

It is believed that once there may have been a Saxon church on the site. However, the only firm evidence of the origin of the present building comes

St Mary Magdelene, Trimdon – a premier's church?

from a detailed archaeological assessment of 1993, which indicates that this is basically a Norman church dating from the 12$^{th}$ century. It is a well-proportioned building with a neat south porch and an integrated bell-cote. The well-dressed stone work gives it an elegant and harmonious appearance.

Inside there is a similar impression of consistency of style, most probably due to the fact that St Mary Magdalene's has not been subject to much modification over the centuries. It appears that, as none of its patrons were powerful or wealthy enough to secure its long-term endowment, the church had largely fallen into disrepair by the early 19$^{th}$ century. Although some restoration work was carried out, it was not until 1883/4 that major repairs were undertaken and a north aisle and vestry added. The 20$^{th}$ century, however, was kinder to the church.

The interior is small, neat and intimate, with three arcades separating the north aisle from the nave. The whitewashed walls, the tinted windows and the high raftered roof produce a feeling of light and airiness. However, it is the arch leading to the chancel that really catches the eye, clearly separating as it does the almost square nave from the narrow chancel. This remains as the most outstanding indication of the Norman origins of the church. It has an unusual horseshoe form said to be matched by only one other of its kind, in France. This was apparently a subject of discussion between the respective prime ministers of the UK and France, Mr Blair and Mr Jospin, during their visit to the church in July 1998.

St Mary Magdalene's is an oasis of peace and tranquillity. It is evident that it is now lovingly cared for and maintained, and the sensitive illumination of the building at night reinforces its significance within the community.

### *Among the other features of interest are:*

❖ The carved oak reredos behind the main altar with the mosaic representations of the Virgin Mary and the Infant Jesus in the centre, St Cuthbert on the right (holding the head of King Oswald), and on the left a bishop, possibly that other great northern saint, Aidan.

❖ The small, round-headed window on the south side of the chancel which may once have been a leper window to allow the afflicted to witness services. The window is now occupied with a stained-glass depiction of St Mary Magdalene.

❖ The modern stained-glass window by Bridget Jones, in the south side of the chancel, on the theme of the Good Samaritan and the concept of bringing healing to the nations of the world.

❖ The interesting collection of kneelers showing various tapestry designs.

### *Information available in the church:*

❶ *A brief history of St Mary Magdalene Church Trimdon*, John Errington, John Burton & Revd John Williamson.

❶ *The Beckwith family vault*, Revd John Williamson.

## Walk 26(a), Trimdon Village and Trimdon Colliery: 7 miles

On leaving the church porch **(A)** turn left and exit through the graveyard. Continue down the side road with the village green and the main road on your left. When your path converges with the main road, ignore the road going off to the left and continue in the signposted direction of Hurworth Burn and Hartlepool. After a further 50 metres or so, cross over the road to visit Trimdon Village Cemetery.

> *Trimdon Village East Cemetery was consecrated as a burial ground in 1862. The cemetery is particularly noted for the memorial to 74 miners who lost their lives in a coal mining disaster in 1882. The ages of many of the dead serve as a poignant reminder of the human cost of coal. In 1991 the memorial was re-dedicated by the then Bishop of Durham, the Rt Revd David Jenkins, who also dedicated part of the cemetery for the internment of ashes, burials there having ceased in 1960. Although this area is in the heart of the Durham coalfield, Trimdon Village itself did not have a mine. The colliery concerned, which closed in 1968, was at nearby Trimdon Grange.*

After visiting the cemetery, continue down the main road for about 1600 metres until, as the road bears to the right, a metalled track appears on the left. Cross over with care, and go down the short length of track past a concrete block to arrive at the corner of a field. (At the time of writing, proceedings were in progress with a view to diverting and creating footpaths in this area and users should be alert for changes. However, the right of way is currently diagonally across the field.) Walk towards the telegraph pole in the centre of the field and proceed to a gap in the hedge, beyond which farm buildings are visible. Continue in the same direction across the next field to join a track that leads past a caravan storage park. At the entrance to the compound, just before the farm gate, take the track that goes off to the left. Follow the track as it bears round Dropswell Farm, and goes left to pass between two barns and through a metal gate **(B)**.

Follow the broad farm track as it ascends with a hedge on your right. The hedge bears away at a corner as you continue climbing gradually on the track. As the track levels out, and where two hedges converge at the next field corner, look out for a metal gateway on your right. Go through the gateway and turn immediately left to continue ahead, now with a hedge on your left. Proceed down the side of the field as far as the field boundary, and go through a gap in the hedge about 15 metres from the right of the corner. Continue ahead with the hedge still on your left. At the next field boundary go through the clear gap and again continue straight ahead, to climb up the side of the field. Make for the plantation ahead and enter via the waymarked stile. Walk the short distance through the plantation and follow the waymark onto a farm track near some stables. Cross the track and descend a few metres to cross a waymarked stile next to a gate. Bear left, walk for about 100 metres with trees on your left and look for a waymark on the fence in front of some conifers. At this point you need to turn right to follow the right of way across the field to find a stile in the hedge opposite. This stile takes you onto a track with part of the Hurworth Burn Reservoir visible over the hedge in front of you. Turn left and follow the track as it makes its way to a bridge over the reservoir **(C)**.

(If and when a new path is approved, it will exit at the metal gate near this bridge).

Cross the bridge over the reservoir. Continue on the broad track on the other side as it turns right between the hawthorn hedges, with the reservoir now just visible on the right. Go through a gate and continue on the path as it bears left to come parallel to the railway embankment on your right. Cross a stile next to a gate, turn right and walk a few metres to join the surfaced track of a disused railway line, now the Wynyard to Station Town Cycleway. Turn left and walk along the cycleway for about 400 metres, until you arrive at a cutting with steps up the embankments on both sides **(D)**.

Go up the steps on the left-hand side and cross the waymarked stile. Proceed straight ahead, with a fence on your left, until you reach the field boundary where you take the waymarked stile next to a metal gate. Walk up the farm track for about 75 metres and cross a waymarked stile in the hedge on your right. Continue ahead, with the hedgerow on your left, and take the waymarked stile at the field boundary onto a farm track near the entrance to White Hurworth farm. Turn right and walk down the track, which can be quite muddy, and after about 100 metres the track divides and you take the left-hand track. Continue along the broad vehicular track for about 1½ miles as it winds between the fields to pass a cottage and some old farm buildings before reaching Hurworth Bryan Farm **(E)**.

Leave the main track as it turns right at the entrance to the farm, and continue straight ahead onto a rougher track. Proceed along this track for a further 500 metres or so, towards the white cottage and farm buildings of Langdale. At the end of a short hedge on your left, cross over the stile on your left and proceed down the path (between the wire fences) to exit over another stile with the farm buildings on your left. Walk ahead for a few metres to join a farm track at Langdale Cottage. Turn right (definitely not left!) and follow the track past some allotments to a road at Trimdon Colliery. Cross the road, turn left and walk some 20 metres to a public footpath sign. Turn right and pass the waymarked stile next to the gateway. Follow the track as it winds down to a footbridge **(F)**.

Cross the bridge and walk ahead in the same direction with a hedge on your right. At the field boundary continue into a wood and, ignoring paths off, proceed ahead. On leaving the wood the path passes between two hedges for a short distance before exiting onto a road via a waymarked stile. Turn right and, after a short distance, leave the road at a bend to take a public footpath as indicated on the right. Cross the stile next to the metal gate and follow the vehicular track as it winds down to a pond. Bear left and go through a metal barrier and continue on the path as it skirts around the other side of the pond. At the field boundary, the path turns left. Follow the path as

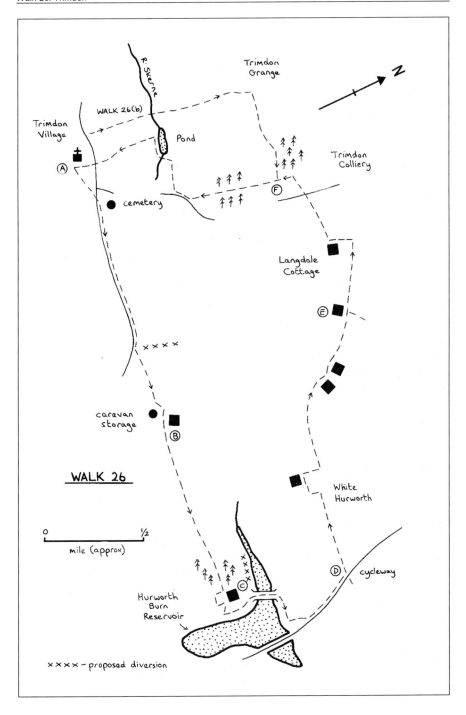

R. Skerne

Trimdon
Grange

WALK 26(b)

Trimdon
Village

Pond

Trimdon
Colliery

Ⓐ

● cemetery

Ⓕ

Langdale
Cottage

Ⓔ

× × × ×

caravan
storage

Ⓑ

**WALK 26**

White
Hurworth

0 ½
mile (approx)

Ⓓ   cycleway

Ⓒ

Hurworth
Burn
Reservoir

× × × × – proposed diversion

it climbs, with the field boundary on your right, towards houses ahead at Trimdon Village. Take the stile on the right just before the white bungalow, and then cross another stile immediately on your left. Follow the path onto the road at the church and the end of the walk.

## Walk 26(b) Trimdon Village and Trimdon Grange: 2½ miles

On leaving the church porch turn right, go through the gate and follow the path down to the road. Cross the road with care and walk up to the Fox and Hounds pub. Turn right at the public footpath sign just before the pub, and follow the path through a gap stile into the field. Walk down the field to take a stile next to a gateway in the bottom left-hand corner. Descend with an old hedgerow on your left to cross a footbridge over the River Skerne – modest-looking at this stage, but apparently the longest inland river in Britain. Continue ahead over a stile and follow the clear path as it gradually climbs between two fields. The path then exits onto a metalled path at Trimdon Grange. Continue straight ahead, cross Hopper Terrace, and after a few metres bear right at a fork in the path to follow the path across the green. Pass Alnwick Avenue on your left and turn right at the wooden fencing in front of the houses to make your way into the recreation ground. Continue in the same direction, and just beyond the second football pitch cross the stile to follow the clear path as it bears left across a field. After passing some large stones near a culvert at the field boundary, bear right and follow the path with the trees on your left. At the corner of the wood take the right fork to descend a few metres to a sturdy footbridge. Now follow Walk 26(a) from **(F)**.

# Walk 27: Escomb

## *Saxons, sidewalks and stud*

**Location:** St John the Evangelist's Church (NY189302) is in Escomb, which is 2 miles west of Bishop Auckland. Escomb is on a minor road running north off the B6282.

**Distance:** 3 miles.

**Map:** OS Explorer 305: Bishop Auckland.

**Terrain:** Mainly on the level on riverside, woodland and field paths with one short, steep ascent.

**Church:** St John the Evangelist.

**Car parking:** On the road near the church.

## The Church

This ancient church is located in its well-maintained, almost circular, churchyard in the centre of the former mining village of Escomb, near Bishop Auckland, surrounded by maturing 1960s housing. Externally, you see a small, compact two-chamber building which, initially, has perhaps an austere almost fortress-like appearance. Yet this simple building dates back to around 675 and has stood almost unaltered since that time. It is not known who built the church or why it was built in Escomb. The circular church-yard, together with the dimensions and ground plan of the building, suggest an Irish-Celtic influence. A counter-view holds that it was built by stonemasons brought from northern France, in 666, by St Wilfrid. Often referred to as Escomb Saxon Church, its importance is recognised by Pevsner (*The Buildings of England: County Durham*) who describes it as "one of the most important and moving survivals of the architecture of the time of Bede and one of only three complete Saxon churches surviving in Britain".

Much of the stonework was foraged from the Roman camp at Binchester, two miles away. Interesting features reflecting the Roman origins can still be detected. For example, some stones have criss-cross incisions known as "diamond broaching", a characteristic of Roman stonework which was to have a plaster covering. When stones with existing Roman inscriptions were used, they were usually laid upside down, possibly to eliminate any Roman influence and drive off evil spirits. The tall height of the nave, relative to its length and width, is typical of the early churches of the Northumbrian type constructed in Saxon England.

Entrance is through the 13th-century porch on the south wall into the high narrow nave. Before looking for specific architectural features, you might like to follow a suggestion in the church's *Guide for Pilgrims* booklet. Take a little time to look around and see the church with your own eyes to sense something of the "feel" of the place. Apart from the antiquity of the building, there has been a Christian presence here for over 1,300 years.

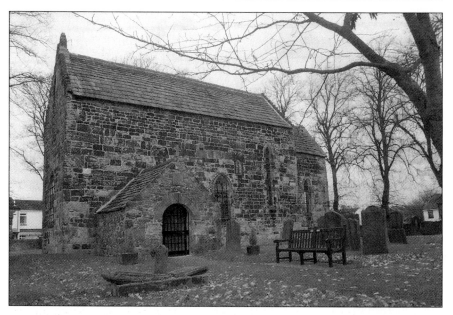

Escomb Saxon church

Above are the exposed, main cross beams, possibly dating back to the 10th century. One of the most striking features is the chancel arch, constructed of Roman stone work and believed to have been reassembled from a Roman archway. The stones supporting the arch are laid in alternative horizontal and vertical positions, the so-called "long and short stonework". The five smaller windows, two each on the south and north nave walls and one on the west wall, are Saxon. They are set, splayed, in the 60 centimetre thick walls to let in as much light as possible.

Most of the structure, except for additional windows, remains substantially unaltered. This is probably, at least in part, because no great saint has been associated with the church. There is no known early dedication – and the Prince Bishops of Durham, who were lords of the manor, would not have been concerned with rebuilding in a tiny, isolated settlement.

In 1863 a new parish church and graveyard were built nearby and the status of the Saxon church was reduced to a chapel. It soon became neglected, and quickly fell into ruin. Fortunately, at a time of growing interest in antiquarian matters, this state of affairs was recognised and funds were raised which enabled major roof and other repairs to be carried out – happily with no "Victorianisation" by the conscientious restorers.

The next 100 years saw a period of gradual neglect of the church, mainly as a result of its reduced status, which was exacerbated during the 1960s by a decline in the fortunes of Escomb village. However, thanks to the enthusiasm of local people, it was decided to restore the church and to furnish it so that it could be used for regular worship. New heating and lighting systems were installed and a new altar, plus floor coverings and oak pews were provided. In 1970, St John's was restored to the status of parish church. The former Victorian church, now itself redundant, was demolished in 1971.

Sensitive improvements have continued. A new organ was dedicated in 1978, and new kneelers have been introduced. Hence, after more than 1,300 years, Escomb Saxon Church continues as a living reminder of the Christian heritage of Northumbria.

### Among the other features of interest are:

❖ The octagonal stone font, thought to be 10th or 11th century. The shape of the bowl, which allowed for the total immersion of infants, suggests an earlier date.

❖ The small consecration cross, carved into the stonework near the chancel arch behind the pulpit. Its shape suggests Celtic influence.

❖ A stone cross, standing behind the altar. The probable date is 9th century although it has been tentatively suggested that it might be earlier, possibly part of a preaching cross used by Celtic missionaries, and predating the church.

❖ Outside, in the middle of the south wall, a Saxon sundial, consisting of a monster head surmounting a serpent. Its meaning is not known for certain, but it seems to be an example of Christian use of pre-Christian symbolism to illustrate the new beliefs.

❖ In the churchyard, close to the porch, two medieval gravestones with skulls and crossbones. These motifs were originally used as a symbol of resurrection, but since being pirated by pirates they are now thought of as having sinister connotations.

❖ From the churchyard looking towards the south wall can be seen, as Simon Jenkins (*England's Thousand Best Churches*) points out, "a gallery of English fenestration: a window each to Saxon, Norman and Gothic traditions, each struggling to admit more light without losing security or wall stability".

### Information available in the church:

❶ *The Saxon Church Escomb, A Guide for Pilgrims*, Revd N.Beddow.

❶ *The Saxon Church Escomb*, M.A. & J.D.Whitehead.

❶ *Interpreting the Saxon Sundial at Escomb*, Nicholas Beddow.

❶ Information cards on the important features in the church.

## The Walk

Leave the church grounds **(A)**, turn left and walk down the road. Bear right to come to Dunelm Chare. Carry on and take the public footpath to the right just beyond the children's play area. Follow the path, crossing a waymarked stile and soon the River Wear comes into view. Bear right to cross the waymarked stile and continue on the path with the river on your left. You are now on the

Weardale Way footpath. Carry on via a series of waymarked stiles over the fields, then bear right to cross the waymarked footbridge into a wooded area. Turn left and walk ahead for a short distance then turn right, as indicated by the waymark on a bench, and walk up between the trees to arrive at a waymarked stile. Cross the stile and turn right to go uphill, with the fence on your right. After passing under telephone wires, carry straight on. Go through the gap in the fence and cross the railway line. This line runs from Eastgate,through Barnard Castle, to Darlington and beyond, and was one of the first passenger and mineral lines in the world. Continue in the same direction. Go through the gap at the side of a metal gate and walk between hedges on the wider path. Pass Primrose Villa (1874) on your right and, immediately after the modern bungalow Glen-lea, turn right onto the public footpath (the sign is partly concealed by a hawthorn hedge) **(B)**.

The next 800 metres or so goes along a gravelled public footpath. Initially, there are houses and gardens on your left. At the end of the houses, at a crossing of paths, carry on in the same direction, now between fields. The footpath emerges onto a road. Turn right and walk 15 metres, then cross to the pavement in front of The Gables. Walk ahead a few metres, turn left and proceed straight ahead using the pavement on the opposite side of the road. After 500 metres, a notice on your right indicates that you are in California **(C)**.

Very soon you pass Sakama Stud on your right. Continue along the pavement (or should we be calling it the sidewalk?). Just beyond the last house on your left (which has a "California" sign on the wall), take the public footpath on the right alongside the overhead power lines for a short distance to reach a waymarked stile. Cross the stile, and bear slightly right as indicated, to walk over the field towards the white house ahead. Cross the waymarked stile and carry on in the same direction, again aiming for the white house. Cross the waymarked stile, turn right and walk ahead with the railway and the white house on your left. Exit over a stile **(D)**.

Bear left to cross the bridge over the railway. Walk ahead to join a farm track and pass Orchard House. Follow the track as it bends to the right. About 50 metres beyond the bend, look out for the unmarked footpath going off left towards the trees ahead. Take this path, which passes through a gateway and in a short while bears left towards the small Escomb Lake, formed by gravel workings, in front of the river ahead of you. Follow the path as it bears right and passes allotments on your left, to emerge via a gate onto a track that leads in a short distance to a street. Walk straight ahead along the street for a few metres past The Saxon Inn (a useful refreshment stop) to the church and the end of the walk.

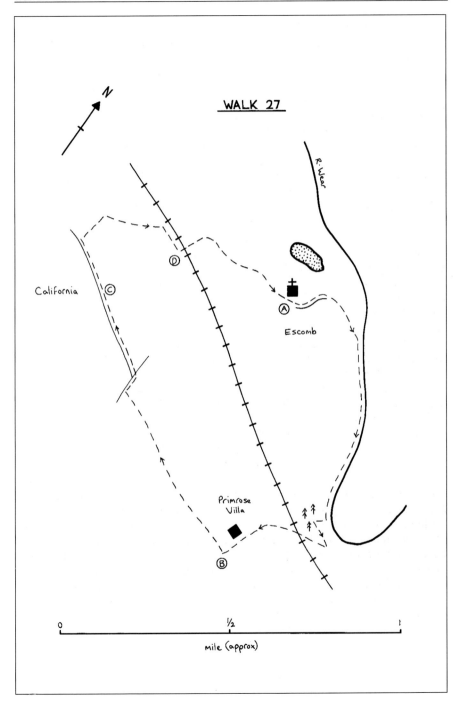

# Walk 28: Romaldkirk and Cotherstone

*Pew mouse, remembered spouse and Friends' house*

**Location:** St Romald's Church (NY995221) is in Romaldkirk which is on the B6277, 5 miles north-west of Barnard Castle.

**Distance:** 7 miles.

**Map:** OS Outdoor Leisure 31: North Pennines Teesdale and Weardale.

**Terrain:** Mostly on the level along a former railway and field and riverside paths, with one short steep ascent from the riverbank.

**Churches:** St Romald, Romaldkirk; St Cuthbert, Cotherstone; Quaker Meeting House, Cotherstone.

**Car parking:** There is parking by (but not on) the village greens, beside the church.

## The Churches

### St Romald, Romaldkirk

St Romald's is set in its well-maintained grounds in the village of Romaldkirk. The church grounds overlook the three village greens which form such a delightful centrepiece to this small attractive settlement. Romaldkirk lies in Teesdale, halfway between Barnard Castle and Middleton-in-Teesdale. The church is large and has been called the "Cathedral of the Dale" – not to be confused with Staindrop (see Walk 29) which is sometimes described as the "Cathedral of the Dales". The answer to the question "why such a large church for such a small village?" is probably simply because the St Romald's parish once served a much greater area than it does today. The dedication to St Romald is certainly unusual – and possibly unique. According to some sources, St Romald was the son of a Northumbrian king and regarded locally as a saint, but nothing of certainty is known about him.

The present church is built on the site of a Saxon church. It is thought that this, along with most of the surrounding district, was laid waste by Malcolm, King of Scotland, around 1086. Rebuilding of the church started around 1155, with the nave and arcaded north aisle, and there were additions and extensions around 1240 and 1360-70. The west tower was added in the 15th century. What is seen now is a sturdy, battlemented west tower, separate nave and chancel, and north and south transepts – all from different periods but presenting a uniform, quite grand appearance in mellow stone.

Inside, the mixture of styles in both architecture and furnishings combine into a harmonious blend of peaceful solidity. There is the ancient stonework of the walls and arcades, light from large windows, and solid pews in the nave. In a major restoration in 1927 the box pews were removed, and replaced with new pews made by Thompson of Kilburn (the "Mouse-man") that had the firm's trademark of a little carved mouse on them. There is interesting tracery in the main east window and the windows in the transepts – in

St Romald, Romaldkirk – the "Cathedral of the Dale"

particular the much admired tracery of the south transept window contrasts with the almost unfinished appearance of that of the main east window. The nave leads into the chancel, rather unusually, by steps down to the lower mosaic floor, laid by Italian craftsman in a restoration in 1890-94. Behind the altar, the carved reredos is the work of the "Mouse-man".

In parishes like Romaldkirk, until reforms instituted by Elizabeth I, it was quite usual for incumbents to have a variety of other livings and to be non-resident, paying other priests to carry out their duties for them. A good (or bad!) example is William Knight, appointed in 1535, who held seven livings, three canonries, three archdeaconries and one prebendaryship!

There is much of interest to see in the church. The explanatory cards near many of the important items are helpful and add to the overall feeling of welcome given to visitors to the "Cathedral of the Dale".

### Among the other features of interest are:

❖ The drum-shaped stone font near the entrance door on the south side. It might be Norman, but could possibly be a 13th-century addition crafted to fit in with the style of the building. The distinctive cover is a replacement for one made in 1728.

❖ The lower section of the original three-decker pulpit of 1728, near the west wall, which includes the reader's pew (left), the clerk's pew (centre) and the women's churching pew (used for a service of thanksgiving for childbirth) on the left. Also, the present pulpit, at the top of the nave on the right, which consists of the imposing upper tier and the stairs from the

1728 original. The original, intact, pulpit stood for 200 years from its completion in 1728 to its dismantling in the restoration of 1927.

❖ On the west wall of the north aisle, a stained-glass window depicting the baptism of Christ in the River Jordan by John the Baptist. This was given by members of the Smythe family of Sunderland in memory of their parents. The local area, specially Cotherstone, was regarded as a health resort, particularly by Sunderland families, some of whom owned cottages for holidays or retirement.

❖ On the north wall of the north transept is a splendid effigy of Hugh Fitz Henry, Lord of Bedale, Ravensworth and Cotherstone. He died in 1305 from wounds suffered in Edward I's Scottish war. The effigy lies on a plain, raised, altar tomb. It shows the figure in chain mail lying, not crossed-legged, but in a rare straight legged position and displays better than any other in England the protective mail on the thighs. The Fitzhugh family of Cotherstone Castle took their name from Hugh Fitz Henry and later became patrons of the parish.

❖ In the south transept, near the east wall, a new light wood chair made in 2000 to replace one previously stolen. This blends in with the plain altar table to form the furnishings of the St Thomas Chantry Chapel.

### *Information available in the church:*

❶ Hand-held information board.

❶ *St Romald's Church, Romaldkirk in Teesdale,* Canon John E. Lee.

❶ *St Romald's Church, Romaldkirk: The Organ,* Hector C. Pass.

### St Cuthbert, Cotherstone

This fairly small church provides an interesting contrast with the "Cathedral of the Dale", St Romald's at Romaldkirk. St Cuthbert's was built in 1881 as a chapel-of-ease to St Romald's. The railway had come to Cotherstone in 1868 and subsequently there was an increase in population whose housing needs were met by the develop-

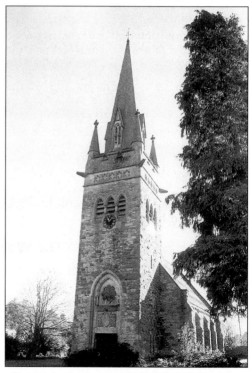

The dominating tower of St Cuthbert, Cotherstone

ment of Victorian terraces and villas. There was also some early tourism in Cotherstone. Before St Cuthbert's was built, the Christian presence was represented by a Methodist chapel of 1872, built following a visit by John Wesley, and a Quaker Meeting House from 1797. George Fox, the founder of the Society of Friends, visited Cotherstone in1653.

As a building, St Cuthbert's is a little unusual in style, with a tall, dominating narrow west tower and a single-chamber nave and chancel with a fairly steep sloping roof. The overall height of the tower was increased by the addition of a spire, given by her husband, in memory of Dame Elizabeth Scott who died in 1911.

Entrance is through a door at the west end. Inside there are stone walls and exposed beams with wooden roof cladding. The nave is furnished with solid pews and the nave windows are mostly plain glass with attractive yellow borders. The walls are mostly unadorned, save for a small number of memorial tablets. There is a plain, narrow chancel arch leading the eye to the stained-glass east window. All combining to produce an overall homely, simplicity.

### Among the other features of interest are:

❖ The stained-glass window on the north wall of the nave by Kempe (see Walk 15, Simonburn).

❖ The small reredos with, inset, the painting of the Last Supper.

❖ The stained-glass window on the south wall of the chancel, by Kempe, in memory of a well travelled minister.

### Quaker Meeting House, Cotherstone

This is a small, unpretentious building in a quite isolated position on the outskirts of the village. It is approached across a field path, from which can be seen on the side of the building the name "Society of Friends' Meeting House". Quaker meetings have been held here for over 200 years. Land was acquired in 1796 and the first meeting was held in April 1797. You can peep into the windows on the south side to see the simple meeting room with its plain benches. In the graveyard, in the Quaker fashion, are small, equally proportioned headstones.

## The Walk

Leave St Romald's churchyard **(A)** and turn right to walk up the road through the village. Just before the junction, pass the village hall dedicated to King Edward VII. Turn left in the direction of Barnard Castle and walk along the pavement. You need to follow the signs for the Tees Railway Walk. At the first junction take the road on the right and proceed uphill for 300 metres or so to reach the access point to the railway walk on the left. **(B)**.

Go through the gate onto the former railway, now a grassy track, and walk straight ahead in the direction of Cotherstone. Thereafter, for the next 2¼ miles, carry on, passing a series of gates and Tees Railway Walk signs. Shortly after crossing the River Balder, the tall spire of Cotherstone Church comes into view on your left. Carry on until you reach the sign "Romaldkirk 2½". Go through the gate onto the road and bear left to walk along the road for 200 metres, to arrive at Cotherstone Church **(C)**.

After leaving the church turn right and walk the short distance to the road junction. Cross the main road, bear left, and in a few metres bear right and walk past the cottages on your right with the green and stream on your left. Turn right onto the narrow path running between The Coach House and The Green. At the end of the path exit onto a narrow metalled lane. Turn left and walk 10 metres to go through the gate, onto the public footpath on the right. Walk straight ahead with the fence/hedge on your left to the end of the field and go through the gate to arrive at the Society of Friends' Meeting House. The graveyard is through the gate on your right. **(D)**.

After visiting the graveyard return back through the gate, turn right and exit the grounds via the narrow gap (with two metal bars). Walk ahead, then bear slightly right to a waymarked gate in the corner of the field. Go through the gate and walk between the trees with a stream on your right, and in a short while turn right to go over a footbridge and up the steps to cross a waymarked stile. Carry on to cross another (quite high) stile and continue with the fence and trees on your left and a stream running below, passing helpful waymark signs on two of the trees. At the field boundary go through the gateway on the left and then continue in the same direction as before, with a hedge/wall on your right. A farm building comes into view ahead. Just before reaching the farm, you arrive at a waymark post indicating that you are joining the Teesdale Way walk **(E)**.

Go diagonally left in the direction of the waymark on the wall below and follow the path as it gradually descends towards the River Tees. Cross a stile and a footbridge and walk ahead to enter, via a stile, into woods. Climb the steps and proceed through the woods, with crags on your left, for 200 metres or so to cross a waymarked stile and climb gradually away from the river. Eventually you emerge from the woods and climb to join a farm track. Turn right and walk ahead. Where the well-defined path bears left, go straight ahead, following the direction indicated by the Teesdale Way waymark on a tree stump on your right. Continue ahead, now fairly high above the banks of the Tees, via a waymarked gate and a stile, and cross a farm lane to come to a lone grave on your right which is worth inspecting. Carry on, crossing a stile, to pass some old poultry sheds and cross another stile. After a few metres, turn sharp right at the waymark on the fence to go down steps and follow the path down to a metalled lane and a grassy area known locally as The Hag. Cross the lane to reach a footbridge over the River Balder, just before it flows into the Tees **(F)**.

Cross the footbridge and carry on the Teesdale Way with the River Tees on your right. Follow the path as it runs close to the river and keep to the path as it climbs to a waymarked stile. Cross the stile and walk straight ahead along

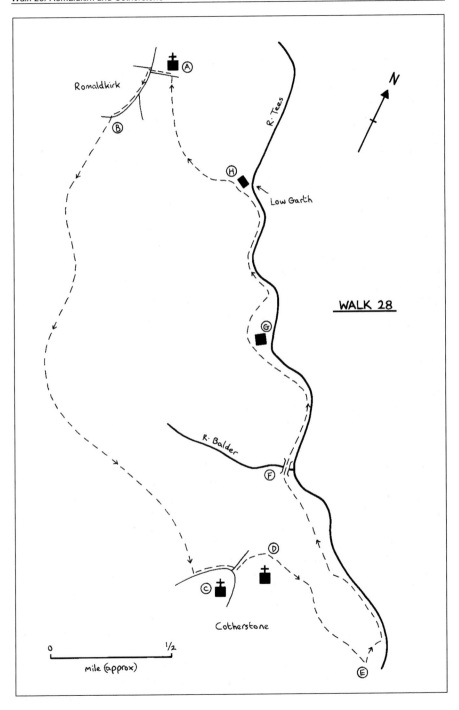

the faint green path to go over a waymarked stile. Continue, with the fence on your left, and go down steps to a stream. Cross the stream by the sturdy looking stepping stones (the first one, however, is wobbly). Climb a few metres to cross a waymarked stile. Walk ahead for 100 metres or so and then bear left to climb between the trees, then right and up the slope towards the roof of the building you can see ahead. Go through the waymarked gateway onto a farm lane with a wall on your left and continue, via a gate, to walk straight ahead. At the top of the field, pass an attractive house and turn right to go through a gate **(G)**.

Continue ahead past the cottages on your right and follow the waymark direction to go through a gate. Carry on to cross a waymarked stile and proceed straight ahead. At the end of the field, cross the stile and bear right to go down to a stile next to a metal gate. Descend and continue ahead with the river on your right. The path becomes stony, veers away from the river, and then swings back. This section can be a little tricky; the stones do not make for easy walking. Eventually reach a waymarked stile. Bear slightly right to follow the path towards the farm ahead. Skirt the abandoned buildings of Low Garth farm on your right and cross the waymarked stile **(H)**.

Follow the farm track as it goes straight ahead then bears left. Do not go to the end of the track. Instead, about 100 metres before the track exits from the field, bear right and walk uphill to a small waymarked gate in the hawthorn hedge. Go through the gate and bear diagonally left to cross the field on the faint path to come to a gate in the hedge. Go through the gate, bear slightly left and walk through the small copse of trees to a waymarked gate. Go through the gate and proceed along the track with a wall on the right. Continue ahead and emerge onto a lane between houses, and walk the few metres to the church and the end of the walk.

# Walk 29: Staindrop

*Eminent effigy, bishop's beck and winding walls*

**Location:** St Mary's Church (NZ131206) is in Staindrop about 6 miles from Barnard Castle on the A688 Barnard Castle to West Auckland road.

**Distance:** 5½ miles.

**Maps:** OS Explorer 304: Darlington & Richmond.

**Terrain:** Largely on the level on footpaths over fields with numerous stiles.

**Church:** St Mary, Staindrop.

**Car parking:** There is limited parking by the east gate of the church near the bridge over the Langley Beck on the A688. There is also parking to the west of the church and by the village green.

## The Church

This church stands proudly in a dominant position at the east end of Staindrop, an elongated village of interlinked greens. Externally it presents a solid central core with slightly lower extensions to the north, south and east, all crowned by a sturdy west tower. The eye is drawn to the generous collection of windows with their attractive tracery. There is evidence that a Saxon church on this site was gradually extended into what Pevsner (*The Buildings of England: Durham*) describes as a "large and impressive medieval parish church, and one of the most interesting in the county". Some helpful models in the church illustrate the various stages in its historical development.

St Mary, Staindrop – a splendid cathedral-like church

However, the existence of a church of such dimension in this area of Durham is undoubtedly due to the benevolence of the Nevilles and the Vanes, lords of nearby Raby Castle (see below).

The church is entered via a south-west porch with an unusual stone arched ceiling. Once inside, the castle connection is immediately clear in the form of an imposing and slightly awesome row of effigies against the west wall. Henry Neville, the 5th Earl of Westmorland (died 1564), and two of his three wives, lie serenely above a number of niches containing smaller effigies of their children, all beautifully carved in oak and so blackened by age that it looks like marble. Beyond is the striking tomb of Ralph Neville, the 1st Earl (1364-1423), with his two wives, described by Simon Jenkins (*England's Thousand Best Churches*) as "one of the most notable alabaster tombs in the country".

Not to be outdone, the Vanes are represented in the north-west corner of the church by various effigies and wall tablets under their titles of Darlington and Cleveland. There are also several hatchments displaying the family coat of arms on the north wall. However, the chancel is the real domain of the Vanes, with numerous wall tablets commemorating various generations of the family.

The grandeur of St Mary's has earned it the epithet "the Cathedral of the Dales", the emphasis on the plural "dales" possibly putting it ahead of its rival at Romaldkirk (see Walk 28). Contributing undoubtedly to its medieval prestige was the fact that the Bishop of Durham, Thomas Langley, granted permission in 1408 for the establishment of a college on land adjacent to the church. The college fell victim to the Reformation process during the reign of Edward VI (1537-1553), but some remnants of its 15th-century furnishings remain in the form of the splendidly carved misericords in the chancel and the dark oak chest at the west end of the central aisle.

There are many fascinating things to see in St Mary's and you are certainly made to feel welcome in this well-maintained and active church. Meanwhile the village of Staindrop also merits a visit in its own right.

### Among the other features of interest are:

❖ The late 15th-century Egglestone marble font at the west end.

❖ The 14th-century chancel screen, believed to be the only pre-Reformation screen surviving in Durham.

❖ The fine chancel floor of Frosterley marble.

❖ Three stained-glass windows by Kempe (see Walk 15, Simonburn): the St Columba, Madonna and St Chad window in the east wall of the north transept; the St John the Baptist and Holy Family window in the north wall of the chancel; and the window in the south-east wall of the nave showing Mary of Bethania, Mary Magdalene and Martha. Look out for the Kempe wheatsheaf logo!

## Information available in the church:

ⓘ Hand-held information board.

ⓘ Information board on a pillar at the west end.

ⓘ *St Mary's Staindrop, an illustrated history and guide.*

> *Raby Castle, built in the 14<sup>th</sup> century, remained for many centuries the family seat of the Neville family – Earls of Westmorland and generous patrons of the church. However, they forfeited their land because of their involvement in the ill-fated Rising of the North in 1569, one of several Counter-Reformation intrigues. In 1626, Raby Castle, together with Barnard Castle, was purchased by Sir Henry Vane whose grandson was given the title of Baron Barnard in 1698. For a time, the family held the titles of Earls of Darlington and Dukes of Cleveland. The Vanes, too, ensured that St Mary's was well endowed and their descendant today, the 11<sup>th</sup> Baron Barnard, remains patron of the church.*

# The Walk

On leaving the church **(A)** turn left and follow the path behind the east end of the church where, to the north, you will see the mausoleum of the Dukes of Cleveland and their families. Exit onto the main road via a gate. Turn left and walk across the aptly named Church Bridge. Turn left again and walk on the permitted path along the side of the Langley Beck for a short distance to the footbridge. The name of the beck recalls the 15<sup>th</sup>-century Bishop who played a significant role in the development of Staindrop church. On your right are the walls, which stretch for several miles around the extensive park land of the Raby Estate (the castle and grounds are open to visitors at times indicated on the main gate on the A688). Cross the footbridge, turn right and walk up the lane for about 400 metres. Follow the lane as it turns left between a high wall and a barn, just before an open space with two driveways. At the end of the lane turn right, and proceed along the pavement across the green and then past the cottages on your right, which include the police house. At the end of the green, take the narrow public footpath immediately to the right of the house bearing the number 54 **(B)**.

Follow the path through a tight gap in a wall and between a fence and a hedge. Cross the stile on your right at the end of the hedge, turn left and walk ahead to go over another stile next to a gate. Continue in the same direction along the field edge to cross a stone stile. Bear right to meet the Raby Park estate wall once again. Now proceed ahead with the wall on your right for about 1,200 metres, going over several stone stiles and passing through gates at two neat, estate lodges. At the second lodge, turn left down the track to leave the estate wall behind you and to arrive at the B6279. Turn right and walk up the road for a few metres and cross over the road with care, to go through a gate next to a public footpath sign. Walk up the field with the hedge on your left. At the top of the field turn right and continue along the field boundary, to exit over a stile at the next corner. Continue ahead with the hedge on your left to join a metalled track at the entrance to Scaife Farm **(C)**.

Turn left through the gateway and keep on the main track, passing the farmhouse on your left to arrive at a field edge. Go straight ahead down the field (usually starting through the gap in the electric fence at the field edge), over a burn, to a waymarked gate to the right of a large tree. Continue in the same direction over the next field and through another gate. Take care at this stage to do what might be called a"V" turn: that is, turn right and walk some 10 metres towards a metal gate, then turn sharp left to pick up the right of way which goes across the middle of the field. The farmer usually provides a helpful tractor line through the crop. Walk towards the right-hand side of a short line of trees which soon appears ahead and go through a metal gate at the field boundary. Continue ahead with the hedge on your right, through a gateway and onto a metalled lane. Turn right and follow the lane as it gradually climbs the rise. Stop at the top to get your breath back and to admire the view, where you should be able to pick out the church tower to the north-east. Proceed a short distance and just before Snotterton Hall farm, leave the lane to take a waymarked stile on your left **(D)**.

Walk a short distance over the paddock, cross the stile, turn almost immediately right and go through the small gate in the wall. Turn left and make your way down the fairly steep bank to the Sudburn Beck. Do not cross the burn (unless you want to picnic near the footbridge) but instead turn left, go through the gate and follow the Sudburn Beck downstream. Proceed close to the bank side over a succession of stiles, some of which can be rather tricky, until you go over a stone stile by a gate and exit onto the A688. Cross the road with care to the signposted footpath opposite. Descend the steps, go over the stile, and continue once more along the side of the beck over a further succession of similar stiles, until you exit onto a minor road via a stone stile to the left of Cleatlam Bridge **(E)**.

Cross the road with care to go over the stone stile opposite. Walk diagonally left across the field, between the telegraph post and the tree, to take the waymarked gated stile. Continue diagonally in the same direction towards the church tower which should be visible behind the trees and cross a small stone bridge and a stile. Proceed ahead again in the same diagonal direction to cross a stile next to a metal gate in the right-hand field boundary. Follow the track as it bears left at the vehicle testing station onto a lane which leads to the village green. Turn right to pass Scarth Memorial Hall (1875) and the former Wesleyan Chapel (1869) and walk a few metres to the information board containing interesting details of the history and buildings of Staindrop. Continue down the slip road to join the main road, cross over with care, turn right, walk along the pavement passing the Methodist Church (1861) to return to St Mary's Church and the end of the walk.

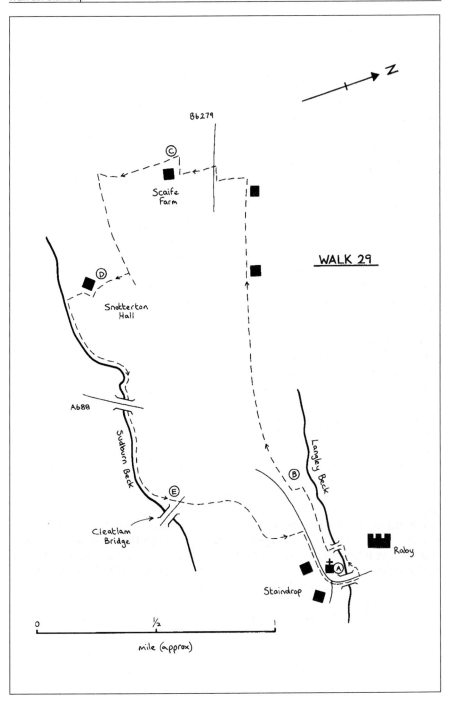

# Walk 30: Barnard Castle, Egglestone Abbey and Whorlton

## *Bernard, bridges and Bowes*

**Location:** St Mary's Church (NZ051163) is in Barnard Castle, 15 miles west of Darlington on the A67.

**Map:** OS Outdoor Leisure 31: North Pennines and OS Explorer 304: Darlington & Richmond.

**Distance:** Walk 30(a), Barnard Castle, Egglestone Abbey and Whorlton: 9 miles; Walk 30(b), Barnard Castle and Egglestone Abbey: 3½ miles.

**Terrain:** The walks are almost entirely on footpaths, on the level, on either side of the River Tees.

**Churches:** St Mary, Barnard Castle; Egglestone Abbey; St Mary, Whorlton; St Mary RC Church, Barnard Castle.

**Car parking:** There are a number of public car parks in Barnard Castle, including a long stay car park close to the church which can be reached by turning left off Newgate at St Mary's RC Church.

---

## The Churches

### St Mary, Barnard Castle

The church stands close to the Market Cross of 1747, on a busy corner in the historic market town of Barnard Castle. It was founded at the beginning of the 12$^{th}$ century, as a chapel for the nearby castle built by Bernard de Balliol which gave its name to the town. St Mary's remained a daughter church of the parish church of the village of Gainford, some eight miles away, until 1866 when it became a separate parish with its own vicar.

Externally the best views are from the south side of the building. The enlargement of the church from a single-chamber Norman edifice to its present imposing size is evident, and the embattlements with their different levels are particularly striking. The 12$^{th}$-century south doorway with its zig-zag bandings was probably the original entrance, re-sited to its present position. Close to it is an elaborately carved chest tomb, on the north side of which is the effigy of George Hopper in his 18$^{th}$-century costume.

The tower has had a chequered history. The original tower of 1270 became unstable due to the vibration of the bells and was strengthened and raised in 1772. However, by 1868 and the addition of further bells it was once again declared to be unsafe, leading to its demolition and replacement by the present tower. Entry to the church is now gained through the north door in the base of the tower, and inside is what the guidebook refers to as a "monumental chamber". Here are numerous wall plaques and monuments, which were transferred from the walls of the church at the time of the 1868 restoration. The benefit of this is obvious in the uncluttered nature of the nave, chancel and transepts.

A well-designed oak screen, a memorial to the First World War, provides access to the church itself. The wide nave is divided by pillars and arcades from north and south aisles, at the end of which are two small transepts. The central nave leads via six steps to the narrow chancel, which has two deeply recessed Norman windows possibly relics of the 12th-century church.

This is a very welcoming church in which there is clearly much to explore, and where you are even invited to turn on the lights at your convenience. As the church guidebook says, "Many centuries of loving care of countless hearts and hands have given us a priceless heritage in this ancient building".

### Among the other features of interest are:

❖ The effigy of Robert de Mortham, a 14th-century vicar of Gainford, over the chest tomb in one of the recesses in the north transept.

❖ The 14th-century sculpture of St Anthony of Egypt. Patron saint (among other things) of swineherds, he is almost hidden behind two large boars. It is believed to have been part of a town gateway at one time.

❖ The exceptionally large and imposing baptismal font of Tees marble in the north transept, which has been dated 1485.

❖ The 15th-century chancel arch, with what is thought to be the head of King Edward IV at the bottom of the left-hand side of the arch and the head of King Richard III on the right-hand side.

❖ The stained-glass window of Christ in the south wall of the chancel by Kempe (see Walk 15, Simonburn).

### Information available in the church:

**❶** *The Parish Church of Saint Mary Barnard Castle*, C.Lilley.

George Hopper's elaborate tombstone at St Mary, Barnard Castle

## Egglestone Abbey

The ruins of Egglestone Abbey, its church and cloisters, are now under the jurisdiction of English Heritage and are open to visitors, free of charge, at any reasonable time. The abbey was founded in the 1190s by the Premonstratensians, a French order of monks. However, it failed to flourish in comparison to other northern abbeys. Closed at the time of the Reformation it then had mixed fortunes, part of it being converted into a manor hall before serving as an abode for local workers in the 1880s.

The ruins of Egglestone Abbey

What remains today is a splendid collection of ruined walls and archways, standing proudly in well laid out grounds on a promontory overlooking the River Tees. A number of information boards help to locate the church, cloisters and chapter house, as well as some interesting grave slabs and the tomb of Ralph Bowes of Streatlam. This is an atmospheric setting and a pleasant place in which to pause and ponder in the course of this long walk.

## St Mary, Whorlton

This church, tucked into a corner just off the village green of this delightful village, is generally closed except for services, although it may be possible to collect a key (for example, by arrangement with the Vicar at Barnard Castle). It is a small building, consisting of a nave and chancel with a slender octagonal spire at the south-west end. The entrance porch on the south side has a king's head on either side of the doorway, a convenient stone bench and two attractive windows. Unusually, there is a stone font just outside the doorway. Inside it has a high timbered ceiling with carved heads supporting the

St Mary, Whorlton – a peaceful place to pause

beams. There are a number of dedicated stained-glass windows and in the chancel there is a memorial chair to the Bishop of Cape Town, who consecrated the church in 1853. In addition, there are some rather imposing choir stalls. Here there is certainly a very peaceful atmosphere both within and without.

## St Mary RC Church, Barnard Castle

The church is generally closed except for services, however, it is worth pausing to visit the tombs of John Bowes and his wife Josephine behind the south-east end of the church. John Bowes, a public-spirited businessman and an MP, was descended from an old Teesdale family and he lived at Streatlam Castle with his French wife. They generously decided to build a museum for the public, and they spent fifteen years in building up a magnificent collection of paintings and furnishings from all over Europe. The foundation stone of the Josephine and John Bowes Museum was laid in 1869, but they were both to die before the museum was opened in 1892. Josephine died in 1874, after which John commenced the building of a memorial chapel in the grounds of the museum where both he and his wife would be buried. However, after John's death in 1885 it was found that the original plan was too expensive and the location impracticable. Hence the decision to build St Mary's a short distance from the entrance to the Bowes Museum. The foundation stone was laid in 1926 and the church was officially opened in 1928, at which time the remains of John and Josephine were transferred from Gibside Chapel to the tombs they now occupy.

# The Walks

## Walk 30(a), Barnard Castle, Egglestone Abbey and Whorlton: 9 miles

After visiting the church **(A)**, turn left towards the Market Cross and left again to follow the road down to the river. As the main road bears right, keep straight ahead and cross the River Tees by the footbridge. Turn immediately left and follow the river downstream along the path. As the track forks by some cottages, take the narrower path to the left to continue with the river on your left. Soon you come to a metalled road leading into a caravan park. After about 30 metres follow the waymark sign and turn right. Follow the road as it bears round the caravans and climbs towards the exit of the caravan park. Very soon after passing the last caravan go over a waymarked stile on the left, which indicates that you are now on the Teesdale Way. Follow the grassy track straight across the field and turn right a few metres before a gateway. Walk up the field edge with the hedge on your left, to pass the side of a house and exit onto a minor road **(B)**.

Turn left, and after a few hundred metres look out for a stile on your right next to a metal gate. Cross the stile, proceed ahead and walk round the two sides of the field edge, with the hedge and then a plantation on your right. At the edge of the plantation bear right down a well worn track. Follow the track and, as it descends and bears to the left, look out for a waymark post on your right. Leave the main track and turn right to pass with care through a tight gap in the hedge and go over a concealed footbridge. Bear left and continue straight ahead, keeping to the lower path at a waymark sign. Up to your right you will soon see the ruins of Egglestone Abbey and to the left the old pack-horse Bow Bridge. Continue ahead to exit onto a minor road. Turn right, follow the road a short distance to a junction and turn right to visit Egglestone Abbey **(C)**.

After visiting the abbey return down the metalled drive to the minor road, turn right and walk a few hundred metres to Abbey Bridge **(D)**.

Do not cross the bridge, but just beyond it take the public footpath "Teesdale Way" which winds its way down to the river. Proceed along the clear path with the river on your left until eventually it takes you over a stile, across a small burn and up some steps into a field. Bear left, continue round the field edge and then take the waymarked stile into the woods. Follow the clear path and exit via a gate, at a junction of a minor road and a private road. Turn left down the private road to follow the sign "Teesdale Way Public Footpath". On the right is Rokeby Park, setting for Sir Walter Scott's ballad "Rokeby". After a few hundred metres the road bears right and passes the confluence of the Tees and the Greta, the oft painted "Meeting of the Waters". Continue along the road as it crosses a bridge over the Greta. After a short distance, as it makes its way through pasture land, the road becomes more of a track and a fine dwelling, which incorporates Mortham Tower, comes into sight on the right. About 100 metres before the entrance to the

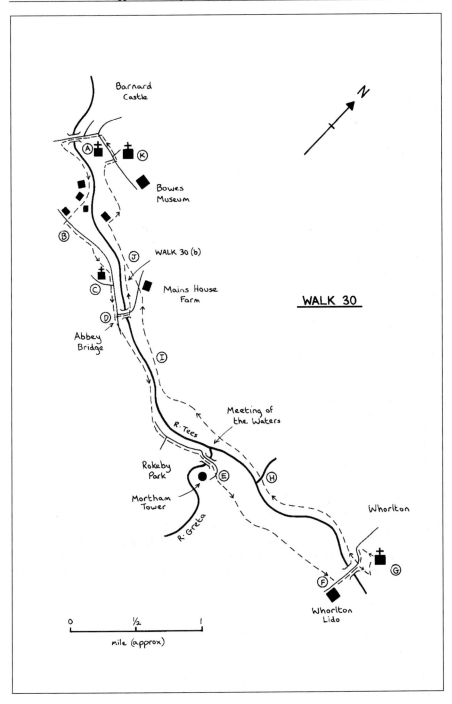

house, as the track bears right, leave the track to go left in the direction of a Teesdale Way sign **(E)**.

Proceed ahead and cross the waymarked stile in the wire fence. Continue over two fields with a wire fence/hedge on your right. Cross a waymarked stile and follow the clear path as it bears left round the field edge with a wood now on your left. After about 200 metres, at a partially concealed waymark on the fence, turn right to continue round the same field, with a stone wall now forming the field boundary on your left. At the next corner go through the waymarked gate and continue along the edge of the next field, with the stone wall now on your right. After passing through a waymarked metal gate, bear diagonally left across the grazing land. Pass a small enclosure with a waymark and descend to a stone stile just beyond a gate. Cross the stile and join a minor road, a few metres past the entrance to Whorlton Lido **(F)**.

Turn left and cross the suspension bridge over the River Tees. Follow the road as it climbs away from the river and then, as it bears sharp left, leave the road to take a waymarked footpath on the right through a gap in the wall. Follow the track for about 25 metres, go up the steps and immediately take the left-hand fork to climb further away from the river. In a few metres, just before a gate, turn right on a pathway, walk past a sewage plant and turn left up the pathway to go through a kissing gate. Follow the grassy path over a stile and through another kissing gate into the churchyard of St Mary at Whorlton **(G)**.

After viewing St Mary's, leave by the lych-gate, turn right and then immediately left to pass in front of the village hall, previously an independent chapel (1840) to meet a minor road. Turn left and after about 200 metres take the public footpath off to the right. At the end of the property fence go through a waymarked gate. You are now high above the River Tees and to return to Barnard Castle you now need to follow the river upstream. The path is generally well waymarked, often with Teesdale Way markers, however, you may care for some guidance! After passing through three field boundaries and a short wooded section with their respective gates/stiles, you arrive at open pasture land. Continue ahead to follow the line of trees on your left and gradually bear left to take a stile next to a waymarked gate. Proceed across two more stiles and then, about halfway across the next field, look carefully for a waymarked stile by a gate marked "no entry". Cross the stile and follow the narrow path at the edge of the trees, with the wire fence on your right. Take care where a stone wall appears on your right and the bank drops steeply away to your left. Go down the steps to cross a footbridge over a burn **(H)**.

Go up the steps and over the waymarked stone stile into pasture land. Go straight ahead and cross three more field boundaries with their respective stiles. At the third boundary, resist the temptation to descend to the left towards The Meeting of the Waters and continue straight ahead to take a high stile slightly to the right of a gate. Proceed in the same direction to a waymark at a trough, to the left of a big tree. Walk diagonally left to cross a stone stile in the wall and continue in the same direction to take a waymarked stile in the corner of the next field. Walk along the field edge, with a stone wall on your left, to cross another waymarked stile. Continue along the field edge for about 100 metres, and then leave to follow the waymark to a stile on the left across the wire fence at the edge of the wood **(I)**.

Cross the stile and follow the path as it works its way through the edge of the wood, to exit at a waymarked stile and gateway. Continue in the same direction, now with the wood on your left. Soon go through a gate and walk straight ahead with farm buildings ahead on your right. Go through the small gate in the corner of the field boundary and go down the stone stile to exit, with care, onto the road. Turn right and walk some 50 metres to take the public footpath on the left opposite Mains House Farm. Go through the gate and follow the grassy track towards the river to go over a waymarked stile next to a gate **(J)**.

Proceed ahead with Egglestone Abbey now on the left over the river. Go through another waymarked gateway and continue in the same direction as the river bank gets closer and a wooden fence appears on your right. Take the gates past the sewage works and then bear slightly right in the direction of the waymark, towards a ruined barn. Turn right just before the barn and climb up the field to cross a stone stile next to waymarked gate. Bear diagonally left up the green path to the top right-hand corner of the rugby field. Continue along the path as it gently climbs behind the sports fields and Bowes Museum comes into view on your right. Take the stile next to the gate onto a stony track, and bear right through a gate and up the metalled Parsons Lonnen to meet a main road. Cross the road with care, bear left and walk a few metres to St Mary's RC Church **(K)**.

Walk up the church steps and bear right round the outside of the church to visit the tombs of John and Josephine Bowes. Return to the main road, turn right and continue along the pavement for a few hundred metres, back to the parish church and the end of the walk.

## Walk 30(b), Barnard Castle and Egglestone Abbey: 3½ miles

Follow Walk 30(a) as far as Abbey Bridge **(D)**. Turn left and cross the bridge. After a few metres, leave the road by a gap in the wall on your left at the sign "Teesdale Way Public Footpath". Follow the clear path between the trees to go through a waymarked kissing gate. Continue ahead in the same direction until you reach a waymarked stile next to a gate where a track converges from the right. Now follow Walk 30(a) from **(J)** back to the parish church and the end of the walk.

# Bibliography

Betjeman, J. (second edition,1993), *Sir John Betjeman's Guide to English Parish Churches*, Harper Collins.

Cole, Grenville S. (1996), *Arms and the Man,* Lady Armstrong.

Collins, Philip (2000), *The Corpus of Kempe Stained Glass in the United Kingdom and Ireland*, The Kempe Trust.

Colls, Robert and Lancaster, Bill, eds. (2001), *Newcastle upon Tyne: A Modern History*, Phillimore.

Evetts, Phyl, ed. (2001), *Leonard Evetts: Master Designer*, Leonard Evetts Publishing Fund.

Faulkner, Thomas and Greg, Andrew (2001), *John Dobson, Architect of the North East*, Tyne Bridge Publishing.

Friar, Stephen (second edition, 2000), *A Companion to the English Parish Church,* Chancellor Press.

Hall, Marshall (1973), *The Artists of Northumbria*, Marshall Hall Associates.

Hodgson, John (1827), *History of Northumberland*, Frank Graham (facsimile edition, 1973).

Jenkins, Simon (1999), *England's Thousand Best Churches*, Allen Lane The Penguin Press.

Moorman, J.R.H. (third edition, 1986), *A History of the Church in England*, A&C Black.

Pevsner, Nikolaus (1985), *The Buildings of England: County Durham* (second edition revised by Elizabeth Williamson), Penguin Books.

Pevsner, Nikolaus and Richmond, Ian (1992), *The Buildings of England: Northumberland* (second edition revised by John Grundy, Grace McCombie, Peter Ryder, Humphrey Welfare), Penguin Books.

Ridley, Nancy (second edition, 1982), *Northumbrian Heritage*, Robert Hale.

Salter, Mike (1997), *The Old Parish Churches of Northumberland*, Folly Publications.

Tomlinson, W.W. (1888), *Comprehensive Guide to Northumberland*, W.H. Robinson, (reprint of 11th edition, 1968), David & Charles Reprints.

# Also of Interest:

### LAKELAND CHURCH WALKS

*Peter Donaghy and John Laidler*

*Foreword by Simon Jenkins – author of "England's 1000 Best Churches".* This is the first walking guide based on Lakeland churches. Over 50 churches open to visitors, with many photographs. Trace the impact of famous people, patrons and personalities such as Wordsworth, Ruskin, the Dacres, Lady Anne Clifford, the Beauty of Buttermere and even Tarzan! *£8.95*

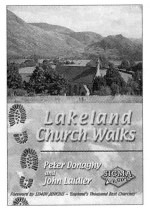

### NORTH NOTTINGHAMSHIRE CHURCH WALKS

*Alan & Janet Nash*

There are so many ancient churches in north Nottinghamshire that once you've seen one of the gems, your boots just keep you marching southward. There are 74 churches featured in this book and the walks are journeys of exploration as the authors describe the magnificent living history that forms the nucleus of many of the villages that are visited. *£8.95*

### DORSET CHURCH WALKS

*Diana Pé*

Take a glimpse into the past – the absorbing history of each church reveals much about the lives of those who lived in the surrounding area. Enjoy a tremendous diversity of walking opportunities: from exhilarating routes by the spectacularly beautiful Dorset coast to peaceful walks around the golden town of Sherborne and in the Vale of Blackmore. Explore Dorset's exceptional literary heritage at sites associated with Thomas Hardy and William Barnes and many others. *£7.95*

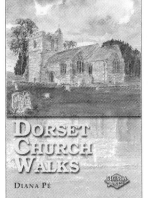

All of our books – including several others for Northumbria – are available through booksellers and online from Amazon.co.uk. For a free catalogue, please contact: **SIGMA LEISURE, 5 ALTON ROAD, WILMSLOW, CHESHIRE SK9 6AR.**

Phone & Fax: 01625-531035    E-mail: info@sigmapress.co.uk

New book announcements – plus updates on all of our published books can be found on our comprehensive web site: **www.sigmapress.co.uk**

# The Churches Conservation Trust

The Churches Conservation Trust cares for 325 churches of outstanding historic, architectural or archaeological importance.

- The Trust warmly welcomes visitors throughout the year to its churches which are scattered throughout England

- The Trust was set up in 1969 to preserve and repair churches which are no longer needed for regular worship

- Many of our churches are hidden gems, beautifully set and ideal for discovering on a walk, cycle ride or day out; others can be found in market towns or bustling cities

- All our churches have something special to offer – breathtaking architecture, brilliant stained glass, fascinating monuments, ancient wallpaintings…..

- All are either opened regularly or have keyholders nearby

**For more information** on Trust churches and opening arrangements visit our website at **www.visitchurches.org.uk**

Alternatively, **write to us** at 89 Fleet Street, London EC4Y 1DH for a free copy of Your Starter for 50 booklet and County leaflets (please specify county/ies required).

# www.visitchurches.org.uk

Registered Charity No. 258612